History of the English People, Volume V: Puritan England, 1603-1660

John Richard Green

ESPRIOS.COM
ESPRIOS DIGITAL PUBLISHING

HISTORY
OF
THE ENGLISH PEOPLE
BY
JOHN RICHARD GREEN, M.A.
HONORARY FELLOW OF JESUS COLLEGE, OXFORD

VOLUME V

PURITAN ENGLAND, 1603-1644

1879

CONTENTS

BOOK VI
 CHAPTER VII
THE ENGLAND OF SHAKSPERE. 1593-1603

BOOK VII
PURITAN ENGLAND. 1603-1660

CHAPTER I
ENGLAND AND PURITANISM. 1603-1660

CHAPTER II
THE KING OF SCOTS.

CHAPTER III
THE BREAK WITH THE PARLIAMENT. 1603-1611

CHAPTER IV
THE FAVOURITES. 1611-1625

CHAPTER V
CHARLES I. AND THE PARLIAMENT. 1625-1629

CHAPTER VI
THE PERSONAL GOVERNMENT. 1629-1635

CHAPTER VII
THE RISING OF THE SCOTS. 1635-1640

CHAPTER VIII
THE LONG PARLIAMENT. 1640-1644

CHAPTER VII

THE ENGLAND OF SHAKSPERE

1593-1603

English Literature.

The defeat of the Armada, the deliverance from Catholicism and Spain, marked the critical moment in our political developement. From that hour England's destiny was fixed. She was to be a Protestant power. Her sphere of action was to be upon the seas. She was to claim her part in the New World of the West. But the moment was as critical in her intellectual developement. As yet English literature had lagged behind the literature of the rest of Western Christendom. It was now to take its place among the greatest literatures of the world. The general awakening of national life, the increase of wealth, of refinement, and leisure that characterized the reign of Elizabeth, was accompanied by a quickening of intelligence. The Renascence had done little for English letters. The overpowering influence of the new models both of thought and style which it gave to the world in the writers of Greece and Rome was at first felt only as a fresh check to the revival of English poetry or prose. Though England shared more than any European country in the political and ecclesiastical results of the New Learning, its literary results were far less than in the rest of Europe, in Italy, or Germany, or France. More alone ranks among the great classical scholars of the sixteenth century. Classical learning indeed all but perished at the Universities in the storm of the Reformation, nor did it revive there till the close of Elizabeth's reign. Insensibly however the influences of the Renascence fertilized the intellectual soil of England for the rich harvest that was to come. The court poetry which clustered round Wyatt and Surrey, exotic and imitative as it was, promised a new life for English verse. The growth of grammar-schools realized the dream of Sir Thomas More, and brought the middle-classes, from the squire to the petty tradesman, into contact with the masters of Greece and Rome. The love of travel, which became so remarkable a characteristic of Elizabeth's age, quickened the temper of the wealthier nobles. "Home-keeping youths," says Shakspere in words that mark the time, "have ever homely wits"; and a tour over the Continent became part of the education of a gentleman. Fairfax's version of Tasso, Harrington's version of Ariosto, were signs of the influence which the literature of Italy, the land to which travel led most frequently, exerted on English minds. The classical writers told upon England at large when they were popularized by a crowd of translations. Chapman's noble version of Homer stands high above its fellows, but all the greater poets and historians of the ancient world were turned into English before the close of the sixteenth century.

Historic Literature.

It is characteristic of England that the first kind of literature to rise from its long death was the literature of history. But the form in which it rose marked the difference between the world in which it had perished and that in which it reappeared. During the Middle Ages the world had been without a past, save the shadowy and unknown past of early Rome; and annalist and chronicler told the story of the years which went before as a preface to their tale of the present without a sense of any difference between them. But the religious, social, and political change which passed over England under the New Monarchy broke the continuity of its life; and the depth of the rift between the two ages is seen by the way in which History passes on its revival under Elizabeth from the mediæval form of pure narrative to its modern form of an investigation and reconstruction of the past. The new interest which attached to the bygone world led to the collection of its annals, their reprinting and embodiment in an English shape. It was his desire to give the Elizabethan Church a basis in the past, as much as any pure zeal for letters, which induced Archbishop Parker to lead the way in the first of these labours. The collection of historical manuscripts which, following in the track of Leland, he rescued from the wreck of the monastic libraries created a school of antiquarian imitators, whose research and industry have preserved for us almost every work of permanent historical value which existed before the Dissolution of the Monasteries. To his publication of some of our earlier chronicles we owe the series of similar publications which bear the name of

Camden, Twysden, and Gale. But as a branch of literature, English History in the new shape which we have noted began in the work of the poet Daniel. The chronicles of Stowe and Speed, who preceded him, are simple records of the past, often copied almost literally from the annals they used, and utterly without style or arrangement; while Daniel, inaccurate and superficial as he is, gave his story a literary form and embodied it in a pure and graceful prose. Two larger works at the close of Elizabeth's reign, the "History of the Turks" by Knolles, and Raleigh's vast but unfinished plan of the "History of the World," showed a widening of historic interest beyond the merely national bounds to which it had hitherto been confined.

Euphuism.

A far higher developement of our literature sprang from the growing influence which Italy was exerting, partly through travel and partly through its poetry and romances, on the manners and taste of the time. Men made more account of a story of Boccaccio's, it was said, than of a story from the Bible. The dress, the speech, the manners of Italy became objects of almost passionate imitation, and of an imitation not always of the wisest or noblest kind. To Ascham it seemed like "the enchantment of Circe brought out of Italy to mar men's manners in England." "An Italianate Englishman," ran the harder proverb of Italy itself, "is an incarnate devil." The literary form which this imitation took seemed at any rate ridiculous. John Lyly, distinguished both as a dramatist and a poet, laid aside the tradition of English style for a style modelled on the decadence of Italian prose. Euphuism, as the new fashion has been named from the prose romance of Euphues which Lyly published in 1579, is best known to modern readers by the pitiless caricature in which Shakspere quizzed its pedantry, its affectation, the meaningless monotony of its far-fetched phrases, the absurdity of its extravagant conceits. Its representative, Armado in "Love's Labour's Lost," is "a man of fire-new words, fashion's own knight," "that hath a mint of phrases in his brain; one whom the music of his own vain tongue doth ravish like enchanting harmony." But its very extravagance sprang from the general burst of delight in the new resources of thought and language which literature felt to be at its disposal; and the new sense of literary beauty which it disclosed in its affectation, in its love of a "mint of phrases," and the "music of its own vain tongue," the new sense of pleasure which it revealed in delicacy or grandeur of expression, in the structure and arrangement of sentences, in what has been termed the atmosphere of words, was a sense out of which style was itself to spring.

Sidney.

For a time Euphuism had it all its own way. Elizabeth was the most affected and detestable of Euphuists; and "that beauty in Court which could not parley Euphuism," a courtier of Charles the First's time tells us, "was as little regarded as she that now there speaks not French." The fashion however passed away, but the "Arcadia" of Sir Philip Sidney shows the wonderful advance which prose had made under its influence. Sidney, the nephew of Lord Leicester, was the idol of his time, and perhaps no figure reflects the age more fully and more beautifully. Fair as he was brave, quick of wit as of affection, noble and generous in temper, dear to Elizabeth as to Spenser, the darling of the Court and of the camp, his learning and his genius made him the centre of the literary world which was springing into birth on English soil. He had travelled in France and Italy, he was master alike of the older learning and of the new discoveries of astronomy. Bruno dedicated to him as to a friend his metaphysical speculations; he was familiar with the drama of Spain, the poems of Ronsard, the sonnets of Italy. Sidney combined the wisdom of a grave councillor with the romantic chivalry of a knight-errant. "I never heard the old story of Percy and Douglas," he says, "that I found not my heart moved more than with a trumpet." He flung away his life to save the English army in Flanders, and as he lay dying they brought a cup of water to his fevered lips. He bade them give it to a soldier who was stretched on the ground beside him. "Thy necessity," he said, "is greater than mine." The whole of Sidney's nature, his chivalry and his learning, his thirst for adventures, his freshness of tone, his tenderness and childlike simplicity of heart, his affectation and false sentiment, his keen sense of pleasure and delight, pours itself out in the pastoral medley, forced, tedious, and yet strangely beautiful, of his "Arcadia." In his "Defence of Poetry" the youthful exuberance of the romancer has passed into the earnest vigour and grandiose stateliness of the rhetorician. But whether in the one work or the other, the flexibility, the music, the luminous clearness of Sidney's style remains the same.

The Novelists.

But the quickness and vivacity of English prose was first developed in a school of Italian imitators which appeared in Elizabeth's later years. The origin of English fiction is to be found in the tales and romances with which Greene and Nash crowded the market, models for which they found in the Italian novels. The brief form of these novelettes soon led to the appearance of the "pamphlet"; and a new world of readers was seen in the rapidity with which the stories or scurrilous libels that passed under this name were issued, and the greediness with which they were devoured. It was the boast of Greene that in the eight years before his death he had produced forty pamphlets. "In a night or a day would he have yarked up a pamphlet, as well as in seven years, and glad was that printer that might be blest to pay him dear for the very dregs of his wit." Modern eyes see less of the wit than of the dregs in the books of Greene and his compeers; but the attacks which Nash directed against the Puritans and his rivals were the first English works which shook utterly off the pedantry and extravagance of Euphuism. In his lightness, his facility, his vivacity, his directness of speech, we have the beginning of popular literature. It had descended from the closet to the street, and the very change implied that the street was ready to receive it. The abundance indeed of printers and of printed books at the close of the Queen's reign shows that the world of readers and writers had widened far beyond the small circle of scholars and courtiers with which it began.

Influence of the age.

But to the national and local influences which were telling on English literature was added that of the restlessness and curiosity which characterized the age. At the moment which we have reached the sphere of human interest was widened as it has never been widened before or since by the revelation of a new heaven and a new earth. It was only in the later years of the sixteenth century that the discoveries of Copernicus were brought home to the general intelligence of mankind by Kepler and Galileo, or that the daring of the Buccaneers broke through the veil which the greed of Spain had drawn across the New World of Columbus. Hardly inferior to these revelations as a source of intellectual impulse was the sudden and picturesque way in which the various races of the world were brought face to face with one another through the universal passion for foreign travel. While the red tribes of the West were described by Amerigo Vespucci, and the strange civilization of Mexico and Peru disclosed by Cortes and Pizarro, the voyages of the Portuguese threw open the older splendours of the East, and the story of India and China was told for the first time to Christendom by Maffei and Mendoza. England took her full part in this work of discovery. Jenkinson, an English traveller, made his way to Bokhara. Willoughby brought back Muscovy to the knowledge of Western Europe. English mariners penetrated among the Esquimaux, or settled in Virginia. Drake circumnavigated the globe. The "Collection of Voyages" which was published by Hakluyt in 1582 disclosed the vastness of the world itself, the infinite number of the races of mankind, the variety of their laws, their customs, their religions, their very instincts. We see the influence of this new and wider knowledge of the world, not only in the life and richness which it gave to the imagination of the time, but in the immense interest which from this moment attached itself to Man. Shakspere's conception of Caliban, like the questioning of Montaigne, marks the beginning of a new and a truer, because a more inductive, philosophy of human nature and human history. The fascination exercised by the study of human character showed itself in the essays of Bacon, and yet more in the wonderful popularity of the drama.

The new English temper.

And to these larger and world-wide sources of poetic power was added in England, at the moment which we have reached in its story, the impulse which sprang from national triumph, from the victory over the Armada, the deliverance from Spain, the rolling away of the Catholic terror which had hung like a cloud over the hopes of the new people. With its new sense of security, its new sense of national energy and national power, the whole aspect of

England suddenly changed. As yet the interest of Elizabeth's reign had been political and material; the stage had been crowded with statesmen and warriors, with Cecils and Walsinghams and Drakes. Literature had hardly found a place in the glories of the time. But from the moment when the Armada drifted back broken to Ferrol the figures of warriors and statesmen were dwarfed by the grander figures of poets and philosophers. Amidst the throng in Elizabeth's antechamber the noblest form is that of the singer who lays the "Faerie Queen" at her feet, or of the young lawyer who muses amid the splendours of the presence over the problems of the "Novum Organum." The triumph at Cadiz, the conquest of Ireland, pass unheeded as we watch Hooker building up his "Ecclesiastical Polity" among the sheepfolds, or the genius of Shakspere rising year by year into supremer grandeur in a rude theatre beside the Thames.

Spenser.

The glory of the new literature broke on England with Edmund Spenser. We know little of his life; he was born in 1552 in East London, the son of poor parents, but linked in blood with the Spencers of Althorpe, even then—as he proudly says—"a house of ancient fame." He studied as a sizar at Cambridge, and quitted the University while still a boy to live as a tutor in the north; but after some years of obscure poverty the scorn of a fair "Rosalind" drove him again southwards. A college friendship with Gabriel Harvey served to introduce him to Lord Leicester, who sent him as his envoy into France, and in whose service he first became acquainted with Leicester's nephew, Sir Philip Sidney. From Sidney's house at Penshurst came in 1579 his earliest work, the "Shepherd's Calendar"; in form, like Sidney's own "Arcadia," a pastoral where love and loyalty and Puritanism jostled oddly with the fancied shepherd life. The peculiar melody and profuse imagination which the pastoral disclosed at once placed its author in the forefront of living poets, but a far greater work was already in hand; and from some words of Gabriel Harvey's we see Spenser bent on rivalling Ariosto, and even hoping "to overgo" the "Orlando Furioso" in his "Elvish Queen." The ill-will or the indifference of Burleigh however blasted the expectations he had drawn from the patronage of Sidney or Leicester, and from the favour with which he had been welcomed by the Queen. Sidney, in disgrace with Elizabeth through his opposition to the marriage with Anjou, withdrew to Wilton to write the "Arcadia" by his sister's side; and "discontent of my long fruitless stay in princes' courts," the poet tells us, "and expectation vain of idle hopes" drove Spenser into exile. In 1580 he followed Lord Grey as his secretary into Ireland, and remained there on the Deputy's recall in the enjoyment of an office and a grant of land from the forfeited estates of the Earl of Desmond. Spenser had thus enrolled himself among the colonists to whom England was looking at the time for the regeneration of Munster, and the practical interest he took in the "barren soil where cold and want and poverty do grow" was shown by the later publication of a prose tractate on the condition and government of the island. It was at Dublin or in his castle of Kilcolman, two miles from Doneraile, "under the foot of Mole, that mountain hoar," that he spent the ten years in which Sidney died and Mary fell on the scaffold and the Armada came and went; and it was in the latter home that Walter Raleigh found him sitting "alwaies idle," as it seemed to his restless friend, "among the cooly shades of the green alders by the Mulla's shore" in a visit made memorable by the poem of "Colin Clout's come home again."

The Faerie Queen.

But in the "idlesse" and solitude of the poet's exile the great work begun in the two pleasant years of his stay at Penshurst had at last taken form, and it was to publish the first three books of the "Faerie Queen" that Spenser returned in Raleigh's company to London. The appearance of the "Faerie Queen" in 1590 is the one critical event in the annals of English poetry; it settled in fact the question whether there was to be such a thing as English poetry or no. The older national verse which had blossomed and died in Caedmon sprang suddenly into a grander life in Chaucer, but it closed again in a yet more complete death. Across the Border indeed the Scotch poets of the fifteenth century preserved something of their master's vivacity and colour, and in England itself the Italian poetry of the Renascence had of late found echoes in Surrey and Sidney. The new English drama too was beginning to display its wonderful powers, and the work of Marlowe had already prepared the way for the work of Shakspere. But bright as was the promise of coming song, no great imaginative poem had broken the silence of English literature for nearly two hundred years when Spenser landed at Bristol with the "Faerie Queen." From that moment the stream of English poetry has flowed on without a break. There have been times, as in the years which immediately followed, when England has "become a nest of singing birds"; there have been times when song was scant and poor; but there never has been a time when England was wholly without a singer.

The new English verse has been true to the source from which it sprang, and Spenser has always been "the poet's poet." But in his own day he was the poet of England at large. The "Faerie Queen" was received with a burst of general welcome. It became "the delight of every accomplished gentleman, the model of every poet, the solace of every soldier." The poem expressed indeed the very life of the time. It was with a true poetic instinct that Spenser fell back for the framework of his story on the faery world of Celtic romance, whose wonder and mystery had in fact become the truest picture of the wonder and mystery of the world around him. In the age of Cortes and of Raleigh dreamland had ceased to be dreamland, and no marvel or adventure that befell lady or knight was stranger than the tales which weather-beaten mariners from the Southern Seas were telling every day to grave merchants upon 'Change. The very incongruities of the story of Arthur and his knighthood, strangely as it had been built up out of the rival efforts of bard and jongleur and priest, made it the fittest vehicle for the expression of the world of incongruous feeling which we call the Renascence. To modern eyes perhaps there is something grotesque in the strange medley of figures that crowd the canvas of the "Faerie Queen," in its fauns dancing on the sward where knights have hurtled together, in its alternation of the salvage-men from the New World with the satyrs of classic mythology, in the giants, dwarfs, and monsters of popular fancy who jostle with the nymphs of Greek legend and the damosels of mediæval romance. But, strange as the medley is, it reflects truly enough the stranger medley of warring ideals and irreconcileable impulses which made up the life of Spenser's contemporaries. It was not in the "Faerie Queen" only, but in the world which it pourtrayed, that the religious mysticism of the Middle Ages stood face to face with the intellectual freedom of the Revival of Letters, that asceticism and self-denial cast their spell on imaginations glowing with the sense of varied and inexhaustible existence, that the dreamy and poetic refinement of feeling which expressed itself in the fanciful unrealities of chivalry co-existed with the rough practical energy that sprang from an awakening sense of human power, or the lawless extravagance of an idealized friendship and love lived side by side with the moral sternness and elevation which England was drawing from the Reformation and the Bible.

But strangely contrasted as are the elements of the poem, they are harmonized by the calmness and serenity which is the note of the "Faerie Queen." The world of the Renascence is around us, but it is ordered, refined, and calmed by the poet's touch. The warmest scenes which he borrows from the Italian verse of his day are idealized into purity; the very struggle of the men around him is lifted out of its pettier accidents and raised into a spiritual oneness with the struggle in the soul itself. There are allusions in plenty to contemporary events, but the contest between Elizabeth and Mary takes ideal form in that of Una and the false Duessa, and the clash of arms between Spain and the Huguenots comes to us faint and hushed through the serener air. The verse, like the story, rolls on as by its own natural power, without haste or effort or delay. The gorgeous colouring, the profuse and often complex imagery which Spenser's imagination lavishes, leave no sense of confusion in the reader's mind. Every figure, strange as it may be, is seen clearly and distinctly as it passes by. It is in this calmness, this serenity, this spiritual elevation of the "Faerie Queen," that we feel the new life of the coming age moulding into ordered and harmonious form the life of the Renascence. Both in its conception, and in the way in which this conception is realized in the portion of his work which Spenser completed, his poem strikes the note of the coming Puritanism. In his earlier pastoral, the "Shepherd's Calendar," the poet had boldly taken his part with the more advanced reformers against the Church policy of the Court. He had chosen Archbishop Grindal, who was then in disgrace for his Puritan sympathies, as his model of a Christian pastor; and attacked with sharp invective the pomp of the higher clergy. His "Faerie Queen" in its religious theory is Puritan to the core. The worst foe of its "Red-cross Knight" is the false and scarlet-clad Duessa of Rome, who parts him for a while from Truth and leads him to the house of Ignorance. Spenser presses strongly and pitilessly for the execution of Mary Stuart. No bitter word ever breaks the calm of his verse save when it touches on the perils with which Catholicism was environing England, perils before which his knight must fall "were not that Heavenly Grace doth him uphold and steadfast Truth acquite him out of all." But it is yet more in the temper and aim of his work that we catch the nobler and deeper tones of English Puritanism. In his earlier musings at Penshurst the poet had purposed to surpass Ariosto, but the gaiety of Ariosto's song is utterly absent from his own. Not a ripple of laughter breaks the calm surface of Spenser's verse. He is habitually serious, and the seriousness of his poetic tone reflects the seriousness of his poetic purpose. His aim, he tells us, was to represent the moral virtues, to assign to each its knightly patron, so that its excellence might be expressed and its contrary vice trodden under foot by deeds of arms and chivalry. In knight after knight of the twelve he purposed to paint, he wished to embody some single virtue of the virtuous man in its struggle with the faults and errors which specially beset it; till in Arthur, the sum of the whole company, man might have been seen perfected, in his longing and progress towards the "Faerie Queen," the Divine Glory which is the true end of human effort.

The largeness of his culture indeed, his exquisite sense of beauty, and above all the very intensity of his moral enthusiasm, saved Spenser from the narrowness and exaggeration which often distorted goodness into unloveliness in the Puritan. Christian as he is to the core, his Christianity is enriched and fertilized by the larger temper of the Renascence, as well as by a poet's love of the natural world in which the older mythologies struck their roots. Diana and the gods of heathendom take a sacred tinge from the purer sanctities of the new faith; and in one of the greatest songs of the "Faerie Queen" the conception of love widens, as it widened in the mind of a Greek, into the mighty thought of the productive energy of Nature. Spenser borrows in fact the delicate and refined forms of the Platonist philosophy to express his own moral enthusiasm. Not only does he love, as others have loved, all that is noble and pure and of good report, but he is fired as none before or after him have been fired with a passionate sense of moral beauty. Justice, Temperance, Truth, are no mere names to him, but real existences to which his whole nature clings with a rapturous affection. Outer beauty he believed to spring, and loved because it sprang, from the beauty of the soul within. There was much in such a moral protest as this to rouse dislike in any age, but it is the glory of the age of Elizabeth that, "mad world" as in many ways it was, all that was noble welcomed the "Faerie Queen." Elizabeth herself, says Spenser, "to mine oaten pipe inclined her ear," and bestowed a pension on the poet. In 1595 he brought three more books of his poem to England. He returned to Ireland to commemorate his marriage in Sonnets and the most beautiful of bridal songs, and to complete the "Faerie Queen" amongst love and poverty and troubles from his Irish neighbours. But these troubles soon took a graver form. In 1599 Ireland broke into revolt, and the poet escaped from his burning house to fly to England, and to die broken-hearted in an inn at Westminster.

The Drama.

If the "Faerie Queen" expressed the higher elements of the Elizabethan age, the whole of that age, its lower elements and its higher alike, was expressed in the English drama. We have already pointed out the circumstances which throughout Europe were giving a poetic impulse to the newly-aroused intelligence of men, and this impulse everywhere took a dramatic shape. The artificial French tragedy which began about this time with Garnier was not indeed destined to exert any influence over English poetry till a later age; but the influence of the Italian comedy, which had begun half a century earlier with Machiavelli and Ariosto, was felt directly through the Novelle, or stories, which served as plots for our dramatists. It left its stamp indeed on some of the worst characteristics of the English stage. The features of our drama that startled the moral temper of the time and won the deadly hatred of the Puritans, its grossness and profanity, its tendency to scenes of horror and crime, its profuse employment of cruelty and lust as grounds of dramatic action, its daring use of the horrible and the unnatural whenever they enable it to display the more terrible and revolting sides of human passion, were derived from the Italian stage. It is doubtful how much the English playwrights may have owed to the Spanish drama, which under Lope and Cervantes sprang suddenly into a grandeur that almost rivalled their own. In the intermixture of tragedy and comedy, in the abandonment of the solemn uniformity of poetic diction for the colloquial language of real life, the use of unexpected incidents, the complication of their plots and intrigues, the dramas of England and Spain are remarkably alike; but the likeness seems rather to have sprung from a similarity in the circumstances to which both owed their rise, than from any direct connexion of the one with the other. The real origin of the English drama, in fact, lay not in any influence from without but in the influence of England itself. The temper of the nation was dramatic. Ever since the Reformation, the Palace, the Inns of Court, and the University had been vying with one another in the production of plays; and so early was their popularity that even under Henry the Eighth it was found necessary to create a "Master of the Revels" to supervise them. Every progress of Elizabeth from shire to shire was a succession of shows and interludes. Dian with her nymphs met the Queen as she returned from hunting; Love presented her with his golden arrow as she passed through the gates of Norwich. From the earlier years of her reign the new spirit of the Renascence had been pouring itself into the rough mould of the Mystery Plays, whose allegorical virtues and vices, or scriptural heroes and heroines, had handed on the spirit of the drama through the Middle Ages. Adaptations from classical pieces began to alternate with the purely religious "Moralities"; and an attempt at a livelier style of expression and invention appeared in the popular comedy of "Gammer Gurton's Needle"; while Sackville, Lord Dorset, in his tragedy of "Gorbuduc" made a bold effort at sublimity of diction, and introduced the use of blank verse as the vehicle of dramatic dialogue.

The theatre and the people.

But it was not to these tentative efforts of scholars and nobles that the English stage was really indebted for the amazing outburst of genius which dates from the year 1576, when "the Earl of Leicester's servants" erected the first public theatre in Blackfriars. It was the people itself that created its Stage. The theatre indeed was commonly only the courtyard of an inn, or a mere booth such as is still seen at a country fair. The bulk of the audience sate beneath the open sky in the "pit" or yard; a few covered seats in the galleries which ran round it formed the boxes of the wealthier spectators, while patrons and nobles found seats upon the actual boards. All the appliances were of the roughest sort: a few flowers served to indicate a garden, crowds and armies were represented by a dozen scene-shifters with swords and bucklers, heroes rode in and out on hobby-horses, and a scroll on a post told whether the scene was at Athens or London. There were no female actors, and the grossness which startles us in words which fell from women's lips took a different colour when every woman's part was acted by a boy. But difficulties such as these were more than compensated by the popular character of the drama itself. Rude as the theatre might be, all the world was there. The stage was crowded with nobles and courtiers. Apprentices and citizens thronged the benches in the yard below. The rough mob of the pit inspired, as it felt, the vigorous life, the rapid transitions, the passionate energy, the reality, the lifelike medley and confusion, the racy dialogue, the chat, the wit, the pathos, the sublimity, the rant and buffoonery, the coarse horrors and vulgar bloodshedding, the immense range over all classes of society, the intimacy with the foulest as well as the fairest developements of human temper, which characterized the English stage. The new drama represented "the very age and body of the time, his form and pressure." The people itself brought its nobleness and its vileness to the boards. No stage was ever so human, no poetic life so intense. Wild, reckless, defiant of all past tradition, of all conventional laws, the English dramatists owned no teacher, no source of poetic inspiration, but the people itself.

The early dramatists.

Few events in our literary history are so startling as this sudden rise of the Elizabethan drama. The first public theatre was erected only in the middle of the Queen's reign. Before the close of it eighteen theatres existed in London alone. Fifty dramatic poets, many of the first order, appeared in the fifty years which precede the closing of the theatres by the Puritans; and great as is the number of their works which have perished, we still possess a hundred dramas, all written within this period, and of which at least a half are excellent. A glance at their authors shows us that the intellectual quickening of the age had now reached the mass of the people. Almost all of the new playwrights were fairly educated, and many were university men. But instead of courtly singers of the Sidney and Spenser sort we see the advent of the "poor scholar." The earlier dramatists, such as Nash, Peele, Kyd, Greene, or Marlowe, were for the most part poor, and reckless in their poverty; wild livers, defiant of law or common fame, in revolt against the usages and religion of their day, "atheists" in general repute, "holding Moses for a juggler," haunting the brothel and the alehouse, and dying starved or in tavern brawls. But with their appearance began the Elizabethan drama. The few plays which have reached us of an earlier date are either cold imitations of the classical and Italian comedy, or rude farces like "Ralph Roister Doister," or tragedies such as "Gorbuduc" where, poetic as occasional passages may be, there is little promise of dramatic developement. But in the year which preceded the coming of the Armada the whole aspect of the stage suddenly changes, and the new dramatists range themselves around two men of very different genius, Robert Greene and Christopher Marlowe.

Greene.

Of Greene, as the creator of our lighter English prose, we have already spoken. But his work as a poet was of yet greater importance, for his perception of character and the relations of social life, the playfulness of his fancy, and the liveliness of his style, exerted an influence on his contemporaries which was equalled by that of none but Marlowe and Peele. In spite of the rudeness of his plots and the unequal character of his work, Greene must be regarded as the creator of our modern comedy. No figure better paints the group of young playwrights. He left Cambridge to travel through Italy and Spain, and to bring back the debauchery of the one and the scepticism of the other. In the words of remorse he wrote before his death he paints himself as a drunkard and a roysterer, winning money only by ceaseless pamphlets and plays to waste it on wine and women, and drinking the cup of life to the dregs. Hell and the after-world were the butts of his ceaseless mockery. If he had not feared the judges of the Queen's Courts more than he feared God, he said in bitter jest, he should often have turned cutpurse. He married, and loved his wife, but she was soon deserted; and the wretched profligate found himself again plunged into excesses which he loathed, though he could not live without them. But wild as was the life of Greene, his pen was pure. He is steadily on virtue's side in the love pamphlets and novelettes he poured out in endless succession, and whose plots were dramatized by the school which gathered round him.

Marlowe.

The life of Marlowe was as riotous, his scepticism even more daring, than the life and scepticism of Greene. His early death alone saved him in all probability from a prosecution for atheism. He was charged with calling Moses a juggler, and with boasting that, if he undertook to write a new religion, it should be a better religion than the Christianity he saw around him. But he stood far ahead of his fellows as a creator of English tragedy. Born in 1564 at the opening of Elizabeth's reign, the son of a Canterbury shoemaker, but educated at Cambridge, Marlowe burst on the world in the year which preceded the triumph over the Armada with a play which at once wrought a revolution in the English stage. Bombastic and extravagant as it was, and extravagance reached its height in a scene where captive kings, the "pampered jades of Asia," drew their conqueror's car across the stage, "Tamburlaine" not only indicated the revolt of the new drama against the timid inanities of Euphuism, but gave an earnest of that imaginative daring, the secret of which Marlowe was to bequeath to the playwrights who followed him. He perished at thirty in a shameful brawl, but in his brief career he had struck the grander notes of the coming drama. His Jew of Malta was the herald of Shylock. He opened in "Edward the Second" the series of historical plays which gave us "Cæsar" and "Richard the Third." His "Faustus" is riotous, grotesque, and full of a mad thirst for pleasure, but it was the first dramatic attempt to touch the problem of the relations of man to the unseen world. Extravagant, unequal, stooping even to the ridiculous in his cumbrous and vulgar buffoonery, there is a force in Marlowe, a conscious grandeur of tone, a range of passion, which sets him above all his contemporaries save one. In the higher qualities of imagination, as in the majesty and sweetness of his "mighty line," he is inferior to Shakspere alone.

Shakspere.

A few daring jests, a brawl, and a fatal stab, make up the life of Marlowe; but even details such as these are wanting to the life of William Shakspere. Of hardly any great poet indeed do we know so little. For the story of his youth we have only one or two trifling legends, and these almost certainly false. Not a single letter or characteristic saying, not one of the jests "spoken at the Mermaid," hardly a single anecdote, remain to illustrate his busy life in London. His look and figure in later age have been preserved by the bust over his tomb at Stratford, and a hundred years after his death he was still remembered in his native town; but the minute diligence of the enquirers of the Georgian time was able to glean hardly a single detail, even of the most trivial order, which could throw light upon the years of retirement before his death. It is owing perhaps to the harmony and unity of his temper that no salient peculiarity seems to have left its trace on the memory of his contemporaries; it is the very grandeur of his genius which precludes us from discovering any personal trait in his works. His supposed self-revelation in the Sonnets is so obscure that only a few outlines can be traced even by the boldest conjecture. In his dramas he is all his characters, and his characters range over all mankind. There is not one, or the act or word of one, that we can identify personally with the poet himself.

His actor's life.

He was born in 1564, the sixth year of Elizabeth's reign, twelve years after the birth of Spenser, three years later than the birth of Bacon. Marlowe was of the same age with Shakspere: Greene probably a few years older. His father, a glover and small farmer of Stratford-on-Avon, was forced by poverty to lay down his office of alderman as his son reached boyhood; and stress of poverty may have been the cause which drove William Shakspere, who was already married at eighteen to a wife older than himself, to London and the stage. His life in the capital can hardly have begun later than in his twenty-third year, the memorable year which followed Sidney's death, which preceded the coming of the Armada, and which witnessed the production of Marlowe's "Tamburlaine." If we take the language of the Sonnets as a record of his personal feeling, his new profession as an actor stirred in him only the bitterness of self-contempt. He chides with Fortune "that did not better for my life provide than public means that public manners breed"; he writhes at the thought that he has "made himself a motley to the view" of the gaping apprentices in the pit of Blackfriars. "Thence comes it," he adds, "that my name receives a brand, and almost thence my nature is subdued to that it works in." But the application of the words is a more than doubtful one. In spite of petty squabbles with some of his dramatic rivals at the outset of his career, the genial nature of the newcomer seems to have won him a general love among his fellows. In 1592, while still a mere actor and fitter of old plays for the stage, a fellow-playwright, Chettle, answered Greene's attack on him in words of honest affection: "Myself have seen his demeanour no less civil than he excellent in the quality he professes: besides, divers of worship have reported his uprightness of dealing, which argues his honesty, and his facetious grace in writing, that approves his art." His partner Burbage spoke of him after death as a "worthy friend and fellow"; and Jonson handed down the general tradition of his time when he described him as "indeed honest, and of an open and free nature."

His early work.

His profession as an actor was at any rate of essential service to him in the poetic career which he soon undertook. Not only did it give him the sense of theatrical necessities which makes his plays so effective on the boards, but it enabled him to bring his pieces as he wrote them to the test of the stage. If there is any truth in Jonson's statement that Shakspere never blotted a line, there is no justice in the censure which it implies on his carelessness or incorrectness. The conditions of poetic publication were in fact wholly different from those of our own day. A drama remained for years in manuscript as an acting piece, subject to continual revision and amendment; and every rehearsal and representation afforded hints for change which we know the young poet was far from neglecting. The chance which has preserved an earlier edition of his "Hamlet" shows in what an unsparing way Shakspere could recast even the finest products of his genius. Five years after the supposed date of his arrival in London he was already famous as a dramatist. Greene speaks bitterly of him under the name of "Shakescene" as an "upstart crow beautified with our feathers," a sneer which points either to his celebrity as an actor or to his preparation for loftier flights by fitting pieces of his predecessors for the stage. He was soon partner in the theatre, actor, and playwright; and another nickname, that of "Johannes Factotum" or Jack-of-all-Trades, shows his readiness to take all honest work which came to hand.

His first plays.

With his publication in 1593 of the poem of "Venus and Adonis," "the first heir of my invention," as Shakspere calls it, the period of independent creation fairly began. The date of its publication was a very memorable one. The "Faerie Queen" had appeared only three years before, and had placed Spenser without a rival at the head of English poetry. On the other hand the two leading dramatists of the time passed at this moment suddenly away. Greene died in poverty and self-reproach in the house of a poor shoemaker. "Doll," he wrote to the wife he had abandoned, "I charge thee, by the love of our youth and by my soul's rest, that thou wilt see this man paid; for if he and his wife had not succoured me I had died in the streets." "Oh that a year were granted me to live," cried the young poet from his bed of death, "but I must die, of every man abhorred! Time, loosely spent, will not again be won! My time is loosely spent—and I undone!" A year later the death of Marlowe in a street brawl removed the only rival whose powers might have equalled Shakspere's own. He was now about thirty; and the twenty-three years which elapsed between the appearance of the "Adonis" and his death were filled with a series of masterpieces. Nothing is more characteristic of his genius than its incessant activity. Through the five years which followed the publication of his early poem he seems to have produced on an average two dramas a year. When we attempt however to trace the growth and progress of the poet's mind in the order of his plays we are met in the case of many of them by an absence of certain information as to the dates of their appearance. The facts on which enquiry has to build are extremely few. "Venus and Adonis," with the "Lucrece," must have been written before their publication in 1593-4; the Sonnets, though not published till 1609, were known in some form among his private friends as early as 1598. His earlier plays are defined by a list given in the "Wit's

Treasury" of Francis Meres in 1598, though the omission of a play from a casual catalogue of this kind would hardly warrant us in assuming its necessary non-existence at the time. The works ascribed to him at his death are fixed in the same approximate fashion through the edition published by his fellow-actors. Beyond these meagre facts and our knowledge of the publication of a few of his dramas in his lifetime all is uncertain; and the conclusions which have been drawn from these, and from the dramas themselves, as well as from assumed resemblances with, or references to, other plays of the period, can only be accepted as approximations to the truth.

His earlier comedies.

The bulk of his lighter comedies and historical dramas can be assigned with fair probability to a period from about 1593, when Shakspere was known as nothing more than an adapter, to 1598, when they are mentioned in the list of Meres. They bear on them indeed the stamp of youth. In "Love's Labour's Lost" the young playwright, fresh from his own Stratford, its "daisies pied and violets blue," with the gay bright music of its country ditties still in his ears, flings himself into the midst of the brilliant England which gathered round Elizabeth, busying himself as yet for the most part with the surface of it, with the humours and quixotisms, the wit and the whim, the unreality, the fantastic extravagance, which veiled its inner nobleness. Country-lad as he is, Shakspere shows himself master of it all; he can patter euphuism and exchange quip and repartee with the best; he is at home in their pedantries and affectations, their brag and their rhetoric, their passion for the fantastic and the marvellous. He can laugh as heartily at the romantic vagaries of the courtly world in which he finds himself as at the narrow dulness, the pompous triflings, of the country world which he has left behind him. But he laughs frankly and without malice; he sees the real grandeur of soul which underlies all this quixotry and word-play; and owns with a smile that when brought face to face with the facts of human life, with the suffering of man or the danger of England, these fops have in them the stuff of heroes. He shares the delight in existence, the pleasure in sheer living, which was so marked a feature of the age; he enjoys the mistakes, the contrasts, the adventures, of the men about him; his fun breaks almost riotously out in the practical jokes of the "Taming of the Shrew" and the endless blunderings of the "Comedy of Errors." In these earlier efforts his work had been marked by little poetic elevation, or by passion. But the easy grace of the dialogue, the dexterous management of a complicated story, the genial gaiety of his tone, and the music of his verse promised a master of social comedy as soon as Shakspere turned from the superficial aspects of the world about him to find a new delight in the character and actions of men. The interest of human character was still fresh and vivid; the sense of individuality drew a charm from its novelty; and poet and essayist were busy alike in sketching the "humours" of mankind. Shakspere sketched with his fellows. In the "Two Gentlemen of Verona" his painting of manners was suffused by a tenderness and ideal beauty which formed an effective protest against the hard though vigorous character-painting which the first success of Ben Jonson in "Every Man in his Humour" brought at the time into fashion. But quick on these lighter comedies followed two in which his genius started fully into life. His poetic power, held in reserve till now, showed itself with a splendid profusion in the brilliant fancies of the "Midsummer Night's Dream"; and passion swept like a tide of resistless delight through "Romeo and Juliet."

His historical plays.

Side by side however with these passionate dreams, these delicate imaginings and piquant sketches of manners, had been appearing during this short interval of intense activity a series of dramas which mark Shakspere's relation to the new sense of patriotism, the more vivid sense of national existence, national freedom, national greatness, which gives its grandeur to the age of Elizabeth. England itself was now becoming a source of literary interest to poet and prose-writer. Warner in his "Albion's England," Daniel in his "Civil Wars," embalmed in verse the record of her past; Drayton in his "Polyolbion" sang the fairness of the land itself, the "tracts, mountains, forests, and other parts of this renowned isle of Britain." The national pride took its highest poetic form in the historical drama. No plays seem to have been more popular from the earliest hours of the new stage than dramatic representations of our history.

Marlowe had shown in his "Edward the Second" what tragic grandeur could be reached in this favourite field; and, as we have seen, Shakspere had been led naturally towards it by his earlier occupation as an adapter of stock pieces like "Henry the Sixth" for the new requirements of the stage. He still to some extent followed in plan the older plays on the subjects he selected, but in his treatment of their themes he shook boldly off the yoke of the past. A larger and deeper conception of human character than any of the old dramatists had reached displayed itself in Richard the Third, in Falstaff, or in Hotspur; while in Constance and Richard the Second the pathos of human suffering was painted as even Marlowe had never dared to paint it.

His religious sympathies.

No dramas have done so much for Shakspere's enduring popularity with his countrymen as these historical plays. They have done more than all the works of English historians to nourish in the minds of Englishmen a love of and reverence for their country's past. When Chatham was asked where he had read his English history he answered, "In the plays of Shakspere." Nowhere could he have read it so well, for nowhere is the spirit of our history so nobly rendered. If the poet's work echoes sometimes our national prejudice and unfairness of temper, it is instinct throughout with English humour, with our English love of hard fighting, our English faith in goodness and in the doom that waits upon triumphant evil, our English pity for the fallen. Shakspere is Elizabethan to the core. He stood at the meeting-point of two great epochs of our history. The age of the Renascence was passing into the age of Puritanism. Rifts which were still little were widening every hour, and threatening ruin to the fabric of Church and State which the Tudors had built up. A new political world was rising into being; a world healthier, more really national, but less picturesque, less wrapt in the mystery and splendour that poets love. Great as were the faults of Puritanism, it may fairly claim to be the first political system which recognized the grandeur of the people as a whole. As great a change was passing over the spiritual sympathies of men. A sterner Protestantism was invigorating and ennobling life by its morality, its seriousness, its intense conviction of God. But it was at the same time hardening and narrowing it. The Bible was superseding Plutarch. The "obstinate questionings" which haunted the finer souls of the Renascence were being stereotyped into the theological formulas of the Puritan. The sense of a divine omnipotence was annihilating man. The daring which turned England into a people of "adventurers," the sense of inexhaustible resources, the buoyant freshness of youth, the intoxicating sense of beauty and joy, which created Sidney and Marlowe and Drake, were passing away before the consciousness of evil and the craving to order man's life aright before God.

From this new world of thought and feeling Shakspere stood aloof. Turn as others might to the speculations of theology, man and man's nature remained with him an inexhaustible subject of interest. Caliban was among his latest creations. It is impossible to discover whether his religious belief was Catholic or Protestant. It is hard indeed to say whether he had any religious belief or no. The religious phrases which are thinly scattered over his works are little more than expressions of a distant and imaginative reverence. But on the deeper grounds of religious faith his silence is significant. He is silent, and the doubt of Hamlet deepens his silence, about the afterworld. "To die," it may be, was to him as it was to Claudio, "to go we know not whither." Often as his questionings turn to the riddle of life and death he leaves it a riddle to the last without heeding the common theological solutions around him. "We are such stuff as dreams are made of, and our little life is rounded with a sleep."

His political sympathies.

Nor were the political sympathies of the poet those of the coming time. His roll of dramas is the epic of civil war. The Wars of the Roses fill his mind, as they filled the mind of his contemporaries. It is not till we follow him through the series of plays from "Richard the Second" to "Henry the Eighth" that we realize how profoundly the memory of the struggle between York and Lancaster had moulded the temper of the people, how deep a dread of civil war, of baronial turbulence, of disputes over the succession to the throne, it had left behind it. Men had learned the horrors of the time from their fathers; they had drunk in with their childhood the lesson that such a chaos of weakness and misrule must never be risked again. From such a risk the Crown seemed the one security. With Shakspere as with his fellow-countrymen the Crown is still the centre and safeguard of the national life. His ideal England is an England grouped around a noble king, a king such as his own Henry the Fifth, devout, modest, simple as he is brave, but a lord in battle, a born ruler of men, with a loyal people about him and his enemies at his feet. Socially the poet reflects the aristocratic view of social life which was shared by all the nobler spirits of the Elizabethan time. Coriolanus is the embodiment of a great noble; and the taunts which Shakspere hurls in play after play at the rabble only echo the general temper of the Renascence. But he shows no sympathy with the struggle of feudalism against the Crown. If he paints Hotspur with a fire which proves how thoroughly he could sympathize with the rough, bold temper of the baronage, he suffers him to fall unpitied before Henry the Fourth. Apart however from the strength and justice of its rule, royalty has no charm for him. He knows nothing of the "right divine of kings to govern wrong" which became the doctrine of prelates and courtiers in the age of the Stuarts. He shows in his "Richard the Second" the doom that waits on a lawless despotism, as he denounces in his "Richard the Third" the selfish and merciless ambition that severs a ruler from his people. But the dread of misrule was a dim and distant one. Shakspere had grown up under the reign of Elizabeth; he had known no ruler save one who had cast a spell over the hearts of Englishmen. His thoughts were absorbed, as those of the country were absorbed, in the struggle for national existence which centred round the Queen. "King John" is a trumpet-call to rally round Elizabeth in her fight for England. Again a Pope was asserting his right to depose an English sovereign and to loose Englishmen from their bond of allegiance. Again political ambitions and civil discord woke at the call of religious war. Again a foreign power was threatening England at the summons of Rome, and hoping to master her with the aid of revolted Englishmen. The heat of such a struggle as this left no time for the thought of civil liberties. Shakspere casts aside the thought of the Charter to fix himself on the strife of the stranger for England itself. What he sang was the duty of patriotism, the grandeur of loyalty, the freedom of England from Pope or Spaniard, its safety within its "water-walled bulwark," if only its national union was secure. And now that the nation was at one, now that he had seen in his first years of London life Catholics as well as Protestants trooping to the muster at Tilbury and hasting down Thames to the fight in the Channel, he could thrill his hearers with the proud words that sum up the work of Elizabeth:—

> "This England never did, nor never shall
> Lie at the proud foot of a conqueror,
> But when it first did help to wound itself.
> Now that her princes are come home again,
> Come the three corners of the world in arms,
> And we shall shock them! Nought shall make us rue
> If England to itself do rest but true."

Shakspere's prosperity.

With this great series of historical and social dramas Shakspere had passed far beyond his fellows whether as a tragedian or as a writer of comedy. "The Muses," said Meres in 1598, "would speak with Shakspere's fine-filed phrase, if they would speak English." His personal popularity was now at its height. His pleasant temper and the vivacity of his wit had drawn him early into contact with the young Earl of Southampton, to whom his "Adonis" and "Lucrece" are dedicated; and the different tone of the two dedications shows how rapidly acquaintance ripened into an ardent friendship. Shakspere's wealth and influence too were growing fast. He had property both in Stratford and London, and his fellow-townsmen made him their suitor to Lord Burleigh for favours to be bestowed on Stratford. He was rich enough to aid his father, and to buy the house at Stratford which afterwards became his home. The tradition that Elizabeth was so pleased with Falstaff in "Henry the Fourth" that she ordered the poet to show her Falstaff in love—an order which produced the "Merry Wives of Windsor"—whether true or false, proves his repute as a playwright. As the group of earlier poets passed away, they found successors in Marston, Dekker, Middleton, Heywood, and Chapman, and above all in Ben Jonson. But none of these could dispute the supremacy of Shakspere. The verdict of Meres that "Shakspere among the English is the most excellent in both kinds for the stage," represented the general feeling of his contemporaries. He was at last fully master of the resources of his art. The "Merchant of Venice" marks the perfection of his developement as a dramatist in the completeness of its stage effect, the ingenuity of its incidents, the ease of its movement, the beauty of its higher passages, the reserve and self-control with which its poetry is used, the conception and unfolding of character, and above all the mastery with which character and event are grouped round the figure of Shylock. Master as he is of his art, the poet's temper is still young; the "Merry Wives of Windsor" is a burst of gay laughter; and laughter more tempered, yet full of a sweeter fascination, rings round us in "As You Like It."

His gloom.

But in the melancholy and meditative Jaques of the last drama we feel the touch of a new and graver mood. Youth, so full and buoyant in the poet till now, seems to have passed almost suddenly away. Though Shakspere had hardly reached forty, in one of his Sonnets which cannot have been written at a much later time than this there are indications that he already felt the advance of premature age. And at this moment the outer world suddenly darkened around him. The brilliant circle of young nobles whose friendship he had shared was broken up in 1601 by the political storm which burst in a mad struggle of the Earl of Essex for power. Essex himself fell on the scaffold; his friend and Shakspere's idol, Southampton, passed a prisoner into the Tower; Herbert Lord Pembroke, a younger patron of the poet, was banished from the Court. While friends were thus falling and hopes fading without, Shakspere's own mind seems to have been going through a phase of bitter suffering and unrest. In spite of the ingenuity of commentators, it is difficult and even impossible to derive any knowledge of Shakspere's inner history from the Sonnets; "the strange imagery of passion which passes over the magic mirror," it has been finely said, "has no tangible evidence before or behind it." But its mere passing is itself an evidence of the restlessness and agony within. The change in the character of his dramas gives a surer indication of his change of mood. The fresh joyousness, the keen delight in life and in man, which breathes through Shakspere's early work disappears in comedies such as "Troilus" and "Measure for Measure." Disappointment, disillusion, a new sense of the evil and foulness that underlie so much of human life, a loss of the old frank trust in its beauty and goodness, threw their gloom over these comedies. Failure seems everywhere. In "Julius Cæsar" the virtue of Brutus is foiled by its ignorance of and isolation from mankind; in Hamlet even penetrating intellect proves helpless for want of the capacity of action; the poison of Iago taints the love of Desdemona and the grandeur of Othello; Lear's mighty passion battles helplessly against the wind and the rain; a woman's weakness of frame dashes the cup of her triumph from the hand of Lady Macbeth; lust and self-indulgence blast the heroism of Antony; pride ruins the nobleness of Coriolanus.

His passion plays.

But the very struggle and self-introspection that these dramas betray were to give a depth and grandeur to Shakspere's work such as it had never known before. The age was one in which man's temper and powers took a new range and energy. Sidney or Raleigh lived not one but a dozen lives at once; the daring of the adventurer, the philosophy of the scholar, the passion of the lover, the fanaticism of the saint, towered into almost superhuman grandeur. Man became conscious of the immense resources that lay within him, conscious of boundless powers that seemed to mock the narrow world in which they moved. All through the age of the Renascence one feels this impress of the gigantic, this giant-like activity, this immense ambition and desire. The very bombast and extravagance of the times reveal cravings and impulses before which common speech broke down. It is this grandeur of humanity that finds its poetic expression in the later work of Shakspere. As the poet penetrated deeper and deeper into the recesses of the soul, he saw how great and wondrous a thing was man. "What a piece of work is a man," cries Hamlet; "how noble in reason; how infinite in faculty; in form and moving how express and admirable; in action how like an angel; in apprehension how like a god; the beauty of the world; the paragon of animals!" It is the wonder of man that spreads before us as the poet pictures the wide speculation of Hamlet, the awful convulsion of a great nature in Othello, the terrible storm in the soul of Lear which blends with the very storm of the heavens themselves, the awful ambition that nerved a woman's hand to dabble itself with the blood of a murdered king, the reckless lust that "flung away a world for love." Amid the terror and awe of these great dramas we learn something of the vast forces of the age from which they sprang. The passion of Mary Stuart, the ruthlessness of Alva, the daring of Drake, the chivalry of Sidney, the range of thought and action in Raleigh or Elizabeth, come better home to us as we follow the mighty series of tragedies which began in "Hamlet" and ended in "Coriolanus."

Bacon.

Shakspere's last dramas, the three exquisite works in which he shows a soul at rest with itself and with the world, "Cymbeline," "The Tempest," "Winter's Tale," were written in the midst of ease and competence, in a house at Stratford to which he withdrew a few years after the death of Elizabeth. In them we lose all relation with the world or the time and pass into a region of pure poetry. It is in this peaceful and gracious close that the life of Shakspere contrasts most vividly with that of his greatest contemporary. If the imaginative resources of the new England were seen in the creators of Hamlet and the Faerie Queen, its purely intellectual capacity, its vast command over the stores of human knowledge, the amazing sense of its own powers with which it dealt with them, were seen in the work of Francis Bacon. Bacon was born in 1561, three years before the birth of Shakspere. He was the younger son of a Lord Keeper, as well as the nephew of Lord Burleigh, and even in childhood his quickness and sagacity won the favour of the Queen. Elizabeth "delighted much to confer with him, and to prove him with questions: unto which he delivered himself with that gravity and maturity above his years that her Majesty would often term him 'the young Lord Keeper.'" Even as a boy at college he expressed his dislike of the Aristotelian philosophy, as "a philosophy only strong for disputations and contentions but barren of the production of works for the benefit of the life of man." As a law student of twenty-one he sketched in a tract on the "Greatest Birth of Time" the system of inductive enquiry which he was already prepared to substitute for it. The speculations of the young thinker however were interrupted by his hopes of Court success. But these were soon dashed to the ground. He was left poor by his father's death; the ill-will of the Cecils barred his advancement with the Queen: and a few years before Shakspere's arrival in London Bacon entered as a barrister at Gray's Inn. He soon became one of the most successful lawyers of the time. At twenty-three Bacon was a member of the House of Commons, and his judgement and eloquence at once brought him to the front. "The fear of every man that heard him was lest he should make an end," Ben Jonson tells us. The steady growth of his reputation was quickened in 1597 by the appearance of his "Essays," a work remarkable, not merely for the condensation of its thought and its felicity and exactness of expression, but for the power with which it applied to human life that experimental analysis which Bacon was at a later time to make the key of Science.

His fame at once became great at home and abroad, but with this nobler fame Bacon could not content himself. He was conscious of great powers as well as great aims for the public good: and it was a time when such aims could hardly be realized save through the means of the Crown. But political employment seemed farther off than ever. At the outset of his career in Parliament he irritated Elizabeth by a firm opposition to her demand of a subsidy; and though the offence was atoned for by profuse apologies and by the cessation of all further resistance to the policy of the Court, the law offices of the Crown were more than once refused to him, and it was only after the publication of his "Essays" that he could obtain some slight promotion as a Queen's Counsel. The moral weakness which more and more disclosed itself is the best justification of the Queen in her reluctance—a reluctance so greatly in contrast with her ordinary course—to bring the wisest head in her realm to her Council-board. The men whom Elizabeth employed were for the most part men whose intellect was directed by a strong sense of public duty. Their reverence for the Queen, strangely exaggerated as it may seem to us, was guided and controlled by an ardent patriotism and an earnest sense of religion; and with all their regard for the royal prerogative, they never lost their regard for the law. The grandeur and originality of Bacon's intellect parted him from men like these quite as much as the bluntness of his moral perceptions. In politics, as in science, he had little reverence for the past. Law, constitutional privileges, or religion, were to him simply means of bringing about certain ends of good government; and if these ends could be brought about in shorter fashion he saw only pedantry in insisting on more cumbrous means. He had great social and political ideas to realize, the reform and codification of the law, the civilization of Ireland, the purification of the Church, the union—at a later time—of Scotland and England, educational projects, projects of material improvement, and the like; and the direct and shortest way of realizing these ends was, in Bacon's eyes, the use of the power of the Crown. But whatever charm such a conception of the royal power might have for her successor, it had little charm for Elizabeth; and to the end of her reign Bacon was foiled in his efforts to rise in her service.

The Novum Organum.

Political activity however and Court intrigue left room in his mind for the philosophical speculation which had begun with his earliest years. Amidst debates in Parliament and flatteries in the closet Bacon had been silently framing a new philosophy. It made its first decisive appearance after the final disappointment of his hopes from Elizabeth in the publication of the "Advancement of Learning." The close of this work was, in his own words, "a general and faithful perambulation of learning, with an enquiry what parts thereof lie fresh and waste and not improved and converted by the industry of man; to the end that such a plot, made and recorded to memory, may both minister light to any public designation and also serve to excite voluntary endeavours." It was only by such a survey, he held, that men could be turned from useless studies, or ineffectual means of pursuing more useful ones, and directed to the true end of knowledge as "a rich storehouse for the glory of the Creator and the relief of man's estate." The work was in fact the preface to a series of treatises which were intended to be built up into an "Instauratio Magna," which its author was never destined to complete, and of which the parts that we possess were published in the following reign. The "Cogitata et Visa" was a first sketch of the "Novum Organum," which in its complete form was presented to James in 1621. A year later Bacon produced his "Natural and Experimental History." This, with the "Novum Organum" and the "Advancement of Learning," was all of his projected "Instauratio Magna" which he actually finished; and even of this portion we have only part of the last two divisions. The "Ladder of the Understanding," which was to have followed these and led up from experience to science, the "Anticipations," or provisional hypotheses for the enquiries of the new philosophy, and the closing account of "Science in Practice" were left for posterity to bring to completion. "We may, as we trust," said Bacon, "make no despicable beginnings. The destinies of the human race must complete it, in such a manner perhaps as men looking only at the present world would not readily conceive. For upon this will depend, not only a speculative good, but all the fortunes of mankind, and all their power."

When we turn from words like these to the actual work which Bacon did, it is hard not to feel a certain disappointment. He did not thoroughly understand the older philosophy which he attacked. His revolt from the waste of human intelligence which he conceived to be owing to the adoption of a false method of investigation blinded him to the real value of deduction as an instrument of discovery; and he was encouraged in his contempt for it as much by his own ignorance of mathematics as by the non-existence in his day of the great deductive sciences of physics and astronomy. Nor had he a more accurate prevision of the method of modern science. The inductive process to which he exclusively directed men's attention bore no fruit in Bacon's hands. The "art of investigating nature" on which he prided himself has proved useless for scientific purposes, and would be rejected by modern investigators. Where he was on a more correct track he can hardly be regarded as original. "It may be doubted," says Dugald Stewart, "whether any one important rule with regard to the true method of investigation be contained in his works of which no hint can be traced in those of his predecessors." Not only indeed did Bacon fail to anticipate the methods of modern science, but he even rejected the great scientific discoveries of his own day. He set aside with the same scorn the astronomical theory of Copernicus and the magnetic investigations of Gilbert. The contempt seems to have been fully returned by the scientific workers of his day. "The Lord Chancellor wrote on science," said Harvey, the discoverer of the circulation of the blood, "like a Lord Chancellor."

In spite however of his inadequate appreciation either of the old philosophy or the new, the almost unanimous voice of later ages has attributed, and justly attributed, to the "Novum Organum" a decisive influence on the developement of modern science. If he failed in revealing the method of experimental research, Bacon was the first to proclaim the existence of a Philosophy of Science, to insist on the unity of knowledge and enquiry throughout the physical world, to give dignity by the large and noble temper in which he treated them to the petty details of experiment in which science had to begin, to clear a way for it by setting scornfully aside the traditions of the past, to claim for it its true rank and value, and to point to the enormous results which its culture would bring in increasing the power and happiness of mankind. In one respect his attitude was in the highest degree significant. The age in which he lived was one in which theology was absorbing the intellectual energy of the world. He was the servant too of a king with whom theological studies superseded all others. But if he bowed in all else to James, Bacon would not, like Casaubon, bow in this. He would not even, like Descartes, attempt to transform theology by turning reason into a mode of theological demonstration. He stood absolutely aloof from it. Though as a politician he did not shrink from dealing with such subjects as Church Reform, he dealt with them simply as matters of civil polity. But from his exhaustive enumeration of the branches of human knowledge he excluded theology, and theology alone. His method was of itself inapplicable to a subject where the premisses were assumed to be certain, and the results known. His aim was to seek for unknown results by simple experiment. It was against received authority and accepted tradition in matters of enquiry that his whole system protested; what he urged was the need of making belief rest strictly on proof, and proof rest on the conclusions drawn from evidence by reason. But in theology—all theologians asserted—reason played but a subordinate part. "If I proceed to treat of it," said Bacon, "I shall step out of the bark of human reason, and enter into the ship of the Church. Neither will the stars of philosophy, which have hitherto so nobly shone on us, any longer give us their light."

The certainty indeed of conclusions on such subjects was out of harmony with the grandest feature of Bacon's work, his noble confession of the liability of every enquirer to error. It was his especial task to warn men against the "vain shows" of knowledge which had so long hindered any real advance in it, the "idols" of the

Tribe, the Den, the Forum, and the Theatre, the errors which spring from the systematizing spirit which pervades all masses of men, or from individual idiosyncrasies, or from the strange power of words and phrases over the mind, or from the traditions of the past. Nor were the claims of theology easily to be reconciled with the position which he was resolute to assign to natural science. "Through all those ages," Bacon says, "wherein men of genius or learning principally or even moderately flourished, the smallest part of human industry has been spent on natural philosophy, though this ought to be esteemed as the great mother of the sciences; for all the rest, if torn from this root, may perhaps be polished and formed for use, but can receive little increase." It was by the adoption of the method of inductive enquiry which physical science was to make its own, and by basing enquiry on grounds which physical science could supply, that the moral sciences, ethics and politics, could alone make any real advance. "Let none expect any great promotion of the sciences, especially in their effective part, unless natural philosophy be drawn out to particular sciences; and, again, unless these particular sciences be brought back again to natural philosophy. From this defect it is that astronomy, optics, music, many mechanical arts, and (what seems stranger) even moral and civil philosophy and logic rise but little above the foundations, and only skim over the varieties and surfaces of things." It was this lofty conception of the position and destiny of natural science which Bacon was the first to impress upon mankind at large. The age was one in which knowledge was passing to fields of enquiry which had till then been unknown, in which Kepler and Galileo were creating modern astronomy, in which Descartes was revealing the laws of motion, and Harvey the circulation of the blood. But to the mass of men this great change was all but imperceptible; and it was the energy, the profound conviction, the eloquence of Bacon which first called the attention of mankind as a whole to the power and importance of physical research. It was he who by his lofty faith in the results and victories of the new philosophy nerved its followers to a zeal and confidence equal to his own. It was he above all who gave dignity to the slow and patient processes of investigation, of experiment, of comparison, to the sacrifice of hypothesis to fact, to the single aim after truth, which was to be the law of modern science.

Advance of the Parliament.

While England thus became "a nest of singing birds," while Bacon was raising the lofty fabric of his philosophical speculation, the people itself was waking to a new sense of national freedom. Elizabeth saw the forces, political and religious, which she had stubbornly held in check for half a century pressing on her irresistibly. In spite of the rarity of its assemblings, in spite of high words and imprisonment and dexterous management, the Parliament had quietly gained a power which, at her accession, the Queen could never have dreamed of its possessing. Step by step the Lower House had won the freedom of its members from arrest save by its own permission, the right of punishing and expelling members for crimes committed within its walls, and of determining all matters relating to elections. The more important claim of freedom of speech had brought on from time to time a series of petty conflicts in which Elizabeth generally gave way. But on this point the Commons still shrank from any consistent repudiation of the Queen's assumption of control. A bold protest of Peter Wentworth against her claim to exercise such a control in 1575 was met indeed by the House itself with his committal to the Tower; and the bolder questions which he addressed to the Parliament of 1588, "Whether this Council is not a place for every member of the same freely and without control, by bill or speech, to utter any of the griefs of the Commonwealth," brought on him a fresh imprisonment at the hands of the Council, which lasted till the dissolution of the Parliament and with which the Commons declined to interfere. But while vacillating in its assertion of the rights of individual members, the House steadily claimed for itself a right to discuss even the highest matters of State. Three great subjects, the succession, the Church, and the regulation of trade, had been regarded by every Tudor sovereign as lying exclusively within the competence of the Crown. But Parliament had again and again asserted its right to consider the succession. It persisted in spite of censure and rebuff in presenting schemes of ecclesiastical reform. And three years before Elizabeth's death it dealt boldly with matters of trade. Complaints made in 1571 of the licences and monopolies by which internal and external commerce was fettered were repressed by a royal reprimand as matters neither pertaining to the Commons nor within the compass of their understanding. When the subject was again stirred nearly twenty years afterwards, Sir Edward Hoby was sharply rebuked by "a great personage" for his complaint of the illegal exactions made by the Exchequer. But the bill which he promoted was sent up to the Lords in spite of this, and at the close of Elizabeth's reign the storm of popular indignation which had been roused by the growing grievance nerved the Commons, in 1601, to a decisive struggle. It was in vain that the ministers opposed a bill for the Abolition of Monopolies, and after four days of vehement debate the tact of Elizabeth taught her to give way. She acted with her usual ability, declared her previous ignorance of the existence of the evil, thanked the House for its interference, and quashed at a single blow every monopoly that she had granted.

Growth of Puritanism.

Dexterous as was Elizabeth's retreat, the defeat was none the less a real one. Political freedom was proving itself again the master in the long struggle with the Crown. Nor in her yet fiercer struggle against religious freedom could Elizabeth look forward to any greater success. The sharp suppression of the Martin Marprelate pamphlets was far from damping the courage of the Presbyterians. Cartwright, who had been appointed by Lord Leicester to the mastership of an hospital at Warwick, was bold enough to organize his system of Church discipline among the clergy of that county and of Northamptonshire. His example was widely followed; and the general gatherings of the whole ministerial body of the clergy and the smaller assemblies for each diocese or shire, which in the Presbyterian scheme bore the name of Synods and Classes, began to be held in many parts of England for the purposes of debate and consultation. The new organization was quickly suppressed, but Cartwright was saved from the banishment which Whitgift demanded by a promise of submission, and his influence steadily widened. With Presbyterianism itself indeed Elizabeth was strong enough to deal. Its dogmatism and bigotry were opposed to the better temper of the age, and it never took any popular hold on England. But if Presbyterianism was limited to a few, Puritanism, the religious temper which sprang from a deep conviction of the truth of Protestant doctrines and of the falsehood of Catholicism, had become through the struggle with Spain and the Papacy the temper of three-fourths of the English people. Unluckily the policy of Elizabeth did its best to give to the Presbyterians the support of Puritanism. Her establishment of the Ecclesiastical Commission had given fresh life and popularity to the doctrines which it aimed at crushing by drawing together two currents of opinion which were in themselves perfectly distinct. The Presbyterian platform of Church discipline had as yet been embraced by the clergy only, and by few among the clergy. On the other hand, the wish for a reform in the Liturgy, the dislike of "superstitious usages," of the use of the surplice, the sign of the cross in baptism, the gift of the ring in marriage, the posture of kneeling at the Lord's Supper, was shared by a large number of the clergy and the laity alike. At the opening of Elizabeth's reign almost all the higher Churchmen save Parker were opposed to them, and a motion for their abolition in Convocation was lost but by a single vote. The temper of the country gentlemen on this subject was indicated by that of Parliament; and it was well known that the wisest of the Queen's Councillors, Burleigh, Walsingham, and Knollys, were at one in this matter with the gentry. If their common persecution did not wholly succeed in fusing these two sections of religious opinion into one, it at any rate gained for the Presbyterians a general sympathy on the part of the Puritans, which raised them from a clerical clique into a popular party.

Philip and Ireland.

But if Elizabeth's task became more difficult at home, the last years of her reign were years of splendour and triumph abroad. The overthrow of Philip's hopes in France had been made more bitter by the final overthrow of his hopes at sea. In 1596 his threat of a fresh Armada was met by the daring descent of an English force upon Cadiz. The town was plundered and burned to the ground; thirteen vessels of war were fired in its harbour, and the stores accumulated for the expedition utterly destroyed. In spite of this crushing blow a Spanish fleet gathered in the following year and set sail for the English coast; but as in the case of its predecessor storms proved more fatal than the English guns, and the ships were wrecked and almost destroyed in the Bay of Biscay. Meanwhile whatever hopes remained of subjecting the Low Countries were destroyed by the triumph of Henry of Navarre. A triple league of France, England,

and the Netherlands left Elizabeth secure to the eastward; and the only quarter in which Philip could now strike a blow at her was the great dependency of England in the west. Since the failure of the Spanish force at Smerwick the power of the English government had been recognized everywhere throughout Ireland. But it was a power founded solely on terror, and the outrages and exactions of the soldiery who had been flushed with rapine and bloodshed in the south sowed during the years which followed the reduction of Munster the seeds of a revolt more formidable than any which Elizabeth had yet encountered. The tribes of Ulster, divided by the policy of Sidney, were again united by a common hatred of their oppressors; and in Hugh O'Neill they found a leader of even greater ability than Shane himself. Hugh had been brought up at the English court and was in manners and bearing an Englishman. He had been rewarded for his steady loyalty in previous contests by a grant of the earldom of Tyrone, and in his contest with a rival chieftain of his clan he had secured aid from the government by an offer to introduce the English laws and shire-system into his new country. But he was no sooner undisputed master of the north than his tone gradually changed. Whether from a long-formed plan, or from suspicion of English designs upon himself, he at last took a position of open defiance.

Revolt of Ulster.

It was at the moment when the Treaty of Vervins and the wreck of the second Armada freed Elizabeth's hands from the struggle with Spain that the revolt under Hugh O'Neill broke the quiet which had prevailed since the victories of Lord Grey. The Irish question again became the chief trouble of the Queen. The tide of her recent triumphs seemed at first to have turned. A defeat of the English forces in Tyrone caused a general rising of the northern tribes, and a great effort made in 1599 for the suppression of the growing revolt failed through the vanity and disobedience, if not the treacherous complicity, of the Queen's lieutenant, the young Earl of Essex. His successor, Lord Mountjoy, found himself master on his arrival of only a few miles round Dublin. But in three years the revolt was at an end. A Spanish force which landed to support it at Kinsale was driven to surrender; a line of forts secured the country as the English mastered it; all open opposition was crushed out by the energy and the ruthlessness of the new Lieutenant; and a famine which followed on his ravages completed the devastating work of the sword. Hugh O'Neill was brought in triumph to Dublin; the Earl of Desmond, who had again roused Munster into revolt, fled for refuge to Spain; and the work of conquest was at last brought to a close.

The last years of Elizabeth.

The triumph of Mountjoy flung its lustre over the last days of Elizabeth, but no outer triumph could break the gloom which gathered round the dying Queen. Lonely as she had always been, her loneliness deepened as she drew towards the grave. The statesmen and warriors of her earlier days had dropped one by one from her Council-board. Leicester had died in the year of the Armada; two years later Walsingham followed him to the grave; in 1598 Burleigh himself passed away. Their successors were watching her last moments, and intriguing for favour in the coming reign. Her favourite, Lord Essex, not only courted favour with James of Scotland, but brought him to suspect Robert Cecil, who had succeeded his father at the Queen's Council-board, of designs against his succession. The rivalry between the two ministers hurried Essex into fatal projects which led to his failure in Ireland and to an insane outbreak of revolt which brought him in 1601 to the block. But Cecil had no sooner proved the victor in this struggle at Court than he himself entered into a secret correspondence with the king of Scots. His action was wise: it brought James again into friendly relations with the Queen; and paved the way for a peaceful transfer of the crown. But hidden as this correspondence was from Elizabeth, the suspicion of it only added to her distrust. The troubles of the war in Ireland brought fresh cares to the aged Queen. It drained her treasury. The old splendour of her Court waned and disappeared. Only officials remained about her, "the other of the Council and nobility estrange themselves by all occasions." The love and reverence of the people itself lessened as they felt the pressure and taxation of the war. Of old men had pressed to see the Queen as if it were a glimpse of heaven. "In the year 1588," a bishop tells us, who was then a country boy fresh come to town, "I did live at the upper end of the Strand near St. Clement's church, when suddenly there came a report to us (it was in December, much about five of the clock at night, very dark) that the Queen was gone to Council, 'and if you will see the Queen you must come quickly.' Then we all ran, when the Court gates were set open, and no man did hinder us from coming in. There we came, where there was a far greater company than was usually at Lenten sermons; and when we had staid there an hour and that the yard was full, there being a number of torches, the Queen came out in great state. Then we cried, 'God save your Majesty! God save your Majesty!' Then the Queen turned to us and said, 'God bless you all, my good people!' Then we cried again, 'God bless your Majesty! God bless your Majesty!' Then the Queen said again to us, 'You may well have a greater prince, but you shall never have a more loving prince.' And so looking one upon another a while the Queen departed. This wrought such an impression on us, for shows and pageantry are ever best seen by torchlight, that all the way long we did nothing but talk what an admirable Queen she was, and how we would adventure our lives to do her service." But now, as Elizabeth passed along in her progresses, the people whose applause she courted remained cold and silent. The temper of the age in fact was changing, and isolating her as it changed. Her own England, the England which had grown up around her, serious, moral, prosaic, shrank coldly from this brilliant, fanciful, unscrupulous child of earth and the Renascence.

Elizabeth's death.

But if ministers and courtiers were counting on her death, Elizabeth had no mind to die. She had enjoyed life as the men of her day enjoyed it, and now that they were gone she clung to it with a fierce tenacity. She hunted, she danced, she jested with her young favourites, she coquetted and scolded and frolicked at sixty-seven as she had done at thirty. "The Queen," wrote a courtier a few months before her death, "was never so gallant these many years nor so set upon jollity." She persisted, in spite of opposition, in her gorgeous progresses from country-house to country-house. She clung to business as of old, and rated in her usual fashion "one who minded not to giving up some matter of account." But death crept on. Her face became haggard, and her frame shrank almost to a skeleton. At last her taste for finery disappeared, and she refused to change her dresses for a week together. A strange melancholy settled down on her. "She held in her hand," says one who saw her in her last days, "a golden cup, which she often put to her lips: but in truth her heart seemed too full to need more filling." Gradually her mind gave way. She lost her memory, the violence of her temper became unbearable, her very courage seemed to forsake her. She called for a sword to lie constantly beside her and thrust it from time to time through the arras, as if she heard murderers stirring there. Food and rest became alike distasteful. She sate day and night propped up with pillows on a stool, her finger on her lip, her eyes fixed on the floor, without a word. If she once broke the silence, it was with a flash of her old queenliness. When Robert Cecil declared that she "must" go to bed the word roused her like a trumpet. "Must!" she exclaimed; "is *must* a word to be addressed to princes? Little man, little man! thy father, if he had been alive, durst not have used that word." Then, as her anger spent itself, she sank into her old dejection. "Thou art so presumptuous," she said, "because thou knowest I shall die." She rallied once more when the ministers beside her bed named Lord Beauchamp, the heir to the Suffolk claim, as a possible successor. "I will have no rogue's son," she cried hoarsely, "in my seat." But she gave no sign, save a motion of the head, at the mention of the king of Scots. She was in fact fast becoming insensible; and early the next morning, on the twenty-fourth of March 1603, the life of Elizabeth, a life so great, so strange and lonely in its greatness, ebbed quietly away.

BOOK VII

PURITAN ENGLAND

1603-1660

AUTHORITIES FOR BOOK VII

1603-1660

For the reign of James the First we have Camden's "Annals" of that king, Goodman's "Court of King James I.," Weldon's "Secret History of the Court of James I.," Roger Coke's "Detection," the correspondence in the "Cabala," the letters published under the title of "The Court and Times of James I.," the documents in Winwood's "Memorials of State," and the reported proceedings of the last two Parliaments. The Camden Society has published the correspondence of James with Cecil, and Walter Yonge's "Diary." The letters and works of Bacon, now fully edited by Mr. Spedding, are necessary for any true understanding of the period. Hacket's "Life of Williams" and Harrington's "Nugæ Antiquæ" throw valuable side-light on the politics of the time. But the Stuart system, both at home and abroad, can only fairly be read by the light of the state-papers of this and the following reign, calendars of which are now being published by the Master of the Rolls. It is his employment of these, as well as his own fairness and good sense, which gives value to the series of works which Mr. Gardiner has devoted to this period; his "History of England from the Accession of James the First," his "Prince Charles and the Spanish Marriage," "England under the Duke of Buckingham," and "The Personal Government of Charles the First." The series has as yet been carried to 1637. To Mr. Gardiner also we owe the publication, through the Camden Society, of reports of some of the earlier Stuart Parliaments. Ranke's "History of England during the Seventeenth Century" has the same documentary value as embodying the substance of state-papers in both English and foreign archives, which throw great light on the foreign politics of the Stuart kings. It covers the whole period of Stuart rule. With the reign of Charles the First our historical materials increase. For Laud we have his remarkable "Diary"; for Strafford the "Strafford Letters." Hallam has justly characterized Clarendon's "History of the Rebellion" as belonging "rather to the class of memoirs" than of histories; and the rigorous analysis of it by Ranke shows the very different value of its various parts. Though the work will always retain a literary interest from its nobleness of style and the grand series of character-portraits which it embodies, the worth of its account of all that preceded the war is almost destroyed by the contrast between its author's conduct at the time and his later description of the Parliament's proceedings, as well as by the deliberate and malignant falsehood with which he has perverted the whole action of his parliamentary opponents. With the outbreak of the war he becomes of greater value, and he gives a good account of the Cornish rising; but from the close of the first struggle his work becomes tedious and unimportant. May's "History of the Long Parliament" is fairly accurate and impartial; but the basis of any real account of it must be found in its own proceedings as they have been preserved in the notes of Sir Ralph Verney and Sir Simonds D'Ewes. The last remain unpublished; but Mr. Forster has drawn much from them in his two works, "The Grand Remonstrance" and "The Arrest of the Five Members." The collections of state-papers by Rushworth and Nalson are indispensable for this period. It is illustrated by a series of memoirs, of very different degrees of value, such as those of Whitelock, Ludlow, Sir Philip Warwick, Holles, and Major Hutchinson, as well as by works like Mrs. Hutchinson's memoir of her husband, Baxter's "Autobiography," or Sir Thomas Herbert's memoirs of Charles during his last two years. The Diary of Nehemiah Wallington gives us the common life of Puritanism during this troubled time. For Cromwell the primary authority is Mr. Carlyle's "Life and Letters of Cromwell," an invaluable store of documents, edited with the care of an antiquarian and the genius of a poet. Fairfax may be studied in the "Fairfax Correspondence," and in the documents embodied in Mr. Clements Markham's life of him. Sprigge's "Anglia Rediviva" gives an account of the New Model and its doings. Thurlow's State Papers furnish an immense mass of documents for the period of the

Protectorate; and Burton's "Diary" gives an account of the proceedings in the Protector's second Parliament. For Irish affairs we have a vast store of materials in the Ormond papers and letters collected by Carte; for Scotland we have "Baillie's Letters," Burnet's "Lives of the Hamiltons," and Sir James Turner's "Memoir of the Scotch Invasion." Among the general accounts of this reign we may name Disraeli's "Commentaries of the Reign of Charles I." as prominent on one side, Brodie's "History of the British Empire" and Godwin's "History of the Commonwealth" on the other. Guizot in his three works on "Charles I. and the Revolution," "Cromwell and the Protectorate," and "Richard Cromwell and the Restoration," is accurate and impartial; and the documents he has added are valuable for the foreign history of the time. A good deal of information may be found in Forster's "Lives of the Statesmen of the Commonwealth," and Sandford's "Illustrations of the Great Rebellion."

CHAPTER I

ENGLAND AND PURITANISM

1603-1660

England at the death of Elizabeth.

The death of Elizabeth is one of the turning-points of English history. The age of the Renascence and of the New Monarchy passed away with the Queen. The whole face of the realm had been silently changing during the later years of her reign. The dangers which had hitherto threatened our national existence and our national unity had alike disappeared. The kingdom which had been saved from ruin but fifty years before by the jealousies of its neighbours now stood in the forefront of European powers. France clung to its friendship. Spain trembled beneath its blows. The Papacy had sullenly withdrawn from a fruitless strife with the heretic island. The last of the Queen's labours had laid Ireland at her feet, and her death knit Scotland to its ancient enemy by the tie of a common king. Within England itself the change was as great. Religious severance, the most terrible of national dangers, had been averted by the patience and the ruthlessness of the Crown. The Catholics were weak and held pitilessly down. The Protestant sectaries were hunted as pitilessly from the realm. The ecclesiastical compromise of the Tudors had at last won the adhesion of the country at large. Nor was the social change less remarkable. The natural growth of wealth and a patient good government had gradually put an end to all social anarchy. The dread of feudal revolt had passed for ever away. The fall of the Northern Earls, of Norfolk, and of Essex, had broken the last strength of the older houses. The baronage had finally made way for a modern nobility, but this nobility, sprung as it was from the court of the Tudors, and dependent for its existence on the favour of the Crown, had none of that traditional hold on the people at large which made the feudal lords so formidable a danger to public order.

Growth of social wealth.

If the older claims of freedom had been waived in presence of the dangers which so long beset even national existence, the disappearance of these dangers brought naturally with it a revival of the craving for liberty and self-government. And once awakened such a craving found a solid backing in the material progress of the time, in the upgrowth of new social classes, in the intellectual developement of the people, and in the new boldness and vigour of the national temper. The long outer peace, the tranquillity of the realm, the lightness of taxation till the outbreak of war with Spain, had spread prosperity throughout the land. Even the war failed to hinder the enrichment of the trading classes. The Netherlands were the centre of European trade, and of all European countries England had for more than half-a-century been making the greatest advance in its trade with the Netherlands. As early as in the eight years which preceded Elizabeth's accession and the eight years that followed it, while the trade of Spain with the Low Countries had doubled, and that of France and Germany with them had grown threefold, the trade between England and Antwerp had increased twentyfold. The increase remained at least as great through the forty years that followed, and the erection of stately houses, marriages with noble families, and the purchase of great estates, showed the rapid growth of the merchant class in wealth and social importance. London above all was profiting by the general advance. The rapidity of its growth awoke the jealousy of the royal Council. One London merchant, Thomas Sutton, founded the great hospital and school of the Charter House. Another, Hugh Myddelton, brought the New River from its springs at Chadwell and Amwell to supply London with pure water. Ere many years had gone the wealth of the great capital was to tell on the whole course of English history. Nor was the merchant class alone in this elevation. If the greater nobles no longer swayed the State, the spoil of the Church lands, and the general growth of national wealth, were raising the lesser landowners into a new social power. An influence which was to play a growing part in our history, the influence of the gentry, of the squires—as they were soon to be called—told more and more on English politics. In all but name indeed the leaders of this class were the equals of the peers whom they superseded. Men like the Wentworths in the north, or the

Hampdens in the south, boasted as long a rent-roll and wielded as great an influence as many of the older nobles. The attitude of the Lower House towards the Higher throughout the Stuart Parliaments sprang mainly from the consciousness of the Commons that in wealth as well as in political consequence the merchants and country gentlemen who formed the bulk of their members stood far above the mass of the peers.

Growth of national spirit.

While a new social fabric was thus growing up on the wreck of feudal England, new influences were telling on its developement. The immense advance of the people as a whole in knowledge and intelligence throughout the reign of Elizabeth was in itself a revolution. The hold of tradition, the unquestioning awe which formed the main strength of the Tudor throne, had been sapped and weakened by the intellectual activity of the Renascence, by its endless questionings, its historic research, its philosophic scepticism. Writers and statesmen were alike discussing the claims of government and the wisest and most lasting forms of rule, travellers turned aside from the frescoes of Giorgione to study the aristocratic polity of Venice, and Jesuits borrowed from the schoolmen of the Middle Ages a doctrine of popular rights which still forms the theory of modern democracy. On the other hand the nation was learning to rely on itself, to believe in its own strength and vigour, to crave for a share in the guidance of its own life. His conflict with the two great spiritual and temporal powers of Christendom, his strife at once with the Papacy and the House of Austria, had roused in every Englishman a sense of supreme manhood, which told, however slowly, on his attitude towards the Crown. The seaman whose tiny bark had dared the storms of far-off seas, the young squire who crossed the Channel to flesh his maiden sword at Ivry or Ostend, brought back with them to English soil the daring temper, the sense of inexhaustible resources, which had borne them on through storm and battle-field. The nation which gave itself to the rule of the Stuarts was another nation from the panic-struck people that gave itself in the crash of social and religious order to the guidance of the Tudors. It was plain that a new age of our history must open when the lofty patriotism, the dauntless energy, the overpowering sense of effort and triumph, which rose into their full grandeur through the war with Spain, turned from the strife with Philip to seek a new sphere of activity at home.

The spirit of religion.

What had hindered this force from telling as yet fully on national affairs was the breadth and largeness which characterized the temper of the Renascence. Through the past half-century the aims of Englishmen had been drawn far over the narrow bounds of England itself to every land and every sea; while their mental activity spent itself as freely on poetry and science as on religion and politics. But at the moment which we have reached the whole of this energy was seized upon and concentrated by a single force. For a hundred years past men had been living in the midst of a spiritual revolution. Not only the world about them but the world of thought and feeling within every breast had been utterly transformed. The work of the sixteenth century had wrecked that tradition of religion, of knowledge, of political and social order, which had been accepted without question by the Middle Ages. The sudden freedom of the mind from these older bonds brought a consciousness of power such as had never been felt before; and the restless energy, the universal activity of the Renascence were but outer expressions of the pride, the joy, the amazing self-confidence, with which man welcomed this revelation of the energies which had lain slumbering within him. But his pride and self-reliance were soon dashed by a feeling of dread. With the deepening sense of human individuality came a deepening conviction of the boundless capacities of the human soul. Not as a theological dogma, but as a human fact, man knew himself to be an all but infinite power, whether for good or for ill. The drama towered into sublimity as it painted the strife of mighty forces within the breast of Othello or Macbeth. Poets passed into metaphysicians as they strove to unravel the workings of conscience within the soul. From that hour one dominant influence told on human action: and all the various energies that had been called into life by the age that was passing away were seized, concentrated, and steadied to a definite aim by the spirit of religion.

The Bible.

The whole temper of the nation felt the change. "Theology rules there," said Grotius of England only two years after Elizabeth's death; and when Casaubon was invited by her successor to his court he found both king and people indifferent to pure letters. "There is a great abundance of theologians in England," he says; "all point their studies in that direction." Even a country gentleman, like Colonel Hutchinson, felt the theological impulse. "As soon as he had improved his natural understanding with the acquisition of learning, the first studies he exercised himself in were the principles of religion." It was natural that literature should reflect the tendency of the time; and the dumpy little quartos of controversy and piety which still crowd our older libraries drove before them the classical translations and Italian novelettes of the age of the Renascence. But their influence was small beside that of the Bible. The popularity of the Bible had been growing fast from the day when Bishop Bonner set up the first six copies in St. Paul's. Even then, we are told, "many well-disposed people used much to resort to the hearing thereof, especially when they could get any that had an audible voice to read to them." ... "One John Porter used sometimes to be occupied in that goodly exercise, to the edifying of himself as well as others. This Porter was a fresh young man and of a big stature; and great multitudes would resort thither to hear him, because he could read well and had an audible voice." But the "goodly exercise" of readers such as Porter was soon superseded by the continued recitation of both Old Testament and New in the public services of the Church; while the small Geneva Bibles carried the Scripture into every home, and wove it into the life of every English family.

Its literary influence.

Religion indeed was only one of the causes for this sudden popularity of the Bible. The book was equally important in its bearing on the intellectual developement of the people. All the prose literature of England, save the forgotten tracts of Wyclif, has grown up since the translation of the Scriptures by Tyndale and Coverdale. So far as the nation at large was concerned, no history, no romance, hardly any poetry save the little-known verse of Chaucer, existed in the English tongue when the Bible was ordered to be set up in churches. Sunday after Sunday, day after day, the crowds that gathered round the Bible in the nave of St. Paul's, or the family group that hung on its words in the devotional exercises at home, were leavened with a new literature. Legend and annal, war song and psalm, State-roll and biography, the mighty voices of prophets, the parables of Evangelists, stories of mission journeys, of perils by the sea and among the heathen, philosophic arguments, apocalyptic visions, all were flung broadcast over minds unoccupied for the most part by any rival learning. The disclosure of the stores of Greek literature had wrought the revolution of the Renascence. The disclosure of the older mass of Hebrew literature wrought the revolution of the Reformation. But the one revolution was far deeper and wider in its effects than the other. No version could transfer to another tongue the peculiar charm of language which gave their value to the authors of Greece and Rome. Classical letters therefore remained in the possession of the learned, that is, of the few; and among these, with the exception of Colet and More, or of the pedants who revived a Pagan worship in the gardens of the Florentine Academy, their direct influence was purely intellectual. But the language of the Hebrew, the idiom of the Hellenistic Greek, lent themselves with a curious felicity to the purposes of translation. As a mere literary monument the English version of the Bible remains the noblest example of the English tongue, while its perpetual use made it from the instant of its appearance the standard of our language.

Its social influence.

For the moment however its literary effect was less than its social. The power of the book over the mass of Englishmen showed itself in a thousand superficial ways, and in none more conspicuously than in the influence it exerted on ordinary speech. It formed, we must repeat, the whole literature which was practically accessible to ordinary Englishmen; and when we recall the number of common phrases which we owe to great authors, the bits of Shakspere, or Milton, or Dickens, or Thackeray, which unconsciously interweave themselves in our ordinary talk, we shall better understand the strange mosaic of Biblical words and phrases which coloured English talk two hundred years ago. The mass of picturesque allusion and illustration which we borrow from a thousand books, our fathers were forced to borrow from one; and the borrowing was the easier and the more natural that the range of the Hebrew literature fitted it for the expression of every phase of feeling. When Spenser poured forth his warmest love-notes in the "Epithalamion," he adopted the very words of the Psalmist, as he bade the gates open for the entrance of his bride. When Cromwell saw the mists break over the hills of Dunbar, he hailed the sun-burst with the cry of David: "Let God arise, and let his enemies be scattered. Like as the smoke vanisheth, so shalt thou drive them away!" Even to common minds this familiarity with grand poetic imagery in prophet and apocalypse gave a loftiness and ardour of expression that with all its tendency to exaggeration and bombast we may prefer to the slipshod vulgarisms of to-day.

Its religious influence.

But far greater than its effect on literature or social phrase was the effect of the Bible on the character of the people at large. The Bible was as yet the one book which was familiar to every Englishman; and everywhere its words, as they fell on ears which custom had not deadened to their force and beauty, kindled a startling enthusiasm. The whole moral effect which is produced nowadays by the religious newspaper, the tract, the essay, the missionary report, the sermon, was then produced by the Bible alone; and its effect in this way, however dispassionately we examine it, was simply amazing. The whole nation became a church. The problems of life and death, whose questionings found no answer in the higher minds of Shakspere's day, pressed for an answer not only from noble and scholar but from farmer and shopkeeper in the age that followed him. The answer they found was almost of necessity a Calvinistic answer. Unlike as the spirit of Calvinism seemed to the spirit of the Renascence, both found a point of union in their exaltation of the individual man. The mighty strife of good and evil within the soul itself which had overawed the imagination of dramatist and poet became the one spiritual conception in the mind of the Puritan. The Calvinist looked on churches and communions as convenient groupings of pious Christians; it might be as even indispensable parts of a Christian order. But religion in its deepest and innermost sense had to do not with churches but with the individual soul. It was each Christian man who held in his power the issues of life and death. It was in each Christian conscience that the strife was waged between Heaven and Hell. Not as one of a body, but as a single soul, could each Christian claim his part in the mystery of redemption. In the outer world of worship and discipline the Calvinist might call himself one of many brethren, but at every moment of his inner existence, in the hour of temptation and of struggle, in his dark and troubled wrestling with sin, in the glory of conversion, in the peace of acceptance with God, he stood utterly alone. With such a conception of human life Puritanism offered the natural form for English religion at a time when the feeling with which religion could most easily ally itself was the sense of individuality. The 'prentice who sate awed in the pit of the theatre as the storm in the mind of Lear outdid the storm among the elements passed easily into the Calvinist who saw himself day by day the theatre of a yet mightier struggle between the powers of light and the powers of darkness, and his soul the prize of an eternal conflict between Heaven and Hell.

Growth of Calvinism.

It was thus by its own natural developement that the temper of Englishmen became above all religious, and that their religion took in most cases the form of Calvinism. But the rapid spread of Calvinism was aided by outer causes as well as inner ones. The reign of Elizabeth had been a long struggle for national existence. When Shakspere first trod the streets of London it was a question whether England should still remain England or whether it should sink into a vassal of Spain. In that long contest the creed which Henry and Elizabeth had constructed, the strange compromise of old tradition with new convictions which the country was gradually shaping into a new religion for itself, had done much for England's victory. It had held England together as a people. It had hindered any irreparable severance of the nation into warring churches. But it had done this unobserved. To the bulk of men the victory seemed wholly due to the energy and devotion of Calvinism. Rome had placed herself in the forefront of England's enemies, and it was the Calvinistic Puritan who was the irreconcileable foe of Rome. It was the Puritan who went forth to fight the Spaniard in France or in the Netherlands. It was the Puritan who broke into the Spanish Main, and who singed Philip's beard at Cadiz. It was the Puritan whose assiduous preachings and catechizings had slowly won the mass of the English people to any real acceptance of Protestantism. And as the war drifted on, as the hatred of Spain and resentment at the Papacy grew keener and fiercer, as patriotism became more identified with Protestantism, and Protestantism more identified with hatred of Rome, the side of English religion which lay furthest from all contact with the tradition of the past grew more and more popular among Englishmen.

Puritanism and the people.

To Elizabeth, whether on religious or political grounds, Calvinism was the most hateful of her foes. But it was in vain that she strove by a rigorous discipline to check its advance. Her discipline could only tell on the clergy, and the movement was far more a lay than a clerical one. Whether she would or no, in fact, the Queen's policy favoured the Puritan cause. It was impossible to befriend Calvinism abroad without furthering Calvinism at home. The soldiers and adventurers who flocked from England to fight in the Huguenot camps came back steeped in the Huguenot theology. The exiles who fled to England from France and from the Netherlands spread their narrower type of religion through the towns where they found a refuge. As the strife with Rome grew hotter the government was forced to fill Parliament and the magistracy with men whose zealous Protestantism secured their fidelity in the case of a Catholic rising. But a zealous Protestant was almost inevitably a Calvinist; and to place the administration of the country in Calvinist hands was to give an impulse to Puritanism. How utterly Elizabeth failed was seen at the beginning of her successor's reign. The bulk of the country gentlemen, the bulk of the wealthier traders, had by that time become Puritans. In the first Parliament of James the House of Commons refused for the first time to transact business on a Sunday. His second Parliament chose to receive the communion at St. Margaret's Church instead of Westminster Abbey "for fear of copes and wafer-cakes."

Puritanism in the Church.

The same difficulty met Elizabeth in her efforts to check the growth of Puritanism in the Church itself. At the very outset of her reign the need of replacing the Marian bishops by staunch Protestants forced her to fill the English sees with men whose creed was in almost every case Calvinistic. The bulk of the lower clergy indeed were left without change; but as the older parsons died out their places were mostly filled by Puritan successors. The Universities furnished the new clergy, and at the close of Elizabeth's reign the tone of the Universities was hotly Puritan. Even the outer uniformity on which the Queen set her heart took a Puritan form. The use of the Prayer-book indeed was enforced; but the aspect of English churches and of English worship tended more and more to the model of Geneva. The need of more light to follow the service in the new Prayer-books served as a pretext for the removal of stained glass from the church windows. The communion table stood almost everywhere in the midst of the church. If the surplice was generally worn during the service, the preacher often mounted the pulpit in a Geneva gown. We see the progress of this change in the very chapel of the Primates themselves. The chapel of Lambeth House was one of the most conspicuous among the ecclesiastical buildings of the time; it was a place "whither many of the nobility, judges, clergy, and persons of all sorts, as well strangers as natives, resorted." But all pomp of worship gradually passed away from it. Under Cranmer the stained glass was dashed from its windows. In Elizabeth's time the communion table was moved into the middle of the chapel, and the credence table destroyed. Under James Archbishop Abbott put the finishing stroke on all attempts at a high ceremonial. The cope was no longer used as a special vestment in the communion. The Primate and his chaplains forbore to bow at the name of Christ. The organ and choir were alike abolished, and the service reduced to a simplicity which would have satisfied Calvin.

Puritanism and politics.

Foiled as it was, the effort of Elizabeth to check the spread of Puritanism was no mere freak of religious bigotry. It sprang from a clear realization of the impossibility of harmonizing the new temper of the nation with the system of personal government which had done its work under the Tudors. With the republican and anti-monarchical theories indeed that Calvinism had begotten elsewhere, English Calvinism showed as yet no sort of sympathy. The theories of resistance, of a people's right to judge and depose its rulers, which had been heard in the heat of the Marian persecution, had long sunk into silence. The loyalty of the Puritan gentleman was as fervent as that of his fellows. But with the belief of the Calvinist went necessarily a new and higher sense of political order. The old conception of personal rule, the dependence of a nation on the arbitrary will of its ruler, was jarring everywhere more and more with the religious as well as the philosophic impulses of the time. Men of the most different tendencies were reaching forward to the same conception of law. Bacon sought for universal laws in material nature. Hooker asserted the rule of law over the spiritual world. It was in the same way that the Puritan sought for a divine law by which the temporal kingdoms around him might be raised into a kingdom of Christ. The diligence with which he searched the Scriptures sprang from his earnestness to discover a Divine Will which in all things, great or small, he might implicitly obey. But this implicit obedience was reserved for the Divine Will alone; for human ordinances derived their strength only from their correspondence with the revealed law of God. The Puritan was bound by his religion to examine every claim made on his civil and spiritual obedience by the powers that be; and to own or reject the claim, as it accorded with the higher duty which he owed to God. "In matters of faith," a Puritan wife tells us of her husband, "his reason always submitted to the Word of God; but in all other things the greatest names in the world would not lead him without reason."

Puritanism and the Crown.

It was plain that an impassable gulf parted such a temper as this from the temper of unquestioning devotion to the Crown which the Tudors termed loyalty; for it was a temper not only legal, but even pedantic in its legality, intolerant from its very sense of a moral order and law of the lawlessness and disorder of a personal tyranny, a temper of criticism, of judgement, and, if need be, of stubborn and unconquerable resistance. The temper of the Puritan indeed was no temper of mere revolt. His resistance, if he was forced to resist, would spring not from any disdain of kingly authority, but from his devotion to an authority higher and more sacred than that of kings. He had as firm a faith as the nation at large in the divine right of the sovereign, in the sacred character of the throne. It was in fact just because his ruler's authority had a divine origin that he obeyed him. But the nation about the throne seemed to the Puritan not less divinely ordered a thing than the throne itself; it was the voice of God, inspiring and directing, which spoke through its history and its laws; it was God that guided to wisdom the hearts of Englishmen in Parliament assembled as He guided to wisdom the hearts of kings. Never was the respect for positive law so profound; never was the reverence for Parliaments so great as at the death of Elizabeth. There was none of the modern longing for a king that reigned without governing; no conscious desire shows itself anywhere to meddle with the actual exercise of the royal administration. But the Puritan could only conceive of the kingly power as of a power based upon constitutional tradition, controlled by constitutional law, and acting in willing harmony with that body of constitutional counsellors in the two Houses, who represented the wisdom and the will of the realm.

Puritanism and society.

It was in the creation of such a temper as this that Puritanism gave its noblest gift to English politics. It gave a gift hardly less noble to society at large in its conception of social equality. Their common calling, their common brotherhood in Christ, annihilated in the mind of the Puritans that overpowering sense of social distinctions which characterized the age of Elizabeth. There was no open break with social traditions; no open revolt against the social subordination of class to class. But within these forms of the older world beat for the first time the spirit which was to characterize the new. The meanest peasant felt himself ennobled as a child of God. The proudest noble recognized a spiritual equality in the poorest "saint." The great social revolution of the Civil Wars and the Protectorate was already felt in the demeanour of English gentlemen. "He had a loving and sweet courtesy to the poorest," we are told of one of them, "and would often employ many spare hours with the commonest soldiers and poorest labourers." "He never disdained the meanest nor flattered the greatest." But it was felt even more in the new dignity and self-respect with which the consciousness of their "calling" invested the classes beneath the rank of the gentry. Take such a portrait as that which a turner in Eastcheap, Nehemiah Wallington, has left us of a London housewife, his mother. "She was very loving," he says, "and obedient to her parents, loving and kind to her husband, very tender-hearted to her children, loving all that were godly, much misliking the wicked and profane. She was a pattern of sobriety unto many, very seldom was seen abroad except at church; when others recreated themselves at holidays and other times, she would take her needlework and say 'here is my recreation.' ... God had given her a pregnant wit and an excellent memory. She was very ripe and perfect in all stories of the Bible, likewise in all the stories of the Martyrs, and could readily turn to them; she was also perfect and well seen in the English Chronicles, and in the descents of the kings of England. She lived in holy wedlock with her husband twenty years, wanting but four days."

Puritanism and human conduct.

Where the new conception of life told even more powerfully than on politics or society was in its bearing on the personal temper and conduct of men. There was a sudden loss of the passion, the caprice, the subtle and tender play of feeling, the breadth of sympathy, the quick pulse of delight, which had marked the age of Elizabeth; but on the other hand life gained in moral grandeur, in a sense of the dignity of manhood, in orderliness and equable force. The larger geniality of the age that had passed away was replaced by an intense tenderness within the narrower circle of the home. Home, as we conceive it now, was the creation of the Puritan. Wife and child rose from mere dependants on the will of husband or father, as husband and father saw in them saints like himself, souls hallowed by the touch of a divine Spirit and called with a divine calling like his own. The sense of spiritual fellowship gave a new tenderness and refinement to the common family affections. "He was as kind a father," says a Puritan wife of her husband, "as dear a brother, as good a master, as faithful a friend as the world had." The wilful and lawless passion of the Renascence made way for a manly purity.

"Neither in youth nor riper years could the most fair or enticing woman draw him into unnecessary familiarity or dalliance. Wise and virtuous women he loved, and delighted in all pure and holy and unblameable conversation with them, but so as never to excite scandal or temptation. Scurrilous discourse even among men he abhorred; and though he sometimes took pleasure in wit and mirth, yet that which was mixed with impurity he never could endure." A higher conception of duty coloured men's daily actions. To the Puritan the wilfulness of life, in which the men of the Renascence had revelled, seemed unworthy of life's character and end. His aim was to attain self-command, to be master of himself, of his thought and speech and acts. A certain gravity and reflectiveness gave its tone to the lightest details of his converse with the world about him. His temper, quick as it might naturally be, was kept under strict control. In his discourse he was on his guard against talkativeness and frivolity, striving to be deliberate in speech, and "ranking the words beforehand." His life was orderly and methodical, sparing of diet and self-indulgence; he rose early; "he never was at any time idle, and hated to see any one else so." The new sobriety and self-restraint showed itself in a change of dress. The gorgeous colours and jewels of the Renascence disappeared. The Puritan squire "left off very early the wearing of anything that was costly, yet in his plainest negligent habit appeared very much a gentleman."

Puritanism and culture.

The loss of colour and variety in costume reflected no doubt a certain loss of colour and variety in life itself. But as yet Puritanism was free from any break with the harmless gaieties of the world about it. The lighter and more elegant sides of the Elizabethan culture harmonized well enough with the temper of the Calvinist gentleman. The figure of such a Puritan as Colonel Hutchinson stands out from his wife's canvas with the grace and tenderness of a portrait by Vandyck. She dwells on the personal beauty which distinguished his youth, on "his teeth even and white as the purest ivory," "his hair of brown, very thick-set in his youth, softer than the finest silk, curling with loose great rings at the ends." Serious as was his temper in graver matters, the young squire of Owthorpe was fond of hawking, and piqued himself on his skill in dancing and fence. His artistic taste showed itself in a critical love of "paintings, sculpture, and all liberal arts," as well as in the pleasure he took in his gardens, "in the improvement of his grounds, in planting groves and walks and forest-trees." If he was "diligent in his examination of the Scriptures," "he had a great love for music and often diverted himself with a viol, on which he played masterly."

Milton.

The strength however of the religious movement lay rather among the middle and professional classes than among the gentry; and it is in a Puritan of this class that we find the fullest and noblest expression of the new influence which was leavening the temper of the time. John Milton is not only the highest but the completest type of Puritanism. His life is absolutely contemporaneous with his cause. He was born when it began to exercise a direct influence over English politics and English religion; he died when its effort to mould them into its own shape was over, and when it had again sunk into one of many influences to which we owe our English character. His earlier verse, the pamphlets of his riper years, the epics of his age, mark with a singular precision the three great stages in its history. His youth shows us how much of the gaiety, the poetic ease, the intellectual culture of the Renascence, lingered in a Puritan home. Scrivener and "precisian" as his father was, he was a skilled musician, and the boy inherited his father's skill on lute and organ. One of the finest outbursts in the scheme of education which he put forth at a later time is a passage in which he vindicates the province of music as an agent in moral training. His home, his tutor, his school were all rigidly Puritan; but there was nothing narrow or illiberal in his early training. "My father," he says, "destined me while yet a little boy to the study of humane letters; which I seized with such eagerness that from the twelfth year of my age I scarcely ever went from my lessons to bed before midnight." But to the Greek, Latin, and Hebrew he learned at school, the scrivener advised him to add Italian and French. Nor were English letters neglected. Spenser gave the earliest turn to the boy's poetic genius. In spite of the war between playwright and precisian, a Puritan youth could still in Milton's days avow his love of the stage, "if Jonson's learned sock be on, or sweetest Shakspere, Fancy's child, warble his native woodnotes wild," and gather from the "masques and antique pageantry" of the court-revel hints for his own "Comus" and "Arcades." Nor does any shadow of the coming struggle with the Church disturb the young scholar's reverie, as he wanders beneath "the high embowed roof, with antique pillars massy proof, and storied windows richly dight, casting a dim religious light," or as he hears "the pealing organ blow to the full-voiced choir below, in service high and anthem clear."

Milton's enjoyment of the gaiety of life stands in bright contrast with the gloom and sternness which strife and persecution fostered in Puritanism at a later time. In spite of a "certain reservedness of natural disposition," which shrank from "festivities and jests, in which I acknowledge my faculty to be very slight," the young singer could still enjoy the "jest and youthful jollity" of the world around him, its "quips and cranks and wanton wiles"; he could join the crew of Mirth, and look pleasantly on at the village fair, where "the jocund rebecks sound to many a youth and many a maid, dancing in the chequered shade." There was nothing ascetic in Milton's look, in his slender, vigorous frame, his face full of a delicate yet serious beauty, the rich brown hair which clustered over his brow; and the words we have quoted show his sensitive enjoyment of all that was beautiful. But his pleasures were "unreproved." From coarse or sensual self-indulgence the young Puritan turned with disgust: "A certain reservedness of nature, an honest haughtiness and self-esteem, kept me still above those low descents of mind." He drank in an ideal chivalry from Spenser, though his religion and purity disdained the outer pledge on which chivalry built up its fabric of honour. "Every free and gentle spirit," said Milton, "without that oath, ought to be born a knight." It was with this temper that he passed from his London school, St. Paul's, to Christ's College at Cambridge, and it was this temper that he preserved throughout his University career. He left Cambridge, as he said afterwards, "free from all reproach, and approved by all honest men," with a purpose of self-dedication "to that same lot, however mean or high, towards which time leads me and the will of heaven."

The narrowness of Puritanism.

Even in the still calm beauty of a life such as this we catch the sterner tones of the Puritan temper. The very height of the Puritan's aim, the intensity of his moral concentration, brought with them a loss of the genial delight in all that was human which gave its charm to the age of Elizabeth. "If ever God instilled an intense love of moral beauty into the mind of any man," said the great Puritan poet, "he has instilled it into mine." "Love Virtue," closed his "Comus," "she alone is free!" But this passionate love of virtue and of moral beauty, if it gave strength to human conduct, narrowed human sympathy and human intelligence. Already in Milton we note "a certain reservedness of temper," a contempt for "the false estimates of the vulgar," a proud withdrawal from the meaner and coarser life around him. Great as was his love for Shakspere, we can hardly fancy him delighting in Falstaff. In minds of a less cultured order, this moral tension ended, no doubt, in a hard unsocial sternness of life. The ordinary Puritan "loved all that were godly, much misliking the wicked and profane." His bond to other men was not the sense of a common manhood, but the recognition of a brotherhood among the elect. Without the pale of the saints lay a world which was hateful to them, because it was the enemy of their God. It is this utter isolation from the "ungodly" that explains the contrast which startles us between the inner tenderness of the Puritans and the ruthlessness of so many of their actions. Cromwell, whose son's death (in his own words) went to his heart "like a dagger, indeed it did!" and who rode away sad and wearied from the triumph of Marston Moor, burst into horse-play as he signed the death-warrant of the king.

Its extravagance.

A temper which had lost sympathy with the life of half the world around it could hardly sympathize with the whole of its own life. Humour, the faculty which above all corrects exaggeration and extravagance, died away before the new stress and strain of existence. The absolute devotion of the Puritan to a Supreme Will tended more and more to rob him of all sense of measure and proportion in common matters. Little things became great things in the glare of religious zeal; and the godly man learnt to shrink from a surplice, or a mince-pie at Christmas, as he shrank from impurity or a lie. Nor was this all. The self-restraint and sobriety which marked the Calvinist limited itself wholly to his outer life. In his inner soul sense, reason, judgement, were too often overborne by the terrible reality of invisible things. Our first glimpse of Oliver Cromwell is as a young country squire and farmer in the marsh-levels around Huntingdon and St. Ives, buried from time to time in a deep melancholy, and haunted by fancies of coming death. "I live in Meshac," he writes to a friend, "which they say signifies Prolonging; in Kedar, which signifies Darkness; yet the Lord forsaketh me not." The vivid sense of a Divine Purity close to such men made the life of common men seem sin. "You know what my manner of life has been," Cromwell adds. "Oh, I lived in and loved darkness, and hated light. I hated godliness." Yet his worst sin was probably nothing more than an enjoyment of the natural buoyancy of youth, and a want of the deeper earnestness which comes with riper years. In imaginative tempers, like that of Bunyan, the struggle took a more picturesque form. John Bunyan was the son of a poor tinker at Elstow in Bedfordshire, and even in childhood his fancy revelled in terrible visions of Heaven and Hell. "When I was but a child of nine or ten years old," he tells us, "these things did so distress my soul, that then in the midst of my merry sports and childish vanities, amidst my vain companions, I was often much cast down and afflicted in my mind therewith; yet could I not let go my sins." The sins he could not let go were a love of hockey and of dancing on the village green; for the only real fault which his bitter self-accusation discloses, that of a habit of swearing, was put an end to at once and for ever by a rebuke from an old woman. His passion for bell-ringing clung to him even after he had broken from it as a "vain practice"; and he would go to the steeple-house and look on, till the thought that a bell might fall and crush him in his sins drove him panic-stricken from the door. A sermon against dancing and games drew him for a time from these indulgences; but the temptation again overmastered his resolve. "I shook the sermon out of my mind, and to my old custom of sports and gaming I returned with great delight. But the same day, as I was in the midst of a game of cat, and having struck it one blow from the hole, just as I was about to strike it the second time, a voice did suddenly dart from heaven into my soul, which said, 'Wilt thou leave thy sins and go to Heaven, or have thy sins and go to Hell?' At this I was put in an exceeding maze; wherefore, leaving my cat upon the ground, I looked up to heaven; and was as if I had with the eyes of my understanding seen the Lord Jesus looking down upon me, as being very hotly displeased with me, and as if He did severely threaten me with some grievous punishment for those and other ungodly practices."

Belief in witchcraft.

The vivid sense of a supernatural world which breathes through words such as these, the awe and terror with which it pressed upon the life of men, found their most terrible expression in the belief in witchcraft. The dread of Satanic intervention indeed was not peculiar to the Puritan. It had come down from the earliest ages of the Christian Church, and had been fanned into a new intensity at the close of the Middle Ages by the physical calamities and moral scepticism which threw their gloom over the world. Joan of Arc was a witch to every Englishman, and the wife of Duke Humphrey of Gloucester paced the streets of London, candle in hand, as a convicted sorceress. But it was not till the chaos and turmoil of the Reformation put their strain on the spiritual imagination of men that the belief in demoniacal possession deepened into a general panic. The panic was common to both Catholics and Protestants; it was in Catholic countries indeed that the persecution of supposed witches was carried on longest and most ruthlessly. Among Protestant countries England was the last to catch the general terror; and the Act of 1541, the first English statute passed against witchcraft, was far milder in tone than the laws of any other European country. Witchcraft itself, where no death could be proved to have followed from it, was visited only with pillory and imprisonment; where death had issued from it, the penalty was the gallows and not the stake. Even this statute was repealed in the following reign. But the fierce religious strife under Mary roused a darker fanaticism; and when Elizabeth mounted the throne preacher after preacher assured her that a multitude of witches filled the land. "Witches and sorcerers," cried Bishop Jewel, "within these few years are marvellously increased within your grace's realm. Your grace's subjects pine away even unto the death; their colour fadeth, their flesh rotteth, their speech is benumbed, their senses are bereft!" Before remonstrances such as these the statute against witchcraft was again enacted; but though literature and the drama show the hold which a belief in satanic agency had gained on the popular fancy, the temper of the times was too bold and self-reliant, its intelligence too keen and restless, its tone too secular, to furnish that atmosphere of panic in which fanaticism is bred.

It was not till the close of the Queen's reign, as hope darkened round Protestantism and the Puritan temper woke a fresh faith in the supernatural, that the belief in witchcraft and the persecution of the unhappy women who were held to be witches became a marked feature of the time. To men who looked on the world about them and the soul within them as battle-fields for a never-ceasing contest between God and the Devil, it was natural enough to ascribe every evil that happened to man, either in soul or body, to the invisible agency of the spirit of ill. A share of his supernatural energies was the bait by which he was held to lure the wicked to their own destruction; and women above all were believed to barter their souls for the possession of power which lifted them above the weakness of their sex. Sober men asserted that the beldame, whom boys hooted in the streets and who groped in the gutter for bread, could blast the corn with mildew and lame the oxen in the plough, that she could smite her persecutors with pains and sickness, that she could rouse storms in the sky and strew every shore with the wrecks of ships and the corpses of men, that as night gathered round she could mount her broomstick and sweep through the air to the witches' Sabbath, to yield herself in body and soul to the demons of ill. The nascent scepticism that startled at tales such as these was hushed before the witness of the Bible, for to question the existence of sorcerer or dæmoniac seemed questioning the veracity of the Scriptures themselves. Pity fell before the stern injunction, "Thou shalt not suffer a witch to live"; and the squire who would have shrunk from any conscious cruelty as from a blow looked on without ruth as the torturers ran needles into the witch's flesh, or swam her in the witch's pool, or hurried her to the witch's stake.

The Protestant defeat.

But the terror with which the Puritan viewed these proofs of a new energy in the powers of ill found a wider sphere of action as he saw their new activity and success in the religious and political world about him. At the opening of Elizabeth's reign every Protestant had looked forward to a world-wide triumph of the Gospel. If Italy and Spain clung blindly to the Papacy, elsewhere, alike on the Danube or the Rhine, on the Elbe or the Seine, the nations of Europe seemed to have risen in irreconcileable revolt against Rome. But the prospect of such a triumph had long since disappeared. At the crisis of the struggle a Catholic reaction had succeeded in holding Protestantism at bay, and after years of fierce combat Rome had begun definitely to win ground. The peaceful victories of the Jesuits were backed by the arms of Spain, and Europe was gradually regained till the policy of Philip the Second was able to aim its blows at the last strongholds of Calvinism in the west. Philip was undoubtedly worsted in the strife. England was saved by its defeat of the Armada. The United Provinces of the Netherlands rose into a great power as well through their own dogged heroism as through the genius of William the Silent. At a moment too when all hope seemed gone France was rescued from the grasp of the Catholic League by the unconquerable energy of Henry of Navarre. But even in its defeat Catholicism gained ground. England alone remained unaffected by its efforts. In the Low Countries the Reformation was finally driven from the Walloon Provinces, from Brabant, and from Flanders. In France Henry the Fourth found himself compelled to purchase Paris by a mass; and the conversion of the king was the beginning of a quiet breaking-up of the Huguenot party. Nobles and scholars alike forsook the cause of heresy, and though Calvinism remained dominant south of the Loire, it lost all hope of winning France as a whole to its side.

Puritan intolerance.

At Elizabeth's death therefore the temper of every earnest Protestant, in England as elsewhere, was that of a man who after cherishing the hope of a crowning victory is forced to look on at a crushing and irremediable defeat. The dream of a Reformation of the universal

Church was utterly at an end. Though the fierce strife of religions seemed for a while to have died down, the borders of Protestantism were narrowing every day, nor was there a sign that the triumph of the Papacy was arrested. Even the older Lutheranism of Germany was threatened; and the minds of men were already presaging the struggle which was to end in the Thirty Years War. Such a struggle could be no foreign strife to the Puritan. The war in the Palatinate kindled a fiercer flame in the English Parliament than all the aggressions of the monarchy; and Englishmen followed the campaigns of Gustavus with even keener interest than the trial of Hampden. We shall see how great a part this sympathy with outer Protestantism played in the earlier struggle between England and the Stuarts: but it played as great a part in determining the Puritan attitude towards religion at home. As hope after hope died into defeat and disaster the mood of the Puritan grew sterner and more intolerant. The system of compromise by which the Tudors had held England together became more and more distasteful to him. To one who looked on himself as a soldier of God and as a soldier who was fighting a losing battle, the struggle with the Papacy was no matter for compromise. It was a struggle between light and darkness, between life and death. No innovation in faith or worship was of small account if it tended in the direction of Rome. The peril in fact was too great to admit of tolerance or moderation. At a moment when all that he hated was gaining ground on all that he loved, the Puritan saw the one security for what he held to be truth in drawing a hard-and-fast line between that truth and what he held to be falsehood.

Hooker.

This dogged concentration of thought and feeling on a single issue told with a fatal effect on his theology. The spirit of the Renascence had been driven for a while from the field of religion by the strife between Catholic and Protestant; and in the upgrowth of a more rigid system of dogma, whether on the one side or on the other, the work of More and Colet seemed to be undone. But no sooner had the strife lost its older intensity, no sooner had a new Christendom fairly emerged from the troubled waters, than the Renascence again made its influence felt. Its voice was heard above all in Richard Hooker, a clergyman who had been Master of the Temple, but had been driven by his distaste for the controversies of its pulpit from London to a Wiltshire vicarage at Boscombe, which he exchanged at a later time for the parsonage of Bishopsbourne among the quiet meadows of Kent. During the later years of Elizabeth he built up in these still retreats the stately fabric of his "Ecclesiastical Polity." The largeness of temper which marked all the nobler minds of his day, the philosophic breadth which is seen as clearly in Shakspere as in Bacon, was united in Hooker with a grandeur and stateliness of style which raised him to the highest rank among English prose-writers. Divine as he was, his spirit and method were philosophical rather than theological. Against the ecclesiastical dogmatism of Presbyterian or Catholic he set the authority of reason. He abandoned the narrow ground of Scriptural argument to base his conclusions on the general principles of moral and political science, on the eternal obligations of natural law. The Puritan system rested on the assumption that an immutable rule for human action in all matters relating to religion, to worship, and to the discipline and constitution of the Church, was laid down, and only laid down, in the words of Scripture. Hooker urged that a divine order exists not in written revelation only, but in the moral relations, the historical developement, and the social and political institutions of men. He claimed for human reason the province of determining the laws of this order; of distinguishing between what is changeable and unchangeable in them, between what is eternal and what is temporary in the Bible itself. It was easy for him to push on to the field of ecclesiastical controversy where men like Cartwright were fighting the battle of Presbyterianism, to show that no form of Church government had ever been of indispensable obligation, and that ritual observances had in all ages been left to the discretion of churches and determined by the differences of times.

His influence on the Church.

From the moment of its appearance the effect of the "Ecclesiastical Polity" was felt in the broader and more generous stamp which it impressed on the temper of the national Church. Hooker had in fact provided with a theory and placed on grounds of reason that policy of comprehension which had been forced on the Tudors by the need of holding England together, and from which the church, as it now existed, had sprung. But the truth on which Hooker based his argument was of far higher value than his argument itself. The acknowledgement of a divine order in human history, of a divine law in human reason, harmonized with the noblest instincts of the Elizabethan age. Ralegh's efforts to grasp as a whole the story of mankind, Bacon's effort to bring all outer nature to the test of human intelligence, were but the crowning manifestations of the two main impulses of their time, its rationalism and its humanity. Both found expression in the work of Hooker; and coloured through its results the after history of the English Church. The historical feeling showed itself in a longing to ally the religion of the present with the religion of the past, to find a unity of faith and practice with the Church of the Fathers, to claim part in that great heritage of Catholic tradition, both in faith and worship, which the Papacy so jealously claimed as its own. Such a longing seized as much on tender and poetic tempers like George Herbert's as on positive and prosaic tempers, such as that of Laud. The one started back from the bare, intense spiritualism of the Puritan to find nourishment for his devotion in the outer associations which the piety of ages had grouped around it, in holy places and holy things, in the stillness of church and altar, in the pathos and exultation of prayer and praise, in the awful mystery of sacraments. The narrow and external mood of the other, unable to find standing ground in the purely personal relation between man and God which formed the basis of Calvinism, fell back on the consciousness of a living Christendom, preserving through the ages a definite faith and worship, and which, torn and rent as it seemed, was soon to resume its ancient unity.

The Arminians.

While the historical feeling which breathes in Hooker's work took form in the new passion for tradition and ceremonialism, the appeal which it addressed to human reason produced a school of philosophical thinkers whose timid upgrowth was almost lost in the clash of warring creeds about them, but who were destined—as the latitudinarians of later days—to make as deep an impression as their dogmatic rivals on the religious thought of their countrymen. As yet however this rationalizing movement hovered on the borders of the system of belief which it was so keenly to attack; it limited itself rather to the work of moderating and reconciling, to recognizing with Calixtus the pettiness of the points of difference which parted Christendom and the greatness of its points of agreement, or to revolting with Arminius from the more extreme tenets of Calvin and Calvin's followers and pleading like him for some co-operation on man's part with the work of grace. As yet Arminianism was little more than a reaction against a system that contradicted the obvious facts of life, a desire to bring theology into some sort of harmony with human experience; but it was soon to pass by a fatal necessity into a wider variance, and to gather round it into one mass of opposition every tendency of revolt which time was disclosing against the Calvinism which now reigned triumphant in Protestant theology.

The doctrinal bigotry of Puritanism.

From the belief in humanity or in reason which gave strength to such a revolt the Puritan turned doggedly away. In the fierce white light of his idealism human effort seemed weakness, human virtue but sin, human reason but folly. Absorbed as he was in the thought of God, craving for nothing less than a divine righteousness, a divine wisdom, a divine strength, he grasped the written Bible as the law of God and concentrated every energy in the effort to obey it. The dogma of justification, the faith that without merit or act of man God would save and call to holiness His own elect, was the centre of his creed. And with such a creed he felt that the humanity of the Renascence, the philosophy of the thinker, the comprehension of the statesman, were alike at war. A policy of comprehension seemed to him simply a policy of faithlessness to God. Ceremonies which in an hour of triumph he might have regarded as solaces to weak brethren, he looked on as acts of treason in this hour of defeat. Above all he would listen to no words of reconciliation with a religious system in which he saw nothing but a lie, nor to any pleas for concession in what he held to be truth. The craving of the Arminian for a more rational theology he met by a fiercer loyalty to the narrowest dogma. Archbishop Whitgift had striven to force on the Church of England a set of articles which embodied the tenets of an extreme Calvinism; and one of the wisest acts of Elizabeth had been to disallow them.

But hateful as Whitgift on every other ground was to the Puritans, they never ceased to demand the adoption of his Lambeth Articles.

Its hatred of sectaries.

And as he would admit no toleration within the sphere of doctrine, so would the Puritan admit no toleration within the sphere of ecclesiastical order. That the Church of England should both in ceremonies and in teaching take a far more distinctively Protestant attitude than it had hitherto done, every Puritan was resolved. But there was as yet no general demand for any change in the form of its government, or of its relation to the State. Though the wish to draw nearer to the mass of the Reformed Churches won a certain amount of favour for the Presbyterian form of organization which they had adopted, as an obligatory system of Church discipline Presbyterianism had been embraced by but a few of the English clergy, and by hardly any of the English laity. Nor was there any tendency in the mass of the Puritans towards a breach in the system of religious conformity which Elizabeth had constructed. On the contrary, what they asked was for its more rigorous enforcement. That Catholics should be suffered under whatever pains and penalties to preserve their faith and worship in a Protestant Commonwealth was abhorrent to them. Nor was Puritan opinion more tolerant to the Protestant sectaries who were beginning to find the State Church too narrow for their enthusiasm. Elizabeth herself could not feel a bitterer abhorrence of the "Brownists" (as they were called from the name of their founder Robert Brown) who rejected the very notion of a national Church, and asserted the right of each congregation to perfect independence of faith and worship. To the zealot whose whole thought was of the fight with Rome, such an assertion seemed the claim of a right to mutiny in the camp, a right of breaking up Protestant England into a host of sects too feeble to hold Rome at bay. Cartwright himself denounced the wickedness of the Brownists; Parliament, Puritan as it was, passed in 1593 a statute against them; and there was a general assent to the stern measures of repression by which Brown himself was forced to fly to the Netherlands. Two of his fellow-congregationalists were seized and put to death on charges of sedition and heresy. Of their followers many, as we learn from a petition in 1592, were driven into exile, "and the rest which remain in her Grace's land greatly distressed through imprisonment and other great troubles." The persecution in fact did its work. "As for those which we call Brownists," wrote Bacon, "being when they were at the most a very small number of very silly and base people, here and there in corners dispersed, they are now, thanks to God, by the good remedies that have been used, suppressed and worn out; so that there is scarce any news of them." The execution of three Nonconformists in the following year was in fact followed by the almost utter extermination of their body. But against this persecution no Puritan voice was raised.

Its wish for reforms.

All in fact that the bulk of the Puritans asked was a change in the outer ritual of worship which should correspond to the advance towards a more pronounced Protestantism that had been made by the nation at large during the years of Elizabeth's reign. Their demands were as of old for the disuse of "superstitious ceremonies." To modern eyes the points which they selected for change seem trivial enough. But they were in fact of large significance. To reject the sign of the Cross in baptism was to repudiate the whole world of ceremonies of which it was a survivor. The disuse of the surplice would have broken down the last outer difference which parted the minister from the congregation, and manifested to every eye the spiritual equality of layman and priest. Kneeling at the Communion might be a mere act of reverence, but formally to discontinue such an act was emphatically to assert a disbelief in the sacramental theories of Catholicism. During the later years of Elizabeth reverence for the Queen had hindered any serious pressure for changes to which she would never assent; but a general expectation prevailed that at her death some change would be made. Even among men of secular stamp there was a general conviction of the need of some concession to the religious sentiment of the nation. They had clung to the usages which the Puritans denounced so long as they were aids in hindering a religious severance throughout the land. But whatever value the retention of such ceremonies might have had in facilitating the quiet passage of the bulk of Englishmen from the old worship to the new had long since passed away. England as a whole was Protestant; and the Catholics who remained were not likely to be drawn to the national Church by trifles such as these. Instead of being the means of hindering religious division, the usages had now become means of creating it. It was on this ground that statesmen who had little sympathy with the religious spirit about them pleaded for the purchase of religious and national union by ecclesiastical reforms. "Why," asked Bacon, "should the civil state be purged and restored by good and wholesome laws made every three years in Parliament assembled, devising remedies as fast as time breedeth mischief, and contrariwise the ecclesiastical state still continue upon the dregs of time, and receive no alteration these forty-five years or more?"

CHAPTER II

THE KING OF SCOTS

Such was the temper of England at the death of Elizabeth; and never had greater issues hung on the character of a ruler than hung on the character of her successor. Had he shared the sympathy with popular feeling which formed the strength of the Tudors, time might have brought peaceably about that readjustment of political forces which the growth of English energies had made a necessity. Had he possessed the genius of a great statesman, he might have distinguished in the mingled mass of impulses about him between the national and the sectarian, and have given scope to the nobleness of Puritanism while resolutely checking its bigotry. It was no common ill-fortune that set at such a crisis on the throne a ruler without genius as without sympathy, and that broke the natural progress of the people by a conflict between England and its kings.

James Stuart.

Throughout the last days of Elizabeth most men had looked forward to a violent struggle for the Crown. The more bigoted Catholics supported the pretensions of Isabella, the eldest daughter of Philip the Second of Spain. The house of Suffolk, which through the marriage of Lady Catharine Grey with Lord Hertford was now represented by their son, Lord Beauchamp, still clung to its parliamentary title under the will of Henry the Eighth. Even if the claim of the house of Stuart was admitted, there were some who held that the Scottish king, as an alien by birth, had no right of inheritance, and that the succession to the crown lay in the next Stuart heiress, Arabella Stuart, a granddaughter of Lady Lennox by her younger son, Darnley's brother. But claims such as these found no general support. By a strange good fortune every great party in the realm saw its hopes realized in King James. The mass of the Catholics, who had always been favourable to a Scottish succession, were persuaded that the son of Mary Stuart would at least find toleration for his mother's co-religionists; and as they watched the distaste for Presbyterian rule and the tendency to comprehension which James had already manifested, they listened credulously to his emissaries. On the other hand the Puritans saw in him the king of a Calvinistic people, bred in a Church which rejected the ceremonies that they detested and upheld the doctrines which they longed to render supreme, and who had till now, whatever his strife might have been with the claims of its ministers, shown no dissent from its creed or from the rites of its worship. Nor was he less acceptable to the more secular tempers who guided Elizabeth's counsels. The bulk of English statesmen saw too clearly the advantages of a union of the two kingdoms under a single head to doubt for a moment as to the succession of James. If Elizabeth had refused to allow his claim to be formally recognized by Parliament she had pledged herself to suffer no detriment to be done to it there; and in her later days Cecil had come forward to rescue the young king from his foolish intrigues with English parties and Catholic powers, and to assure him of support. No sooner in fact was the Queen dead than James Stuart was owned as king by the Council without a dissentient voice.

His youth.

To James himself the change was a startling one. He had been a king indeed from his cradle. But his kingdom was the smallest and meanest of European realms, and his actual power had been less than that of many an English peer. For years he had been the mere sport of warring nobles who governed in his name. Their rule was a sheer anarchy. For a short while after Mary's flight Murray showed the genius of a born master of men; but at the opening of 1570 his work was ended by the shot of a Hamilton. "What Bothwellhaugh has done," Mary wrote joyously from her English prison at the news, "has been done without order of mine: but I thank him all the more for it." The murder in fact plunged Scotland again into a chaos of civil war which, as the Queen shrewdly foresaw, could only tend to the after-profit of the Crown. A year later the next regent, the child-king's grandfather, Lord Lennox, was slain in a fray at Stirling; and it was only when the regency passed into the strong hand of Morton at the close of 1572, and when England intervened in the cause of order, that the land won a short breathing-space. Edinburgh, the last fortress held in Mary's name, surrendered to a force sent by Elizabeth; its captain, Kirkaldy of Grange, was hanged for treason in the market-place; and the stern justice of Morton forced peace upon the warring lords. But hardly five years had passed when a union of his rivals and their adroit proclamation of the boy-king put an end to Morton's regency and gave a fresh aim to the factions who were tearing Scotland to pieces. To get hold of the king's person, to wield in his name the royal power, became the end of their efforts. The boy was safe only at Stirling; and even at Stirling a fray at the gate all but transferred him from the Erskines to fresh hands. It was in vain that James sought security in a bodyguard; or strove to baffle the nobles by recalling a cousin, Esme Stuart, from France, and giving him the control of affairs. A sudden flight back to Stirling only saved him from seizure at Doune; and a few months later, as James hunted at Ruthven, he found the hand of the Master of Glamis on his bridle-rein. "Better bairns greet than bearded men," was the gruff answer to his tears, as his favourite fled into exile and the boy-king saw himself again a tool in the hands of the lords.

His purpose.

Such was the world in which James had grown to manhood; a world of brutal swordsmen, in whose hands the boy who shrank from the very sight of a sword seemed helpless. But if the young king had little physical courage, morally he proved fearless enough. He drew confidence in himself from a sense of his intellectual superiority to the men about him. From his earliest years indeed James showed a precocious cleverness; and as a child he startled grave councillors by his "discourse, walking up and down in the Lady Mar's hand, of knowledge and ignorance." It was his amazing self-reliance which enabled him to bear the strange loneliness of his life. He had nothing in common with the turbulent nobles whose wild cries he had heard from the walls of Stirling Castle, as they slew his grandfather in the streets of the town below. But he had just as little sympathy with the spiritual or political world which was springing into life around his cradle. The republican Buchanan was his tutor, and he was bred in the religious school of Knox; but he shrank instinctively from Calvinism with its consecration of rebellion, its assertion of human equality, its declaration of the responsibility of kings, while he detected and hated the republican drift of the thinkers of the

Renascence. In later years James denounced the chronicles of both Buchanan and Knox as "infamous invectives," and would have had their readers punished "even as it were their authors risen again." His temper and purpose were in fact simply those of the kings who had gone before him. He was a Stuart to the core; and from his very boyhood he set himself to do over again the work which the Stuarts had done.

The work of the Stuarts.

Their work had been the building up of the Scottish realm, its change from a medley of warring nobles into an ordered kingdom. Never had freedom been bought at a dearer price than it was bought by Scotland in its long War of Independence. Wealth and public order alike disappeared. The material prosperity of the country was brought to a standstill. The work of civilization was violently interrupted. The work of national unity was all but undone. The Highlanders were parted by a sharp line of division from the Lowlanders, while within the Lowlands themselves feudalism overmastered the Crown. The nobles became almost wholly independent. The royal power, under the immediate successors of Bruce, sank into insignificance. From the walls of Stirling the Scotch kings of that earlier time looked out on a realm where they could not ride thirty miles to north or to south save at the head of a host of armed men. With James the First began the work of building the monarchy up again from this utter ruin; but the wresting of Scotland from the grasp of its nobles was only wrought out in a struggle of life and death. Few figures are more picturesque than the figures of the young Scotch kings as they dash themselves against the iron circle which girds them round in their desperate efforts to rescue the Crown from serfdom. They carry their life in their hands; a doom is on them; they die young and by violent deaths. One was stabbed by plotters in his bedchamber. Another was stabbed in a peasant's hut where he had crawled for refuge after defeat. Another was slain by the bursting of a cannon. The fourth James fell more nobly at Flodden. The fifth died of a broken heart on the news of Solway Moss. But hunted and slain as they were, the kings clung stubbornly to the task they had set themselves.

The Stuarts and the Reformation.

They stood almost alone. The Scottish people was too weak as yet to form a check on the baronage; and the one force on which the Crown could reckon was the force of the Church. To enrich the Church, to bind its prelates closely to the monarchy by the gift of social and political power, was the policy of every Stuart. A greater force than that of the Church lay in the dogged perseverance of the kings themselves. Little by little their work was done. The great house of Douglas was broken at last. The ruin of lesser houses followed in its train, and under the fifth of the Jameses Scotland saw itself held firmly in the royal grasp. But the work of the Stuarts was hardly done when it seemed to be undone again by the Reformation. The prelates were struck down. The nobles were enormously enriched. The sovereign again stood alone in the face of the baronage. It was only by playing on their jealousies and divisions that Mary Stuart could withstand the nobles who banded themselves together to overawe the Crown. Once she broke their ranks by her marriage with Darnley; and after the ill-fated close of this effort she strove again to break their ranks by her marriage with Bothwell. Again the attempt failed; and Mary fled into lifelong exile, while the nobles, triumphant at last in the strife with the Crown, governed Scotland in the name of her child.

James and the nobles.

It was thus that in his boyhood James looked on the ruin of all that his fathers had wrought. But the wreck was not as utter as it seemed. Even in the storm of the Reformation the sense of royal authority had not wholly been lost; the craving for public order, and the conviction that order could only be found in obedience to the sovereign, had in fact been quickened by the outbreak of faction; and the rule of Murray and Morton had shown how easily the turbulent nobles could be bent by an energetic use of the royal power. Lonely and helpless as he seemed, James was still king, and he was a king who believed in his kingship. The implicit faith in his own divine right to rule the greatest in the land gave him a strength as great as that of the regents. At seventeen he was strong enough to break the yoke of the Douglases and to drive them over the English border. At eighteen he could bring the most powerful of the Protestant nobles, the Earl of Gowrie, to the block. A year later indeed the lords were back again; for the Armada was at hand, and Elizabeth distrusted the young king, who was intriguing at Paris and Madrid. English help brought back the exiles; "there was no need of words," James said bitterly to the lords as they knelt before him with protestations of loyalty; "weapons had spoken loud enough." But their return was far from undoing his work. Elizabeth's pledges as to the succession, James's alliance with her against the Armada, restored the friendship of England; and once secure against English intervention the king had little difficulty in resuming his mastery at home. A significant ceremony showed that the strife with the nobles was at an end. James summoned them to Edinburgh, and called on them to lay aside their feuds with one another. The pledge was solemnly given, and each noble, "holding his chief enemy by the hand," walked in his doublet to the market-cross of the city, while the people sang aloud for joy.

The Scotch people.

The policy of the Stuarts had at last reached its end, and James was master of the great houses that had so long overawed the Crown. But he was farther than ever from being absolute master of his realm. Amidst the turmoil of the Reformation a new force had come to the front. This was the Scottish people itself. Till now peasant and burgher had been of small account in the land. The towns were little more than villages. The peasants, scattered thinly over valley and hillside and winning a scant subsistence from a thankless soil, were too few and too poor to be a political force. They were of necessity dependent on their lords; and in the centuries of feudal anarchy which followed the War of Independence the strife of lord against lord made their life a mere struggle for existence. To know neither rest nor safety, to face danger every hour, to plough the field with arms piled carefully beside the furrow, to watch every figure that crossed the hillside in doubt whether it were foe or friend, to be roused from sleep by the slogan of the Highlander or the cry of the borderer as they swept sheep and kye from every homestead in the valley, to bear hunger and thirst and cold and nakedness, to cower within the peel-tower or lurk in the moorland while barn and byre went up in pitiless flame, to mount and ride at a lord's call on forays as pitiless, this was the rough school in which the Scotch peasant was trained through two hundred years. But it was a school in which he learned much. Suffering that would have degraded a meaner race into slaves only hardened and ennobled the temper of the Scotchman. It was from these ages of oppression and lawlessness that he drew the rugged fidelity, the dogged endurance, the shrewdness, the caution, the wariness, the rigid thrift, the noble self dependence, the patience, the daring, which have distinguished him ever since. Nowhere did the Reformation do a grander work than in Scotland, but it was because nowhere were the minds of men so prepared for its work. The soil was ready for the seed. The developement of a noble manhood brought with it the craving for a spiritual and a national existence, and at the call of the Reformation the Scotch people rose suddenly into a nation and a Church.

Knox.

One well-known figure embodied the moral strength of the new movement. In the king's boyhood, amidst the wild turmoil which followed on Murray's fall, an old man bent with years and toil might have been seen creeping with a secretary's aid to the pulpit of St. Giles. But age and toil were powerless over the spirit of John Knox. In the pulpit "he behoved to lean at his first entry: but ere he had done with his sermon he was so active and vigorous that he was like to ding the pulpit into blads and fly out of it." It was in vain that men strove to pen the fiery words of the great preacher. "In the opening up of his text," says a devout listener, "he was moderate; but when he entered into application he made me so grue and tremble that I could not hold a pen to write." What gave its grandeur to the doctrine of Knox was his resolute assertion of a Christian order before which the social and political forces of the world about him shrank into insignificance. The meanest peasant, once called of God, felt within him a strength that was stronger than the might of nobles, and a wisdom that was wiser than the statecraft of kings. In that mighty elevation of the masses which was embodied in the Calvinist doctrines of election and grace lay the germs of the modern principles of human equality. The fruits of such a teaching soon showed themselves in a new attitude of the people. "Here," said

Morton, over the grave of John Knox, "here lies one who never feared nor flattered any flesh"; and if Scotland still reverences the memory of the reformer it is because at that grave her peasant and her trader learned to look in the face of nobles and kings and "not be ashamed."

The Kirk and the people.

The moral power which Knox created was to express itself through the ecclesiastical forms which had been devised by the genius of Calvin. The new force of popular opinion was concentrated and formulated in an ordered system of kirk-sessions and presbyteries and provincial synods, while chosen delegates formed the General Assembly of the Kirk. In this organization of her churches, Scotland saw herself for the first time the possessor of a really representative system, of a popular government. In her Parliaments the peasant had no voice, the burgher a feeble and unimportant one. They were in fact but feudal gatherings of prelates and nobles, whose action was fettered by the precautions of the Crown. Of real parliamentary life, such as was seen across the border, not a trace could be found in the assemblies which gathered round the Scottish kings; but a parliamentary life of the keenest and intensest order at once appeared among the lay and spiritual delegates who gathered to the General Assembly of the Kirk. Not only did Presbyterianism bind Scotland together as it had never been bound before by its administrative organization, but by the power it gave the lay elders in each congregation, and by the summons of laymen in an overpowering majority to the earlier Assemblies, it called the people at large to a voice, and as it turned out a decisive voice, in the administration of affairs. If its government by ministers gave it the outer look of an ecclesiastical despotism, no Church constitution has proved in practice so democratic as that of Scotland. Its influence in raising the nation at large to a consciousness of its power was shown by the change which passed from the moment of its establishment over the face of Scottish history.

The Kirk and the king.

The sphere of action to which it called the people was in fact not a mere ecclesiastical but a national sphere. Formally the Assembly meddled only with matters of religion; but in the creed of the Calvinist, as in the creed of the Catholic, the secular and the religious world were one. It was the office of the Church to enforce good and to rebuke evil; and social and political life fell alike within her "discipline." Feudalism received its death-blow when the noble who had wronged his wife or murdered his tenant sate humbled before the peasant elders on the stool of repentance. The new despotism which was growing up under the form of the monarchy found a sudden arrest in the challenge of the Kirk. When James summoned the preachers before his Council and arraigned their meetings as without warrant and seditious, "Mr. Andrew Melville could not abide it, but broke off upon the king in so zealous, powerful, and unresistible a manner that howbeit the king used his authority in most crabbed and choleric manner, yet Mr. Andrew bore him down, and uttered the commission as from the mighty God, calling the king but 'God's silly vassal'; and taking him by the sleeve, says this in effect, though with much hot reasoning and many interruptions: 'Sir, we will humbly reverence your Majesty always—namely, in public. But since we have this occasion to be with your Majesty in private, and the truth is that you are brought in extreme danger both of your life and crown, and with you the country and kirk of Christ is like to wreck, for not telling you the truth and giving of you a faithful counsel, we must discharge our duty therein or else be traitors both to Christ and you! And therefore, sir, as divers times before, so now again I must tell you, there are two kings and two kingdoms in Scotland. There is Christ Jesus the King, and his kingdom the Kirk, whose subject James the Sixth is, and of whose kingdom not a king, nor a lord, nor a head, but a member. And they whom Christ hath called to watch over his kirk and govern his spiritual kingdom have sufficient power and authority so to do both together and severally; the which no Christian king nor prince should control and discharge, but fortify and assist, otherwise not faithful servants nor members of Christ!'"

The ministers and the people.

It is idle to set aside words like these as the mere utterances of fanaticism or of priestly arrogance. James and his Council would have made swift work of mere fanatics or of arrogant priests. Why

Melville could withdraw unharmed was because a people stood behind him, a people suddenly wakened to a consciousness of its will, and stern in the belief that a divine duty lay on it to press that will on its king. Through all the theocratic talk of the Calvinist ministers we see a popular power that fronts the Crown. It is the Scotch people that rises into being under the guise of the Scotch Kirk. The men who led it were men with no official position or material power, for the nobles had stripped the Church of the vast endowments which had lured their sons and the royal bastards within the pale of its ministry. The ministers of the new communion were drawn from the burghers and peasantry or at best from the smaller gentry; and nothing in their social position aided them in withstanding the nobles or the Crown. Their strength lay simply in the popular sympathy behind them, in their capacity of rousing national opinion through the pulpit, of expressing it through the Assembly. The claims which such men advanced, ecclesiastical as their garb might be, could not fail to be national in their issues. In struggling against episcopacy they were in fact struggling against any breaking-up or impeding of that religious organization which alone enabled Scotland to withstand the claims of the Crown. In jealously asserting the right of the General Assembly to meet every year and to discuss every question that met it, they were vindicating in the only possible fashion the right of the nation to rule itself in a parliamentary way. In asserting the liberty of the pulpit they were for the first time in the history of Europe recognizing the power of public opinion and fighting for freedom whether of thought or of speech. Strange to modern ears as their language may be, bigoted and narrow as their temper must often seem, it is well to remember the greatness of the debt we owe them. It was their stern resolve, their energy, their endurance that saved Scotland from a civil and religious despotism, and that in saving the liberty of Scotland saved English liberty as well.

Andrew Melville.

The greatest of the successors of Knox was Andrew Melville. Two years after Knox's death Melville came fresh from a training among the French Huguenots to take up and carry forward his work. With less prophetic fire than his master he possessed as fierce a boldness, a greater disdain of secular compromises, a lofty pride in his calling, a bigoted faith in Calvinism that knew neither rest nor delay in its full establishment throughout the land. As yet the system of Presbyterian faith and discipline, with the synods and assemblies in which it was embodied, though it had practically won its hold over southern Scotland, was without legal sanction. The demand of the ministers for a restitution of the Church lands and the resolve of the nobles not to part with their spoil had caused the rejection of the Book of Discipline by the Estates. The same spirit of greed secured the retention of a nominal episcopacy. Though the name of bishops and archbishops appeared "to many to savour of Papistry," bishops and archbishops were still named to vacant dioceses as milch-cows, through whom the revenues of the sees might be drained by the great nobles. Against such "Tulchan-bishops," as they were nicknamed by the people's scorn, a "Tulchan" being a mere calf-skin stuffed with hay by which a cow was persuaded to give her milk after her calf was taken from her, Knox had not cared to protest; he had only taken care that they should be subject to the General Assembly, and deprived of all jurisdiction or authority beyond that of a Presbyterian "Superintendent." His strong political sense hindered a conflict on such a ground with the civil power, and without a conflict it was plain that no change could come. The Regent Morton, Calvinist as he was, supported the cause of Episcopacy, and the fact that bishops formed an integral part of the estates of the realm made any demand for their abolition distasteful to the large mass of men who always shrink from any constitutional revolution.

Presbyterianism established.

But Melville threw aside all compromise. In 1580 the General Assembly declared the office of bishop abolished, as having "no sure warrant, authority, or good ground out of the Word of God." In 1581 it adopted a second Book of Discipline which organized the Church on the pure Calvinistic model and advanced the full Calvinistic claim to its spiritual independence and supremacy within the realm. When the Estates refused to sanction this book the Assembly sent it to every presbytery, and its gradual acceptance secured the organization of the Church. It was at this crisis that the appearance of Esme Stuart brought about the first reaction towards a revival of the royal power; and the Council under the guidance of the favourite struck at once at the preachers who denounced it. But their efforts to "tune the pulpits" were met by a bold defiance. "Though all the kings of the earth should call my words treason," replied one minister who was summoned to the Council-board, "I am ready by good reason to prove them to be the very truth of God, and if need require to seal them with my blood." Andrew Melville, when summoned on the same charge of seditious preaching, laid a Hebrew Bible on the Council-table and "resolved to try conclusions on that only." What the Council shrank from "trying conclusions" with was the popular enthusiasm which backed these protests. When John Durie was exiled for words uttered in the pulpit, the whole town of Edinburgh met him on his return, "and going up the street with bare heads and loud voices sang to the praise of God till heaven and earth resounded."

James and the Kirk.

But it was this very popularity which roused the young king to action. Boy of eighteen as he was, no sooner had the overthrow of the Douglases and the judicial murder of Lord Gowrie freed James from the power of the nobles than he faced this new foe. Theologically his opinions were as Calvinistic as those of Melville himself, but in the ecclesiastical fabric of Calvinism, in its organization of the Church, in its annual assemblies, in its public discussion and criticism of acts of government through the pulpit, he saw an organized democracy which threatened his crown. And at this he struck as boldly as his forefathers had struck at the power of feudalism. The nobles, dreading the resumption of church lands, were with the king; and in 1584 an Act of the Estates denounced the judicial and legislative authority assumed by the General Assembly, provided that no subjects, temporal or spiritual, "take upon them to convocate or assemble themselves together for holding of councils, conventions, or assemblies," and demanded a pledge of obedience from every minister. For the moment the ministers submitted; and James prepared to carry out his victory by a policy of religious balance. The Catholic lords were still strong in northern and western Scotland; and firmly as the King was opposed to the dogmas of

Catholicism he saw the use he might make of the Catholics as a check on the power of the Congregation. It was with this view that he shielded Lord Huntly and the Catholic nobles while he intrigued with the Guises abroad. But such a policy at such a juncture forced England to intervene. At a moment when the Armada was gathering in the Tagus, Elizabeth felt the need of securing Scotland against any revival of Catholicism; and her aid enabled the exiled lords to return in triumph in 1585. For the next ten years James was helpless in their hands. He was forced to ally himself with Elizabeth, to offer aid against the Armada, to make a Protestant marriage, to threaten action against Philip, to attack Huntly and the Catholic lords of the north on a charge of correspondence with Spain and to drive them from the realm. The triumph of the Protestant lords was a triumph of the Kirk. In 1592 the Acts of 1584 were repealed; Episcopacy was formally abolished; and the Calvinistic organization of the Church at last received legal sanction. All that James could save was the right of being present at the General Assembly, and of fixing a time and place for its annual meeting. It was in vain that the young king struggled and argued; in vain that he resolutely asserted himself to be supreme in spiritual as in civil matters; in vain that he showed himself a better scholar and a more learned theologian than the men who held him down. The preachers scolded him from the pulpit and bade him "to his knees" to seek pardon for his vanity; while the Assembly chided him for his "banning and swearing" and sent a deputation to confer with his Queen touching the "want of godly exercise among her maids."

James and Presbyterianism.

The bitter memory of these years of humiliation dwelt with James to the last. They were fiercely recalled, when he mounted the English throne. "A Scottish Presbytery," he exclaimed at the Hampton Court Conference, "as well fitteth with monarchy as God and the Devil." Year after year he watched for the hour of deliverance, and every year brought it nearer. His mother's death gave fresh strength to his throne. The alliance with England, Elizabeth's pledge not to oppose his succession, left him practically heir of the English Crown. Freed from the dread of a Catholic reaction, the Queen was at liberty to indulge in her dread of Calvinism, and to sympathize with the fresh struggle which James was preparing to make against it. Her attitude, as well as the growing certainty of his coming greatness as sovereign of both realms, had no doubt their influence in again strengthening the king's position; and his new power was seen in his renewed mastery over the Scottish lords. But this triumph over feudalism was only the opening of a decisive struggle with Calvinism. If he had defeated Huntly and his fellow-plotters, he refused to keep them in exile or to comply with the demand of the Church that he should refuse their services on the ground of religion. He would be king of a nation, he contended, and not of a part of it. The protest was a fair one; but the real secret of the king's policy towards the Catholics, as of his son's after him, was a "king-craft" which aimed at playing off one part of the nation against another to the profit of the Crown. "The wisdom of the Council," said a defiant preacher, "is this, that ye must be served with all sorts of men to serve your purpose and grandeur, Jew and Gentile, Papist and Protestant. And because the ministers and Protestants in Scotland are over strong and control the King, they must be weakened and brought low."

The struggle with the Church.

It was with this end before him that James set finally to work in 1597. Cool, adroit, firm in his purpose, the young king seized on some wild outbreaks of the pulpit to assert a control over its utterances; a riot in Edinburgh in defence of the ministers enabled him to bring the town to submission by flooding its streets with Highlanders and Borderers; the General Assembly itself was made amenable to royal influence by its summons to Perth, where the cooler temper of the northern ministers could be played off against the hot Presbyterianism of the ministers of the Lothians. It was the Assembly itself which consented to curtail the liberty of preaching and the liberty of assembling in presbytery and synod, as well as to make the king's consent needful for the appointment of every minister. What James was as stubbornly resolved on was the restoration of Episcopacy. He wished not only to bridle but to rule the Church; and it was only through bishops that he could effectively rule it. The old tradition of the Stuarts had looked to the prelates for the support of the Crown, and James saw keenly that the new force which had overthrown them was a force which threatened to overthrow the monarchy itself. It was the people which in its religious or its political guise was the assailant of both. And as their foe was the same, so James argued with the shrewd short-sightedness of his race, their cause was the same. "No bishop," ran his famous adage, "no king!" To restore the episcopate was from this moment his steady policy. But its actual restoration only followed on the failure of a long attempt to bring the Assembly round to a project of nominating representatives of itself in the Estates. The presence of such representatives would have strengthened the moral weight of the Parliament, while it diminished that of the Assembly, and in both ways would have tended to the advantage of the Crown. But, cowed as the ministers now were, no pressure could bring them to do more than name delegates to vote according to their will in the Estates; and as such a plan foiled the king's scheme James was at last driven to use a statute which empowered him to name bishops as prelates with a seat in the Estates, though they possessed no spiritual status or jurisdiction. In 1600 two such prelates appeared in Parliament; and James followed up his triumph by the publication of his "Basilicon Dôron," an assertion of the divine right and absolute authority of kings over all orders of men within their realms.

It is only by recalling the early history of James Stuart that we can realize the attitude and temper of the Scottish Sovereign at the moment when the death of Elizabeth called him to the English throne. He came flushed with a triumph over Calvinism and democracy, but embittered by the humiliations he had endured from them, and dreading them as the deadly enemies of his crown. Raised at last to a greatness of which he had hardly dreamed, he was little likely to yield to a pressure, whether religious or political, against which in his hour of weakness he had fought so hard. Hopes of ecclesiastical change found no echo in a king whose ears were still thrilling with the defiance of Melville and his fellow ministers, and who among all the charms that England presented to him saw none so attractive as its ordered and obedient Church, its synods that met but at the royal will, its courts that carried out the royal ordinances, its bishops that held themselves to be royal officers. Nor were the hopes of political progress likely to meet with a warmer welcome. Politics with a Stuart meant simply a long struggle for the exaltation of the Crown. It was a struggle where success had been won not by a reverence for law or a people's support, but by sheer personal energy, by a blind faith in monarchy and the rights of monarchy, by an unscrupulous use of every weapon which a king possessed. Craft had been met by craft, violence by violence. Justice had been degraded into a weapon in the royal hand. The sacredness of law had disappeared in a strife where all seemed lawful for the preservation of the Crown. By means such as these feudalism had been humbled and the long strife with the baronage brought at last to a close. Strife with the people had yet to be waged. But in whatever forms it might present itself, whether in his new land or his old, it would be waged by James as by his successors in the same temper and with the same belief, a belief that the welfare of the nation lay in the unchecked supremacy of the Crown, and a temper that held all means lawful for the establishment of such a supremacy.

CHAPTER III

THE BREAK WITH THE PARLIAMENT

1603-1611

James the First.

On the sixth of May 1603, after a stately progress through his new dominions, King James entered London. In outer appearance no sovereign could have jarred more utterly against the conception of an English ruler which had grown up under Plantagenet or Tudor. His big head, his slobbering tongue, his quilted clothes, his rickety legs stood out in as grotesque a contrast with all that men recalled of Henry or Elizabeth as his gabble and rhodomontade, his want of personal dignity, his buffoonery, his coarseness of speech, his pedantry, his personal cowardice. Under this ridiculous exterior indeed lay no small amount of moral courage and of intellectual ability. James was a ripe scholar, with a considerable fund of shrewdness, of mother-wit, and ready repartee. His canny humour lights up the political and theological controversies of the time with quaint incisive phrases, with puns and epigrams and touches of irony which still retain their savour. His reading, especially in theological matters, was extensive; and he was already a voluminous author on subjects which ranged from predestination to tobacco. But his shrewdness and learning only left him, in the phrase of Henry the Fourth of France, "the wisest fool in Christendom." He had in fact the temper of a pedant, a pedant's conceit, a pedant's love of theories, and a pedant's inability to bring his theories into any relation with actual facts. It was this fatal defect that marred his political abilities. As a statesman he had shown no little capacity in his smaller realm; his cool humour and good temper had held even Melville at bay; he had known how to wait and how to strike; and his patience and boldness had been rewarded with a fair success. He had studied foreign affairs as busily as he had studied Scotch affairs; and of the temper and plans of foreign courts he probably possessed a greater knowledge than any Englishman save Robert Cecil. But what he never possessed, and what he never could gain, was any sort of knowledge of England or Englishmen. He came to his new home a Scotchman, a foreigner, strange to the life, the thoughts, the traditions of the English people. And he remained strange to them to the last. A younger man might have insensibly imbibed the temper of the men about him. A man of genius would have flung himself into the new world of thought and feeling and made it his own. But James was neither young nor a man of genius. He was already in middle age when he crossed the Border; and his cleverness and his conceit alike blinded him to the need of any adjustment of his conclusions or his prejudices to the facts which fronted him.

The foreign rule.

It was this estrangement from the world of thought and feeling about them which gave its peculiar colour to the rule of the Stuarts. It was not the first time that England had submitted to foreign kings. But it was the first time that England experienced a foreign rule. Foreign notions of religion, foreign maxims of state, foreign conceptions of the attitude of the people or the nobles towards the Crown, foreign notions of the relation of the Crown to the people, formed the policy of James as of his successors. For the Stuarts remained foreigners to the last. Their line filled the English throne for more than eighty years; but like the Bourbons they forgot nothing and they learned nothing. To all influences indeed save English influences they were accessible enough. As James was steeped in the traditions of Scotland, so Charles the First was open to the traditions of Spain. The second Charles and the second James reflected in very different ways the temper of France. But what no Stuart seemed able to imbibe or to reflect was the temper of England. The strange medley of contradictory qualities which blended in the English character, its love of liberty and its love of order, its prejudice and open-mindedness, its religious enthusiasm and its cool good sense, remained alike unintelligible to them. And as they failed to understand England, so in many ways England failed to understand them. It underrated their ability, nor did it do justice to their aims. Its insular temper found no hold on a policy which was far more European than insular. Its practical sense recoiled from the unpractical cleverness that, while it seldom said a foolish thing, yet never did a wise one.

The new policy.

From the first this severance between English feeling and the feeling of the king was sharply marked. If war and taxation had dimmed the popularity of Elizabeth in her later years, England had still a reverence for the Queen who had made her great. But James was hardly over the Border when he was heard expressing his scorn of the character and statecraft of his predecessor. Her policy, whether at home or abroad, he came resolved to undo. Men who had fought side by side with Dutchman and Huguenot against Spaniard and Leaguer heard angrily that the new king was seeking for peace with Spain, that he was negotiating with the Papacy, while he met the advances of France with a marked coolness, and denounced the Hollanders as rebels against their king. It was with scarcely less anger that they saw the stern system of repression which had prevailed through the close of Elizabeth's reign relaxed in favour of the Catholics, and recusants released from the payments of fines. It was clear that both at home and abroad James purposed to withdraw from that struggle with Catholicism which the hotter Protestants looked upon as a battle for God. What the king really aimed at was the security of his throne. The Catholics alone questioned his title; and a formal excommunication by Rome would have roused them to dispute his accession. James had averted this danger by intrigues both with the Papal Court and the English Catholics during the later years of Elizabeth; and his vague assurances had mystified the one and prevented the others from acting. The disappointment of the Catholics when no change followed on the king's accession found vent in a wild plot for the seizure of his person, devised by a priest named Watson; and the alarm this created quickened James to a redemption of his pledges. In July 1603 the leading Catholics were called before the Council and assured that the fines for recusancy would no longer be exacted; while an attempt was made to open a negotiation with Rome and to procure the support of the Pope for the new government. But the real strength of the Catholic party lay in the chance of aid from Spain. So long as the war continued they would look to Spain for succour, and the influence of Spain would be exerted to keep them in antagonism to the Crown. Nor was this the only ground for a cessation of hostilities. The temper of James was peaceful; the royal treasury was exhausted; and the continuance of the war necessitated a close connexion with the Calvinistic and republican Hollanders. At the same time therefore that the Catholics were assured of a relaxation of the penal laws, negotiations for peace were opened with Spain.

James and the Puritans.

However justifiable such steps might be, it was certain that they would rouse alarm and discontent among the sterner Protestants. For a time however it seemed as if concessions on one side were to be balanced by concessions on the other, as if the tolerance which had been granted to the Catholic would be extended to the Puritan. James had hardly crossed the Border when he was met by what was termed the Millenary Petition, from a belief that it was signed by a thousand of the English clergy. It really received the assent of some eight hundred, or of about a tenth of the clergy of the realm. The petitioners asked for no change in the government or organization of the Church, but for a reform of its courts, the removal of superstitious usages from the Book of Common Prayer, the disuse of lessons from the apocryphal books of Scripture, a more rigorous observance of Sundays, and the provision and training of ministers who could preach to the people. Concessions on these points would as yet have satisfied the bulk of the Puritans; and for a while it seemed as if concession was purposed. The king not only received the petition, but promised a conference of bishops and divines in which it should be discussed. Ten months however were suffered to pass before the pledge was redeemed; and a fierce protest from the University of Oxford in the interval gave little promise of a peaceful settlement. The university denounced the Puritan demands as preludes of a Presbyterian system in which the clergy would "have power to bind their king in chains and their prince in links of iron, that is (in their learning) to censure him, to enjoin him penance, to excommunicate him, yea—in case they see cause—to proceed against him as a tyrant."

Hampton Court conference.

The warning was hardly needed by James. The voice of Melville was still in his ears when he summoned four Puritan ministers to meet the Archbishop and eight of his suffragans at Hampton Court in

January 1604. From the first he showed no purpose of discussing the grievances alleged in the petition. He revelled in the opportunity for a display of his theological reading; but he viewed the Puritan demands in a purely political light. He charged the petitioners with aiming at a Scottish presbytery, "where Jack and Tom and Will and Dick shall meet, and at their pleasure censure me and my Council and all their proceedings. Stay," he went on with amusing vehemence, "stay, I pray you, for one seven years before you demand that from me, and if you find me pursy and fat and my windpipe stuffed, I will perhaps hearken to you, for let that government be once up, and I am sure I shall be kept in health." No words could have better shown the new king's unconsciousness that he had passed into a land where parliaments were realities, and where the "censure" of king and council was a national tradition. But neither his theology nor his politics met with any protest from the prelates about him. On the contrary, the bishops declared that the insults James showered on their opponents were inspired by the Holy Ghost. The Puritans however still ventured to question his infallibility, and the king broke up the conference with a threat which disclosed the policy of the Crown. "I will make them conform," he said of the remonstrants, "or I will harry them out of the land!"

The Parliament of 1604.

It is only when we recall the temper of England at the time that we can understand the profound emotion which was roused by threats such as these. Three months after the conference at Hampton Court the members were gathering to the first parliament of the new reign; and the Parliament of 1604 met in another mood from that of any parliament which had met for a hundred years. Under the Tudors the Houses had more than once at great crises in our history withstood the policy of the Crown. But in the main that policy had been their own; and it was the sense of this oneness in aim which had averted any final collision even in the strife with Elizabeth. But this trust in the unity of the nation and the Crown was now roughly shaken. The squires and merchants who thronged the benches at Westminster listened with coldness and suspicion to the self-confident assurances of the king. "I bring you," said James, "two gifts, one peace with foreign nations, the other union with Scotland"; and a project was laid before them for a union of the two kingdoms under the name of Great Britain. "By what laws," asked Bacon, "shall this Britain be governed?" Great in fact as were the advantages of such a scheme, the House showed its sense of the political difficulties involved in it by referring it to a commission. James in turn showed his resentment by passing over the attempts made to commute for a fixed sum the oppressive rights of Purveyance and Wardship. But what the House was really set upon was religious reform; and the first step of the Commons had been the naming of a committee to frame bills for the redress of the more crying ecclesiastical grievances. The influence of the Crown secured the rejection of these bills by the Lords; and the irritation of the Lower House showed itself in an outspoken address to the king. The Parliament, it said, had come together in a spirit of peace. "Our desires were of peace only, and our device of unity." Their aim had been to put an end to the long-standing dissension among the ministers, and to preserve uniformity by the abandonment of "a few ceremonies of small importance," by the redress of some ecclesiastical abuses, and by the establishment of an efficient training for a preaching clergy. If they had waived their right to deal with these matters during the old age of Elizabeth, they asserted it now. "Let your Majesty be pleased to receive public information from your Commons in Parliament, as well of the abuses in the Church as in the civil state and government." Words yet bolder, and which sound like a prelude to the Petition of Right, met the claim of absolutism which was so frequently on the new king's lips. "Your majesty would be misinformed," said the address, "if any man should deliver that the kings of England have any absolute power in themselves, either to alter religion or make any laws concerning the same, otherwise than as in temporal causes, by consent of Parliament."

The Canons of 1604.

The address was met by a petulant scolding, and as the Commons met coldly the king's request for a subsidy the Houses were adjourned. James at once assumed the title to which Parliament had deferred its assent, of King of Great Britain; while the support of the

Crown emboldened the bishops to a fresh defiance of the Puritan pressure. The act of Elizabeth which gave parliamentary sanction to the Thirty-nine Articles compelled ministers to subscribe only to those which concerned the faith and the sacraments, and thus implicitly refused to compel their signatures to the articles which related to points of discipline and Church government. The compromise had been observed from 1571 till now; but the Convocation of 1604 by its canons required the subscription of the clergy to the articles touching rites and ceremonies. The king showed his approval of this step by raising its prime mover, Bancroft, to the vacant See of Canterbury; and Bancroft added to the demand of subscription a requirement of rigid conformity with the rubrics on the part of all beneficed clergymen. In the spring of 1605 three hundred of the Puritan clergy were driven from their livings for a refusal to comply with these demands.

Fresh breach with the Catholics.

If James had come to his new throne with dreams of conciliation and of a greater unity among his subjects, his dream was to be speedily dispelled. At the moment when the persecution of Bancroft announced a final breach between the Crown and the Puritans, a revival of the old rigour made a fresh breach between the Crown and the Catholics. In remitting the fines for recusancy James had never purposed to suffer any revival of Catholicism; and in the opening of 1604 a proclamation which bade all Jesuits and seminary priests depart from the land proved that on its political side the Elizabethan policy was still adhered to. But the effect of the remission of fines was at once to swell the numbers of avowed Catholics. In the diocese of Chester the number of recusants increased by a thousand. Rumours of Catholic conversions spread a panic which showed itself in an act of the Parliament of 1604 confirming the statutes of Elizabeth; and to this James gave his assent. He promised indeed that the statute should remain inoperative; but rumours of his own conversion, which sprang from his secret negotiation with Rome, so angered the king that in the spring of 1605 he bade the judges put it in force, while the fines for recusancy were levied more strictly than before. The disappointment of their hopes, the quick breach of the pledges so solemnly given to them, drove the Catholics to despair.

They gave fresh life to a conspiracy which a small knot of bigots had been fruitlessly striving to bring to an issue since the king's accession. Catesby, a Catholic zealot who had taken part in the rising of Essex, had busied himself during the last years of Elizabeth in preparing for a revolt at the Queen's death, and in seeking for his project the aid of Spain. He was joined in his plans by two fellow-zealots, Winter and Wright; but the scheme was still unripe when James peaceably mounted the throne; and for the moment his pledge of toleration put an end to it. But the zeal of the plotters was revived by the banishment of the priests; and the conspiracy at last took the form of a plan for blowing up both Houses of Parliament and profiting by the terror caused by such a stroke. In Flanders Catesby found a new assistant in his schemes, Guido Fawkes, an Englishman who was serving in the army of the Archduke; and on his return to England he was joined by Thomas Percy, a cousin of the Earl of Northumberland and a pensioner of the king's guard. In May 1604 the little group hired a tenement near the Parliament House, and set themselves to dig a mine beneath its walls.

The Gunpowder Plot.

As yet however they stood alone. The bulk of the Catholics were content with the relaxation of the penal laws; and in the absence of any aid the plotters were forced to suspend their work. It was not till the sudden change in the royal policy that their hopes revived. But with the renewal of persecution Catesby at once bestirred himself; and at the close of 1604 the lucky discovery of a cellar beneath the Parliament House facilitated the execution of this plan. Barrels of gunpowder were placed in the cellar, and the little group waited patiently for the fifth of November 1605, when the Houses were again summoned to assemble. In the interval their plans widened into a formidable conspiracy. It was arranged that on the destruction of the king and the Parliament the Catholics should rise, seize the young princes, use the general panic to make themselves masters of the realm, and call for aid from the Spaniards in Flanders. With this view Catholics of greater fortune, such as Sir Everard Digby and Francis Tresham, were admitted to Catesby's confidence, and supplied money for the larger projects he designed. Arms were bought in Flanders, horses were held in readiness, a meeting of

Catholic gentlemen was brought about under show of a hunting party to serve as the beginning of a rising. Wonderful as was the secrecy with which the plot was concealed, the family affection of Tresham at the last moment gave a clue to it by a letter to Lord Monteagle, his relative, which warned him to absent himself from the Parliament on the fatal day; and further information brought about the discovery of the cellar and of Guido Fawkes, who was charged with its custody. The hunting party broke up in despair, the conspirators, chased from county to county, were either killed or sent to the block; and Garnet, the Provincial of the English Jesuits, was brought to trial and executed. Though he had shrunk from all part in the plot, its existence had been made known to him by way of confession by another Jesuit, Greenway; and horror-stricken as he represented himself to have been, he had kept the secret and left the Parliament to its doom.

The Impositions.

The failure of such a plot necessarily gives strength to a government; and for the moment the Parliament was drawn closer to the king by the deliverance from a common peril. When the Houses again met in 1606 they listened in a different temper to the demand for a subsidy. The needs of the Treasury indeed were great. Elizabeth had left behind her a war expenditure, and a debt of four hundred thousand pounds. The first ceased with the peace, but the debt remained; and the prodigality of James was fast raising the charges of the Crown in time of peace to as high a level as they had reached under his predecessor in time of war. The Commons voted a sum which was large enough to meet the royal debt. The fixed charges of the Crown they held should be met by its ordinary revenues; but James had no mind to bring his expenditure down to the level of Elizabeth's. The growth of English commerce offered a means of recruiting his treasury which seemed to lie within the limits of customary law; and of this he availed himself. The right of the Crown to levy impositions on exports and imports other than those of wool, leather, and tin, had been the last financial prerogative for which the Edwards had struggled. They had been forced indeed to abandon it; but the tradition of such a right lingered on at the royal council-board; and under the Tudors the practice had been to some slight extent revived. A duty on imports had been imposed in one or two instances by Mary, and this impost had been extended by Elizabeth to currants and wine. These instances however were too trivial and exceptional to break in upon the general usage; but a more dangerous precedent had been growing up in the duties which the great trading companies, such as those to the Levant and to the Indies, were allowed to exact from merchants, in exchange—as was held—for the protection they afforded them in far-off and dangerous seas. The Levant Company was now dissolved, and James seized on the duties it had levied as lapsing naturally to the Crown.

Bates's case.

The Parliament at once protested against these impositions; but the prospect of a fresh struggle with the Commons told less with the king than the prospect of a revenue which might free him from dependence on the Commons altogether. His fanatical belief in the rights and power of the Crown hindered all sober judgement of such a question. James cared quite as much to assert his absolute authority as to fill his treasury. In the course of 1606 therefore the case of a Levant merchant called Bates, who refused to pay the imposition, was brought before the Exchequer Chamber. The judgement of the court justified the king's confidence in his claim. It went far beyond the original bounds of the case itself, or the right of the Crown to levy on the ground of protection the dues which had been levied on that ground by the leading companies. It asserted the king's right to levy what customs duties he would. "All customs," said the judges, "are the effects of foreign commerce; but all affairs of commerce and treaties with foreign nations belong to the king's absolute power. He therefore who has power over the cause has power over the effect." The importance of such a decision could hardly be overrated. English commerce was growing fast. English merchants were fighting their way to the Spice Islands, and establishing settlements in the dominions of the Mogul. The judgement gave James a revenue which was certain to grow rapidly, and whose growth would go far to free the Crown from any need of resorting for supplies to Parliament.

The Post-Nati.

But no immediate step was taken to give effect to the judgement; and the Commons contented themselves with a protest against impositions at the close of the session of 1606. When they reassembled in the following year their attention was absorbed by the revival of the questions which sprang from the new relations of Scotland to England through their common king. There was now no question of a national union. The commission to which the whole matter had been referred had reported in favour of the abolition of hostile laws, the establishment of a general free trade between the two kingdoms, and the naturalization as Englishmen of all living Scotchmen who had been born before the king's accession to the English throne. The judges had already given their opinion that all born after it were naturalized Englishmen by force of their allegiance to a sovereign who had become King of England. The constitutional danger of such a theory was easily seen. Had the marriage of Philip and Mary produced a son, every Spaniard and every Fleming would under it have counted as Englishmen, and England would have been absorbed in the mass of the Spanish monarchy. The opinion of the judges in fact implied that nationality hung not on the existence of the nation itself, but on its relation to a king. It was to escape from such a theory that the Commons asked that the question should be waived, and offered on that condition to naturalize all Scotchmen whatever by statute. But James would not assent. To him the assertion of a right inherent in the Crown was far dearer than a peaceful settlement of the matter; the bills for free trade were dropped; and on the adjournment of the Houses a case was brought before the Exchequer Chamber; and the naturalization of the "Post-nati," as Scots born after the king's accession were styled, established by a formal judgement.

James and Scotland.

James had won a victory for his prerogative; but he had won it at the cost of Scotland. To the smaller and poorer kingdom the removal of all obstacles to her commerce with England would have been an inestimable gain. The intercourse which it would have necessitated could hardly have failed in time to bring about a more perfect union.

But as the king's reign drew on, the union of the two realms seemed more distant than ever. Bacon's shrewd question, "Under which laws is this Britain to be governed?" took fresh meaning as men saw James asserting in Scotland an all but absolute authority, and breaking down the one constitutional check which had hitherto hampered him. The energy which he had shown in his earlier combat with the democratic forces embodied in the Kirk was not likely to slacken on his accession to the southern throne. It was in the General Assembly that the new force of public opinion took legislative and administrative form; and even before he crossed the Border James had succeeded in asserting a right to convene and be personally present at the proceedings of the General Assembly. But once King of England he could venture on heavier blows. In spite of his assent to an act legalizing its annual convention, James hindered any meeting of the General Assembly for five successive years by repeated prorogations. The protests of the clergy were roughly met. When nineteen ministers appeared in 1605 at Aberdeen and, in defiance of the prorogation, constituted themselves an Assembly, they were called before the Council, and on refusal to own its jurisdiction banished as traitors from the realm. Of the leaders who remained the boldest were summoned in 1606 with Andrew Melville to confer with the king in England on his projects of change. On their refusal to betray the freedom of the Church they were committed to prison; and an epigram which Melville wrote on the usages of the English communion was seized on as a ground for bringing him before the English Privy Council with Bancroft at its head. But the insolence of the Primate fell on ears less patient than those of the Puritans he had insulted at Hampton Court. As he stood at the council-table Melville seized the Archbishop by the sleeves of his rochet, and shaking them in his manner, called them Popish rags and marks of the beast. He was sent to the Tower, and released after some years of imprisonment only to go into exile.

Submission of the Kirk.

The trial of Scotchmen before a foreign court, the imprisonment of Scotchmen in foreign prisons, were steps that showed the powerlessness of James to grasp the first principles of law; but they were effective for the purpose at which he aimed. They struck terror into the Scotch ministers. Their one weapon lay in the enthusiasm of the people; but, strongly as Scotch enthusiasm might tell on a king at Edinburgh, it was powerless over a king at London. The time had come when James might pass on from merely silencing the General Assembly to the use of it in the enslavement of the Church. Successful as he had been in gagging the pulpits and silencing the Assembly, he had been as yet less successful in his efforts to revive the power of the Crown over the Church by a restoration of Episcopacy. He had nominated a few bishops, and had won back for them their old places in Parliament; but his bishops remained purely secular nobles, unrecognized in their spiritual capacity by the Church, and without any ecclesiastical jurisdiction. It was in vain that James had striven to bring Melville and his fellows to any recognition of prelacy. But with their banishment and imprisonment the field was clear for more vigorous action. Deprived of their leaders, threatened with bonds and exile, deserted by the nobles, ill supported as yet by the mass of the people, to whom the real nature of their struggle was unknown, the Scotch ministers bent at last before the pressure of the Crown. They still shrank indeed from any formal acceptance of episcopacy; but they allowed the bishops to act as perpetual moderators or presidents in the synods of their presbyteries.

Restoration of Scotch Episcopacy.

With such moderators the General Assembly might be suffered to meet. Their influence in fact secured the return of royal nominees to Assemblies which met in 1608 and in 1610; and in the second of these assemblies episcopacy was at last formally recognized by the Scottish Church. The bishops were owned as permanent heads of each provincial synod; the power of ordination was committed to them; the ecclesiastical sentences pronounced by synod or presbytery were henceforth to be submitted for their approval. The new organization of the Church was at once carried out. The vacant sees were filled. Two archbishops were created at St. Andrews and Glasgow, and set at the head of Courts of High Commission for their respective provinces; while three of the prelates were sent to receive consecration in England, and on their return communicated it to their fellow-bishops. With such a measure of success James was fairly content. The prelacy he had revived fell far short of English episcopacy; to the eyes of religious dogmatists such as Laud indeed it seemed little better than the presbyterianism it superseded. But the aim of James was political rather than religious. He had no dislike for presbyterianism as a system of Church-government; what he dreaded was the popular force to which it gave form in its synods and assemblies, and which, in the guise of ecclesiastical independence, was lifting the nation into equality with the Crown. In seizing on the control of the Church through his organized prelacy James held himself to have seized the control of the forces which acted through the Church, and to have won back that mastery of his realm which the Reformation had reft from the Scottish kings.

England and the Prerogative.

What he had really done was to commit the Scotch Crown to a lasting struggle with the religious impulses of the Scottish people. The cause of episcopacy was ruined by his triumph. Belief in bishops ceased to be possible for a Scotchman when bishops were forced on Scotland as mere tools of the royal will. Presbyterianism on the other hand became identified with patriotism. It was no longer an ecclesiastical system; it was the guise under which national freedom and even national existence were to struggle against an arbitrary rule,—against a rule which grew more and more the rule of a foreign king. Nor was the sight of the royal triumph lost on the southern realm. England had no love for presbyters or hatred for bishops; but as she saw the last check on the royal authority broken down over the border she looked the more jealously at the effort which James was making to break down such checks at home. Under Elizabeth proclamations had been sparingly used, and for the most part only to enforce what was already the law. Not only was their number multiplied under James, but their character was changed. They created new offences, imposed new penalties, and directed offenders to be brought before courts which had no legal jurisdiction over them. To narrow indeed the sphere of the common law seemed the special aim of the royal policy; the four counties of the western border had been severed from the rest of England and placed under the jurisdiction of the President and Council of Wales, a court whose constitution and procedure rested on the sheer will of the Crown.

The province of the spiritual courts was as busily enlarged. It was in vain that the judges, spurred no doubt by the old jealousy between civil and ecclesiastical lawyers, entertained appeals against the High Commission, and strove by a series of decisions to set bounds to its limitless claims of jurisdiction or to restrict its powers of imprisonment to cases of schism and heresy. The judges were powerless against the Crown; and James was vehement in his support of courts which were closely bound up with his own prerogative. What work the courts spiritual might be counted on to do, if the king had his way, was plain from the announcement of a civilian named Cowell that "the king is above law by his absolute power," and that "notwithstanding his oath he may alter and suspend any particular law that seemeth hurtful to the public estate."

The claims of the king.

Cowell's book was suppressed on a remonstrance of the House of Commons; but the party of passive obedience grew fast. Even before his accession to the English throne James had formulated his theory of rule in a work on *The True Law of Free Monarchy*, and announced that "although a good king will frame his actions to be according to law, yet he is not bound thereto, but of his own will and for example giving to his subjects." With the Tudor statesmen who used the phrase, "an absolute king" or "an absolute monarchy" meant a sovereign or rule complete in themselves and independent of all foreign or Papal interference. James chose to regard the words as implying the freedom of the monarch from all control by law or from responsibility to anything but his own royal will. The king's theory was already a system of government; it was soon to become a doctrine which bishops preached from the pulpit, and for which brave men laid their heads on the block. The Church was quick to adopt its sovereign's discovery. Some three years after his accession Convocation in its book of Canons denounced as a fatal error the assertion that "all civil power, jurisdiction, and authority were first derived from the people and disordered multitude, or either is originally still in them, or else is deduced by their consent naturally from them; and is not God's ordinance originally descending from him and depending upon him." In strict accordance with the royal theory these doctors declared sovereignty in its origin to be the prerogative of birthright, and inculcated passive obedience to the Crown as a religious obligation. The doctrine of passive obedience was soon taught in the schools. A few years before the king's death the University of Oxford decreed solemnly that "it was in no case lawful for subjects to make use of force against their princes, or to appear offensively or defensively in the field against them." But what gave most force to such teaching were the reiterated expressions of James himself. If the king's "arrogant speeches" woke resentment in the Parliaments to which they were addressed, they created by sheer force of repetition a certain amount of belief in the arbitrary power they challenged for the Crown. One sentence from a speech delivered in the Star Chamber may serve as an instance of their tone. "As it is atheism and blasphemy to dispute what God can do, so," said James, "it is presumption and a high contempt in a subject to dispute what a king can do, or to say that a king cannot do this or that."

Distrust of the king.

"If the practice follow the positions," commented a thoughtful observer on words such as these, "we are not likely to leave to our successors the freedom we received from our forefathers." Their worst effect was in changing the whole attitude of the nation towards the Crown. England had trusted the Tudors, it distrusted the Stuarts. The mood indeed both of king and people had grown to be a mood of jealousy, of suspicion, which, inevitable as it was, often did injustice to the purpose of both. King James looked on the squires and merchants of the House of Commons as his Stuart predecessors had looked on the Scotch baronage. He regarded their discussions, their protests, their delays, not as the natural hesitation of men called suddenly, and with only half knowledge, to the settlement of great and complex questions, but as proofs of a conspiracy to fetter and impede the action of the Crown. The Commons on the other hand listened to the king's hectoring speeches, not as the chance talk of a clever and garrulous theorist, but as proofs of a settled purpose to change the character of the monarchy. In a word, James had succeeded in some seven years of rule in breaking utterly down that mutual understanding between the Crown and its subjects on which all government, save a sheer despotism, must necessarily rest.

Robert Cecil.

It was this mutual distrust which brought about the final breach between the Parliament and the king. The question of the impositions had seemed for a while to have been waived. The Commons had contented themselves with a protest against their levy. James had for two years hesitated in acting on the judgement which asserted his right to levy them. But the needs of the treasury became too great to admit of further hesitation, and in 1608 a royal proclamation imposed customs duties on many articles of import and export. The new duties came in fast; but unluckily the royal debt grew faster. To a king fresh from the penniless exchequer of Holyrood the wealth of England seemed boundless; money was lavished on court-feasts and favourites; and with each year the expenditure of James reached a higher level. It was in vain that Robert Cecil took the treasury into his own hands, and strove to revive the frugal traditions of Elizabeth. The king's prodigality undid his minister's work; and in 1610 Cecil was forced to announce to his master that the annual revenue of the Crown must be supplemented by fresh grants from Parliament. The scheme which Cecil laid before the king and the Commons is of great importance as the last effort of that Tudor policy which had so long hindered an outbreak of strife between the nation and the Crown. Differ as the Tudors might from one another, they were alike in their keen sense of national feeling and in their craving to carry it along with them. Masterful as Henry or Elizabeth might be, what they "prized most dearly," as the Queen confessed, was "the love and goodwill of their subjects." They prized it because they knew the force it gave them. And Cecil knew it too. He had grown up among the traditions of the Tudor rule. He had been trained by his father in the system of Elizabeth. Whether as a minister of the Queen, or as a minister of her successor, he had striven to carry that system into effect. His conviction of the supremacy of the Crown was as strong as that of James himself, but it was tempered by as strong a conviction of the need of the national good-will. He had seen what weight the passionate enthusiasm that gathered round Elizabeth gave to her policy both at home and abroad; and he saw that a time was drawing near when the same weight would be needed by the policy of the Crown.

Protestantism in Germany.

Slowly but steadily the clouds of religious strife were gathering over central Europe. From such a strife, should it once break out in war, England could not hold aloof unless the tradition of its policy was wholly set aside. And so long as Cecil lived, whatever change might take place at home, in all foreign affairs the Elizabethan policy was mainly adhered to. Peace indeed was made with Spain; but a close alliance with the United Provinces, and a more guarded alliance with France, held the ambition of Spain in check almost as effectually as war. The peace in fact set England free to provide against dangers which threatened to become greater than those from Spanish aggression in the Netherlands. Wearily as war in that quarter might drag on, it was clear that the Dutchmen could hold their own, and that all that Spain and Catholicism could hope for was to save the rest of the Low Countries from their grasp. But no sooner was danger from the Spanish branch of the House of Austria at an end than Protestantism had to guard itself against its German branch. The vast possessions of Charles the Fifth had been parted between his brother and his son. While Philip took Spain, Italy, the Netherlands, and the Indies, Ferdinand took the German dominions, the hereditary Duchy of Austria, the Suabian lands, Tyrol, Styria, Carinthia, Carniola. Marriage and fortune brought to the German branch the dependent states of Hungary, Bohemia, Moravia, Silesia; and it had succeeded in retaining the Imperial crown. The wisdom and moderation of Ferdinand and his successor secured tranquillity for Germany through some fifty years. They were faithful to the Peace of Passau, which had been wrested by Maurice of Saxony from Charles the Fifth, and which secured both Protestants and Catholics in the rights and possessions which they held at the moment it was made. Their temper was tolerant; and they looked on quietly while Protestantism spread over Southern Germany and solved all doubtful questions which arose from the treaty in its own favour. The Peace had provided that all church land already secularized should remain so; of the later secularization of other church land it said nothing. It provided that states already Protestant should abide so, but it said nothing of the right of other states to declare themselves Protestant. Doubt however was set aside by religious zeal; new states became Lutheran, and eight great bishoprics of the north were secularized. Meanwhile the new faith was spreading fast over the dominions of the House of Austria. The nobles of their very Duchy embraced it: Moravia, Silesia, Hungary all but wholly abandoned Catholicism. Through the earlier reign of Elizabeth it seemed as if by a peaceful progress of conversion Germany was about to become Protestant.

The Catholic reaction.

German Catholicism was saved by the Catholic revival and by the energy of the Jesuits. It was saved perhaps as much by the strife which broke out in the heart of German Protestantism between Lutheran and Calvinist. But the Catholic zealots were far from resting content with having checked the advance of their opponents. They longed to undo their work. They did not question the Treaty of Passau or the settlement made by it; but they disputed the Protestant interpretation of its silences; they called for the restoration to Catholicism of all church lands secularized, of all states converted from the older faith, since its conclusion. Their new attitude woke little terror in the Lutheran states. The treaty secured their rights, and their position in one unbroken mass stretching across Northern Germany seemed to secure them from Catholic attack. But the Calvinistic states, Hesse, Baden, and the Palatinate, felt none of this security. If the treaty were strictly construed it gave them no right of existence, for Calvinism had arisen since the treaty was signed. Their position too was a hazardous one. They lay girt in on all sides but one by Catholic territories, here by the bishops of the Rhineland with the Spaniards in Franche Comté and the Netherlands to back them, there by Bavaria and by the bishoprics of the Main. Foes such as these indeed the Calvinists could fairly have faced; but behind them lay the House of Austria; and the influence of the Catholic revival was at last telling on the Austrian princes. In 1606 an attempt of the Emperor Rudolf to force Catholicism again on his people woke revolt in the Duchy; and though the troubles were allayed by his removal, his successor Matthias persevered though more quietly in the same anti-Protestant policy.

The Union and the League.

The accession of the House of Austria to the number of their foes created a panic among the Calvinistic states, and in 1608 they joined together in a Protestant Union with Christian of Anhalt at its head. But zeal was at once met by zeal; and the formation of the Union was answered by the formation of a Catholic League among the states about it under Maximilian, the Duke of Bavaria. Both were ostensibly for defensive purposes: but the peace of Europe was at once shaken. Ambitious schemes woke up in every quarter. Spain saw the chance of securing a road along western Germany which would enable her to bring her whole force to bear on the rebels in the Low Countries. France on the other hand had recovered from the exhaustion of her own religious wars, and was eager to take up again the policy pursued by Francis the First and his son, of weakening and despoiling Germany by feeding and using religious strife across the Rhine. In 1610 a quarrel over Cleves afforded a chance for her intervention, and it was only an assassin's dagger that prevented Henry the Fourth from doing that which Richelieu was to do. England alone could hinder a second outbreak of the Wars of Religion; but the first step in such a policy must be a reconciliation between King and Parliament. James might hector about the might of the Crown, but he had no power of acting with effect abroad save through the national good-will. Without troops and without supplies, his threat of war would be ridiculous; and without the backing of such a threat Cecil knew well that mediation would be a mere delusion. Whether for the conduct of affairs at home or abroad it was needful to bring the widening quarrel between the king and the Parliament to a close; and it was with a settled purpose of reconciliation that Cecil brought James to call the Houses again together in 1610.

The Great Contract.

He never dreamed of conciliating the Commons by yielding unconditionally to their demands. Cecil looked on the right to levy impositions as legally established; and the Tudor sovereigns had been as keen as James himself in seizing on any rights that the law could be made to give them. But as a practical statesman he saw that the right could only be exercised to the profit of the Crown if it was exercised with the good-will of the people. To win that good-will it was necessary to put the impositions on a legal footing; while for the conduct of affairs it was necessary to raise permanently the revenue of the Crown. On the Tudor theory of politics these were concessions made by the nation to the king; and it was the Tudor practice to buy such concessions by counter-concessions made by the king to the nation. Materials for such a bargain existed in the feudal rights of the Crown, above all those of marriage and wardship, which were harassing to the people while they brought little profit to the Exchequer. The Commons had more than once prayed for some commutation of these rights, and Cecil seized on their prayer as the ground of an accommodation. He proposed that James should waive his feudal rights, that he should submit to the sanction by Parliament of the impositions already levied, and that he should bind himself to levy no more by his own prerogative, on condition that the Commons assented to this arrangement, discharged the royal debt, and raised the royal revenue by a sum of two hundred thousand a year.

Attitude of the Commons.

Such was the "great contract" with which Cecil met the Houses when they once more assembled in 1610. It was a bargain which the Commons must have been strongly tempted to accept; for heavy as were its terms it averted the great danger of arbitrary taxation, and again brought the monarchy into constitutional relations with Parliament. What hindered their acceptance of it was their suspicion of James. Purveyance and the Impositions were far from being the only grievance against which they came to protest; they had to complain of the increase of proclamations, the establishment of new and arbitrary courts of law, the encroachments of the spiritual jurisdiction; and consent to such a bargain, if it remedied two evils, would cut off all chance of redressing the rest. Were the treasury once full, no means remained of bringing the Crown to listen to their protest against the abuses of the Church, the silencing of godly ministers, the maintenance of pluralities and non-residence, the want of due training for the clergy. Nor had the Commons any mind to pass in silence over the illegalities of the preceding years. Whether they were to give legal sanction to the impositions or no, they were resolute to protest against their levy without sanction of law. James forbade them to enter on the subject, but their remonstrance was none the less vigorous. "Finding that your majesty, without advice or counsel of Parliament, hath lately in time of peace set both greater impositions and more in number than any of your noble ancestors did ever in time of war," they prayed "that all impositions set without the assent of Parliament may be quite abolished and taken away," and that "a law be made to declare that all impositions set upon your people, their goods or merchandise, save only by common consent in Parliament, are and shall be void." As to Church grievances their demands were in the same spirit. They prayed that the deposed ministers might be suffered to preach, and that the jurisdiction of the High Commission should be regulated by statute; in other words, that ecclesiastical like financial matters should be taken out of the sphere of the prerogative and be owned as lying henceforth within the cognizance of Parliament.

Dissolution of the Parliament.

It was no doubt the last demand that roused above all the anger of the king. As to some of the grievances he was ready to make concessions. He had consulted the judges as to the legality of his proclamations, and the judges had pronounced them illegal. It never occurred to James to announce his withdrawal from a claim which he now knew to be wholly against law, and he kept the opinion of the judges secret; but it made him ready to include the grievance of proclamations in his bargain with the Commons, if they would grant a larger subsidy. The question of the court of Wales he treated in the same temper. But on the question of the Church, of Church reform, or of ecclesiastical jurisdiction, he would make no concession whatever. He had just wrought his triumph over the Scottish Kirk; and had succeeded, as he believed, in transferring the control of its spiritual life from the Scottish people to the Crown. He was not likely to consent to any reversal of such a process in England itself. The claim of the Commons had become at last a claim that England through its representatives in Parliament should have a part in the direction of its own religious affairs. Such a claim sprang logically from the very facts of the Reformation. It was by the joint action of the Crown and Parliament that the actual constitution of the English Church had been established; and it seemed hard to deny that the same joint action was operative for its after reform. But it was in vain that the Commons urged their claim. Elizabeth had done wisely in resisting it, for her task was to govern a half-Catholic England with a Puritan Parliament; and in spite of constitutional forms the Queen was a truer representative of national opinion in matters of religion than the House of Commons. In her later years all had changed; and the Commons who fronted her successor were as truly representative of the religious opinion of the realm as Elizabeth had been. But James saw no ground for changing the policy of the Crown. The control of the Church and through it of English religion lay within the sphere of his prerogative, and on this question he was resolute to make a stand. The Commons were as resolute as the king. The long and intricate bargaining came on both sides to an end; and in February 1611 the first Parliament of James was dissolved.

CHAPTER IV

THE FAVOURITES

1611-1625

England and the Crown.

The dissolution of the first Stuart Parliament marks a stage in our constitutional history. With it the system of the Tudors came to an end. The oneness of aim which had carried nation and government alike through the storms of the Reformation no longer existed. On the contrary the aims of the nation and the aims of the government were now in open opposition. The demand of England was that all things in the realm, courts, taxes, prerogatives, should be sanctioned and bounded by law. The policy of the king was to reserve whatever he could within the control of his personal will. James in fact was claiming a more personal and exclusive direction of affairs than any English sovereign that had gone before him. England, on the other hand, was claiming a greater share in its own guidance than it had enjoyed since the Wars of the Roses. Nor were the claims on either side speculative or theoretical. Differences in the theory of government or on the relative jurisdiction of Church and State might have been left as of old to the closet and the pulpit. But the opposition between the Crown and the people had gathered itself round practical questions, and round questions that were of interest to all. Every man's conscience was touched by the question of religion. Every man's pocket was touched by the question of taxation. The strongest among human impulses, the passion of religious zeal and that of personal self-interest, nerved Englishmen to a struggle with the Crown. What gave the strife a yet more practical bearing was the fact that James had provided the national passion with a constitutional rallying-point. There was but one influence which could match the reverence which men felt for the Crown, and that was the reverence that men felt for the Parliament; nor had that reverence ever stood at a greater height than at the moment when James finally broke with the Houses. The dissolution of 1611 proclaimed to the whole people a breach between two powers which it had hitherto looked upon as one. Not only did it disperse to every corner of the realm a crowd of great landowners and great merchants who formed centres of local opposition to the royal system, but it carried to every shire and every borough the news that the Monarchy had broken with the Great Council of the realm.

James his own minister.

On Cecil his failure fell like a sentence of doom. Steeped as he was in the Tudor temper, he could not understand an age when the Tudor system had become impossible; the mood of the Commons and the mood of the king were alike unintelligible to him. He could see no ground for the failure of the Great Contract save that "God had not blessed it." But he had little time to wonder at the new forces which were rising about him, for only a year after the dissolution, in May 1612, he died, killed by overwork. With him died the last check on the policy of James. So long as Cecil lived the Elizabethan tradition, weakened and broken as it might be, lived with him. In foreign affairs there was still the conviction that the Protestant states must not be abandoned in any fresh struggle with the House of Austria. In home affairs there was still the conviction that the national strength hung on the establishment of good-will between the nation and the Crown. But traditions such as these were no longer to hamper the policy of the king. To him Cecil's death seemed only to afford an opportunity for taking further strides towards the establishment of a purely personal rule. For eight years James had borne with the check of a powerful minister. He was resolved now to have no real minister but himself. Cecil's amazing capacity for toil, as well as his greed of power, had already smoothed the way for such a step. The great statesman had made a political solitude about him. Of his colleagues some had been removed by death, some set aside by his jealousy. Ralegh lay in prison; Bacon could not find office under the Crown. And now that Cecil was removed, there was no minister whose character or capacity seemed to give him any right to fill his place. James could at last be his own minister. The treasury was put into commission. The post of secretary was left vacant, and it was announced that the king would be his own Secretary of State. Such an arrangement soon broke down, and the great posts of state were again filled with men of whose dependence James felt sure. But whoever might nominally hold these offices, from the moment of Cecil's death the actual direction of affairs was in the hands of the king.

The Council set aside.

Another constitutional check remained in the royal Council. As the influence of Parliament died down during the Wars of the Roses, that of the Council took to some extent its place. Composed as it was not only of ministers of the Crown but of the higher nobles and hereditary officers of state, it served under Tudor as under Plantagenet as an efficient check on the arbitrary will of the sovereign. Even the despotic temper of Henry VIII. had had to reckon with his Council; it had checked act after act of Mary; it played a great part in the reign of Elizabeth. In the administrative tradition indeed of the last hundred years the Council had become all-important to the Crown. It brought it in contact with public opinion, less efficiently, no doubt, but more constantly than the Parliament itself; it gave to its acts an imposing sanction and assured to them a powerful support; above all it provided a body which stood at every crisis between the nation and the monarchy, which broke the shock of any conflict, and which could stand forth as mediator, should conflict arise, without any loss of dignity on the part of the sovereign. But to the practical advantages or to the traditional weight of such a body James was utterly blind. His cleverness made him impatient of its discussions; his conceit made him impatient of its control; while the foreign traditions which he had brought with him from a foreign land saw in the great nobles who composed it nothing but a possible force which might overawe the Crown. One of his chief aims therefore had been to lessen the influence of the Council. So long as Cecil lived this was impossible, for the practical as well as the conservative temper of Cecil would have shrunk from so violent a change. But he was no sooner dead than James hastened to carry out his plans. The lords of the Council found themselves of less and less account. They were practically excluded from all part in the government; and the whole management of affairs passed into the hands of the king or of the dependent ministers who from this time became mere agents of the king's will.

The Favourites.

Such a personal rule as this, concentrating as it does the whole business of government in a single man, requires for its actual conduct the entire devotion of the ruler to public affairs. The work of Ferdinand of Aragon or of Frederick the Great was the work of galley-slaves. It was work which had broken down the strength of Wolsey, and which was to bow the iron frame of Oliver Cromwell. But James had no mind for work such as this. His intellect was quick, inventive, fruitful in device, eager to plan, and confident in the wisdom of its plans. But he had none of the quality which distinguishes intellectual power from mere cleverness, the capacity not only to plan, but to know what plans can actually be carried out, and by what means they can be carried out. Like all merely clever men, he looked down on the drudgery of details. The posts which he had held vacant were soon filled up; and before many months were over James ceased to be his own Treasurer or his own Secretary of State. But he still claimed the absolute direction of all affairs; he was resolved to be his own chief minister. Even here however he felt the need of a more active and practical mood than his own for giving shape to the schemes with which his brain was fermenting; and he fell back as of old on the tradition of his house. It was so long since England had seen a favourite that the memory of Gaveston or De Vere had almost faded away. But favourites had been part of the system of the Scottish kings. Hemmed in by turbulent barons, unable to find counsellors among the nobles to whom the interests of the Crown were dearer than the interests of their class or their house, Stuart after Stuart had been driven to look for a counsellor and a minister in some dependant, bound to them by ties of personal attachment and of common danger. The Scotch nobles had dealt with such favourites after their manner. One they had hung, others they had stabbed; the last, David Rizzio, had fallen beneath their daggers at Mary's feet. But the notion of a personal dependant through whom his designs might take form for the outer world was as dear to James as to his predecessors, and the death of Cecil was soon followed by the appearance of favourites.

Carr.

There was an æsthetic element in the character of the Stuarts which had shown itself in the poems and architectural skill of those who had gone before James, as it was to show itself in the artistic and literary taste of his successor. In James, grotesque as was his own personal appearance, it took the form of a passionate admiration of manly beauty. It is possible that with the fanciful Platonism of the time he saw in the grace of the outer form evidence of a corresponding fairness in the soul within. If so, he was egregiously deceived. The first favourite whom he raised to honour, a Scotch page named Carr, was as worthless as he was handsome. But his faults passed unheeded. Without a single claim to distinction save the favour of the king, Carr rose at a bound to honours which Elizabeth had denied to Ralegh and to Drake. He was enrolled among English nobles, and raised to the peerage as Viscount Rochester. Young as he was, he at once became sole minister. The lords of the Council found themselves to be mere ciphers. "At the Council-table," writes the Spanish Ambassador only a year after Cecil's death, "the Viscount Rochester showeth much temper and modesty without seeming to press or sway anything; but afterwards the king resolveth all business with him alone." So sudden and complete a revolution in the system of the state would have drawn ill-will on the favourite, even had Rochester shown himself worthy of the king's trust. But he seemed only eager to show his unworthiness. Through the year 1613 all England was looking on with wonder and disgust at his effort to break the marriage of Lord Essex with his wife, Frances Howard. Both had been young when they wedded; the passionate girl soon learned to hate her cold and formal husband; and she yielded readily enough to the seductions of the brilliant favourite. The guilty passion of the two was greedily seized on by the political intriguers of the court. Frances was daughter of a Howard, the Earl of Suffolk; and her father and uncle, the Earl of Northampton, who had already felt the influence of the favourite displacing their own, saw in the girl's shame a chance of winning this influence to their side. With this view they resolved to break the marriage with Essex, and to wed her to Rochester. A charge of impotency was trumped up against Essex as a ground of divorce, and a commission was named for its investigation. The charge was disproved, and with this disproof the case broke utterly down; but a fresh allegation was made that the Earl lay under a spell of witchcraft which incapacitated him from intercourse with his wife, though with her alone. The scandal grew as it became clear that the cause of Lady Essex was backed by the king. The resolute protest of Archbishop Abbot against the proceedings was met by a petulant scolding from James, and when the Commissioners were evenly divided in their judgement the king added two known partizans of the Countess to turn their verdict. By means such as these, after four months of scandal and shame, a sentence of divorce was at last procured, and Lady Essex set free to marry the favourite.

Overbury's murder.

In the foul process of the divorce James had been either dupe or confederate. But throughout the same four months he had been either confederate or dupe in a more terrible tragedy. In his rise to greatness Rochester had been aided by the counsels of Sir Thomas Overbury. Overbury was a young man of singular wit and ability, but he had as few scruples as his master, and he was as ready to lend himself to the favourite's lust as to his ambition. He dictated for him in fact the letters which won the heart of Lady Essex. But if he backed the intrigue, he seems, from whatever cause, to have opposed the project of marriage. So great was his power over Rochester that the Howards deemed it needful to take him out of the way while the divorce was being brought about, and with this end they roused the king's jealousy of this influence over the favourite. James became as resolute to get rid of him as the Howards; he offered him an embassy if he would quit England, and when he refused, he treated his refusal as an offence against the state. Overbury was committed to the Tower, and he remained a close prisoner while the suit took its course. Whether more than imprisonment was designed by the Howards, or what was the part the two Earls played in the deeds that followed, is hard to tell. Still harder is it to tell the part of Rochester or of the king. But behind the web of political intrigue lay a woman's passion, and the part of Lady Essex is clear. Overbury had the secret of her shame to disclose, and she was resolved to silence him by death. A few days after the sentence of divorce was pronounced, he died in his prison, poisoned by her agents. The crime remained unknown; and not a whisper of it broke the king's exultation over his favourite's success. At the close of 1613 the scandal was crowned by the elevation of Rochester to the Earldom of Somerset and his union with Frances Howard. Murderess and adulteress as she was, the girl moved to her bridal through costly pageants which would have fitted the bridal of a queen. The marriage was celebrated in the king's presence. Ben Jonson devised the wedding song. Bacon spent two thousand pounds in a wedding masque. The London Companies offered sumptuous gifts. James himself forced the Lord Mayor to entertain the bride with a banquet in Merchant Taylors' House, and the gorgeous wedding-train wound in triumph from Westminster to the City.

Immorality of the Court.

The shameless bridal was a fitting close to the shameless divorce, as both were outrages on the growing sense of morality. But they harmonized well enough with the profusion and profligacy of the Stuart Court. In spite of Cecil's economy, the treasury was drained to furnish masques and revels on a scale of unexampled splendour. While debts remained unpaid, lands and jewels were lavished on young adventurers whose fair faces caught the royal fancy. Two years back Carr had been a penniless fortune-seeker. Now, though his ostensible revenues were not large, he was able to spend ninety thousand pounds in a single twelvemonth. The Court was as shameless as it was profuse. If the Court of Elizabeth was as immoral as that of her successor, its immorality had been shrouded by a veil of grace and chivalry. But no veil shrouded the degrading grossness of the Court of James. James was no drunkard, but he was a hard drinker, and with the people at large his hard drinking passed for drunkenness. When the Danish king visited England actors in a masque performed at Court were seen rolling intoxicated at his feet. The suit of Lady Essex had shown great nobles and officers of state content to play panders to their kinswoman. A yet more scandalous trial was soon to show them in league with cheats and astrologers and poisoners. James had not shrunk from meddling busily in the divorce or from countenancing the bridal. Before scenes such as these the half-idolatrous reverence with which the sovereign had been regarded throughout the age of the Tudors died away into abhorrence and contempt. Court prelates might lavish their adulation on the virtues and wisdom of the Lord's anointed; but the players openly mocked at the king on the stage, while Puritans like Mrs. Hutchinson denounced the orgies of Whitehall in words as fiery as those with which Elijah denounced the profligacy of Jezebel.

Parliament of 1614.

But profligate and prodigal as was the Court, Somerset had to face the stern fact of an empty Exchequer. The debt was growing steadily. It had now risen to seven hundred thousand pounds, while, in spite of the impositions, the annual deficit had mounted to two hundred thousand. The king had no mind to face the Parliament again; but a little experience of affairs had sobered the arrogance of the favourite, and there still remained counsellors of the same mind as Cecil, who pressed on him the need of reconciling the Houses with the Crown. What at last prevailed on the king were the pledges of some officious meddlers known as "undertakers" who promised to bring about the return to the House of Commons of a majority favourable to the demand of a subsidy. But pledges such as these fell dead before the general excitement which greeted the tidings of a new Parliament. Never had an election stirred so much popular passion as that of 1614. In every case where rejection was possible, the Court candidates were rejected. All the leading members of the country party, or as we should now term it, the Opposition, were again returned. But three hundred of the members were wholly new men; and among them we note for the first time the names of the leaders in the later struggle with the Crown. Calne returned John Pym; Yorkshire sent Thomas Wentworth; St. Germans chose John Eliot. Signs of unprecedented excitement were seen in the vehement cheering and hissing which for the first time marked the proceedings of the Commons. But, excited as they were, their policy was precisely that of the Parliament which had been dissolved three years before. James indeed was farther off from any notion of concession than ever; he had no mind to offer again the Great Contract or even to allow the subject of impositions to be named. But the Parliament was as firm as the king. It refused to grant supplies till it had considered public grievances, and it fixed on the impositions and the abuses of the Church as the first grievances to be redressed. Unluckily the inexperience of the bulk of the House of Commons led it into quarrelling on a point of privilege with the Lords; and though the Houses had sate but two months James seized on the quarrel as a pretext for a fresh dissolution.

Benevolences.

The courtiers mocked at the "addled Parliament," but a statesman would have learned much from the anger and excitement that ran through its stormy debates. During the session the king had been frightened beyond his wont by the tone of the Commons, but the only impressions which remained in his mind were those of wounded pride and stubborn resistance. He sent four of the leading members of the Lower House to the Tower, and fell back on an obstinate resolve to govern without any Parliament at all. The resolve was carried recklessly out through the next seven years. The protests of the Commons James looked on as a defiance of the Crown, and he met them in a spirit of counter-defiance. The abuses which Parliament after Parliament had denounced were not only continued but carried to a greater extent than before. The spiritual courts were encouraged in fresh encroachments. Though the Crown lawyers admitted the illegality of proclamations they were issued in greater numbers than ever. Impositions were strictly levied. But a policy of defiance did little to fill the empty treasury. A large sum was gained by the sale to the Dutch of the towns which had been left by the States in pledge with Elizabeth; but even this supply was exhausted, and a fatal necessity drove James on to a formal and conscious breach of law. Whatever question might exist as to the legality of impositions, no question could exist since the statute of Richard the Third that benevolences were illegal. Nor was there any question that the levy of benevolences would rouse a deep and abiding resentment in the nation at large. Even in the height of the Tudor power Wolsey had been forced to abandon a resource which stirred England to revolt. But the Crown lawyers advised that while the statute forbade the exaction of gifts it left the king free to ask for them; and James resolved to raise money by benevolences. At the close of the Parliament of 1614 therefore letters were sent out to the counties and boroughs in the name of the Council requesting contributions. The letters remained generally unanswered; and in the autumn fresh letters had to be sent out in which the war which now threatened German Protestantism in the Palatinate was used to spur the loyalty of the country to a response. The judges on assize were ordered to press the king's demand. But prayer and pressure failed alike. In the three years which followed the dissolution the strenuous efforts of the sheriffs only raised sixty thousand pounds, a sum less than two-thirds of the value of a single subsidy. Devonshire, Nottinghamshire, and Warwickshire protested against the benevolences, and Somersetshire appealed to the statute which forbade them. It was in vain that the western remonstrants were silenced by threats from the Council, and that the laggard shires were rated for their sluggishness in payment. Two counties, those of Hereford and Stafford, sent not a penny to the last.

Increase of the Peerage.

In his distress for money the king was driven to expedients which widened the breach between the gentry and the Crown. He had refused to part with the feudal rights which came down to him from the Middle Ages, such as his right to the wardship of young heirs and the marriage of heiresses. These were now recklessly used as a means of extortion. Similar abuses of the prerogative alienated the merchant class. London, the main seat of their trade and wealth, was growing fast; and its growth roused terror in the government. In 1611 a proclamation forbade any increase of buildings. But the proclamation remained inoperative till it was seized as a means of extortion. A Commission was issued in 1614 with power to fine all who had disobeyed the king's injunctions, and by its means a considerable sum was gathered into the treasury. All that remained to be done was to alienate the nobles, and this James succeeded in doing by a measure in which political design went hand in hand with the needs of his finance. The Tudors had watched the baronage with jealousy, but they had made no attempt to degrade it. The nobles were sent to the prison and the block, but their rank and honours remained dignities which the Crown was chary to bestow even on the noblest of its servants. During the forty-five years of her reign Elizabeth raised but seven persons to the peerage, and with the exception of Burleigh all of these were of historic descent. The number of lay peers indeed had hardly changed for two centuries; they were about fifty at the accession of Henry the Fifth and counted but sixty at the accession of James. In so small an assembly, where the Crown could count on the unwavering support of ministers, courtiers, and bishops, the royal influence had through the last hundred years been generally supreme. But among the lords of the "old blood," as those whose honours dated from as far back as the Plantagenets were called, there lingered a spirit of haughty independence which, if it had quailed before the Tudors, showed signs of bolder life now the Tudors had gone. It was the policy of James to raise up a new nobility more dependent on the court, a nobility that might serve as a bridle on the older lords, while the increase in the numbers of the baronage which their creation brought about lessened the weight which a peer had drawn from his special and unique position in the realm. Such a policy fell in with the needs of his treasury. Not only could he degrade the peerage by lavishing its honours, but he could degrade it yet more by putting them up to sale. Of the forty-five lay peers whom he added to the Upper House during his reign, a large number were created by sheer bargaining. Baronies were sold to bidders at ten thousand pounds apiece. Ten nobles were created in a batch. Peerages were given to the Scotch dependants whom James brought with him, to Hume and Hay, and Bruce and Ramsay, as well as to his favourites Carr and Villiers. Robartes, of Cornwall, a man who had risen to great wealth through the Cornish mines, complained that he had been forced to take a baronage, for which he had to pay ten thousand pounds to a favourite's use.

The dismissal of Coke.

That this profuse creation of peers was more than the result of passing embarrassment was shown by its continuance under James's successors. Charles the First bestowed no less than fifty-six peerages; Charles the Second forty-eight. But in its immediate application it was no doubt little more than one of those financial shifts by which the king put off from day to day the necessity of again facing the one body which could permanently arrest his effort after despotic rule. There still however remained a body whose tradition was strong enough, if not to arrest, at any rate to check it. The lawyers had been subservient beyond all other classes to the Crown. Their narrow pedantry bent slavishly then, as now, before isolated precedents, while then, as now, their ignorance of general history hindered them from realizing the conditions under which these precedents had been framed, and to which they owed their very varying value. It was thus that the judges had been brought to support James in his case of the Post-Nati or in the levy of impositions. But beyond precedents even the judges refused to go. They had done their best in a case that came before them to restrict the jurisdiction of the ecclesiastical courts within legal and definite bounds, and their effort at once brought down on them the wrath of the king. All that affected the spiritual jurisdiction affected, he said, his prerogative; and whenever any case which affected his prerogative came before a court of justice he asserted that the king possessed an inherent right to be consulted as to the decision upon it. The judges timidly, though firmly, repudiated such a right as unknown to the law. To a king whose notions of law and of courts of law were drawn from those of Scotland, where justice had for centuries been a ready weapon in the royal hand, such a protest was utterly unintelligible. James sent for them to the royal closet. He rated them like schoolboys till they fell on their knees and with a single exception pledged themselves to obey his will. The one exception was the Chief Justice, Sir Edward Coke, a narrow-minded and bitter-tempered man, but of the highest eminence as a lawyer, and with a reverence for the law that overrode every other instinct. He had for some time been forced to evade the king's questions and "closetings" on judicial cases by timely withdrawal from the royal presence. But now that he was driven to answer, he answered well. When any case came before him, he said he would act as it became a judge to act. Coke was at once dismissed from the Council, and a provision which made the judicial office tenable at the king's pleasure, but which had long fallen into disuse, was revived to humble the common law in the person of its chief officer. In November 1616, on the continuance of his resistance, he was deprived of his post of Chief Justice.

The Crown and the Law.

No act of James seems to have stirred a deeper resentment among Englishmen than this announcement of his resolve to tamper with the course of justice. The firmness of Coke in his refusal to consult with the king on matters affecting his prerogative was justified by what immediately followed. As James interpreted the phrase, to consult with the king meant simply to obey the king's bidding as to what the judgement of a court should be. In the case which was then at issue he summoned the judges simply to listen to his decision; and the judges promised to enforce it. The king's course was an outrage on the growing sense of law; but his success was not without useful results. In his zeal to assert his personal will as the source of all power, whether judicial or other, James had struck one of its most powerful instruments from the hands of the Crown. He had broken the spell of the royal courts. If the good sense of Englishmen had revolted against their decisions in favour of the prerogative, the English reverence for law had made men submit to them. But now that all show of judicial independence was taken away, and the judges debased into mere mouthpieces of the king's will, the weight of their judgements came to an end. The nation had bent before their decision in favour of the Post-Nati; it had never a thought of bending before their decision in favour of Ship-money.

Fall of Somerset.

What an impassable gulf lay between the English conception of justice and that of James was shown even more vividly by the ruin of one who stood higher than Coke. At the opening of 1615 Somerset was still supreme. He held the rank of Lord Chamberlain; but he was practically the King's minister in state affairs, domestic or foreign. He was backed since his marriage by the influence of the Howards; and his father-in-law, Suffolk, was Lord Treasurer. He was girt round indeed by rivals and foes. The Queen was jealous of his influence over James; Archbishop Abbot dreaded his intrigues with Spain, intrigues which drew fresh meaning from the Catholic sympathies of the Howards; above all the older Lords of the Council, whom he ousted from any share in the government, watched eagerly for the moment when they hoped to regain their power by his fall. As he moved through the crowd of nobles he heard men muttering "that one man should not for ever rule them all." But Somerset's arrogance only grew with the danger. A new favourite was making way at court, and the king was daily growing colder. But Somerset only rated James for his coldness, demanded the dismissal of the new favourite, and refused to be propitiated by the king's craven apologies. His enemies however had a fatal card to play. In the summer whispers stole about of Overbury's murder, and of Somerset's part in it. The charge was laid secretly before the king, and a secret investigation conducted by his order threw darker and darker light on the story of guilt. Somerset was still unconscious of his peril, and the news that some meaner agents in the crime were arrested found him still with the king and in the seeming enjoyment of his wonted favour. He at once took horse for London to face his foes, and James parted from him with his usual demonstrations of affection. "He would neither eat nor drink," he said, "till he saw him again." He was hardly gone when James added, "I shall never see him more." His ruin in fact was already settled. In a few days he was a prisoner with his wife in the Tower; the agents in the fatal plot were sent to trial and to the gallows; and in May 1616 the young Countess was herself brought before the Lord Steward's Court to avow her guilt. Somerset's daring nature made a more stubborn stand. He threatened the king with disclosures, we know not of what, and when arraigned denied utterly any share in the murder. All however was in vain; and he and the Countess were alike sentenced to death.

If ever justice called for the rigorous execution of the law, it was in the case of Frances Howard. Not only was the Countess a murderess, but her crime passed far beyond the range of common murders. Girl as she was when it was wrought, she had shown the coolness and deliberation of a practised assassin in her lust to kill. Chance foiled her efforts again and again, but she persisted for months, she changed her agents and her modes of death, till her victim was slain. Nor was her crime without profit. She gained by it all she wanted. The secret of her adultery was hidden. There was no one to reveal the perjuries of her divorce. Her ambition and her passion were alike gratified. She became the bride of the man she desired. Her kindred filled the court. Her husband ruled the king. If crime be measured by its relentless purpose, if the guilt of crime be heightened by its amazing success, then no woman that ever stood in the dock was a greater criminal than the wife of Rochester. Nor was this all. The wretched agents in her crime were sent pitilessly to the gallows. The guilt of two of them was at least technically doubtful, but the doubt was not suffered to interfere with their punishment. Only in the one case where no doubt existed, in the case of the woman who had spurred and bribed these tools to their crime, was punishment spared. If life was left to such a criminal, the hanging of these meaner agents was a murder. But this was the course on which James had resolved, and he had resolved on it from the first. There was no more pressure on him. The rivals of Somerset had no need for his blood. The councillors and the new favourite required only his ruin, and James himself was content with being freed from a dependant who had risen to be his master. His pride probably shrank from the shame which the public death of such criminals on such a charge might bring on himself and his crown; his good-nature pleaded for pity, and the claims of justice never entered his head. Before the trial began he had resolved that neither should die, and the sentence of the Earl and the Countess was soon commuted into that of an easy confinement during a few years in the Tower.

Villiers.

The fall of Somerset seemed to restore the old system of rule; and for a short time the Council regained somewhat of its influence. But when the Queen gave her aid in Somerset's overthrow she warned Archbishop Abbot that it was only the investiture of a new favourite with Somerset's power. And a new favourite was already on the scene. It had only been possible indeed to overthrow the Earl by bringing a fresh face into the court. In the autumn of 1614 the son of a Leicestershire knight, George Villiers, presented himself to James. He was poor and friendless, but his personal beauty was remarkable, and it was by his beauty that he meant to make his way with the king. His hopes were soon realized. Queen, Primate, Councillors seized on the handsome youth to pit him against the favourite; in spite of Somerset's struggles he rose from post to post; and the Earl's ruin sealed his greatness. He became Master of the Horse; before the close of 1616 he was raised to the peerage as Viscount Villiers, and gifted with lands to the value of eighty thousand pounds. The next year he was Earl of Buckingham; in 1619 he was made Lord High Admiral; a marquisate and a dukedom raised him to the head of the English nobility. What was of far more import was the hold he gained upon the king. Those who had raised the handsome boy to greatness as a means of establishing their own power found themselves foiled. From the moment when Somerset entered the Tower, Villiers virtually took his place as Minister of State. The councillors soon found themselves again thrust aside. The influence of the new favourite surpassed that of his predecessor. The payment of bribes to him or marriage to his greedy kindred became the one road to political preferment. Resistance to his will was inevitably followed by dismissal from office. Even the highest and most powerful of the nobles were made to tremble at the nod of this young upstart.

His character.

"Never any man in any age, nor, I believe, in any country," says the astonished Clarendon in reviewing his strange career, "rose in so short a time to so much greatness of honour, power, or fortune, upon no other advantage or recommendation than of the beauty or gracefulness of his person." Such, no doubt, was the general explanation of his rise among men of the time; and it would have been well had the account been true. The follies and profusion of a handsome minion pass lightly over the surface of a nation's life. Unluckily Villiers owed his fortune to other qualities besides personal beauty. He was amazingly ignorant, his greed was insatiate, his pride mounted to sheer midsummer madness. But he had no inconsiderable abilities. He was quick of wit and resolute of purpose; he shrank from no labour; his boldness and self-confidence faced any undertaking which was needful for the king's service; he was devoted, heart and soul, to the Crown. Over James his hold was that of a vehement and fearless temper over a mind infinitely better informed, infinitely more thoughtful and reflective, but vague and hesitating amidst all its self-conceit, crowded with theories and fancies, and with a natural bent to the unpractical and unreal. To such a mind the shallow, brilliant adventurer came as a relief. James found all his wise follies and politic moonshine translated for him into positive fact. He leant more and more heavily on an adviser who never doubted and was always ready to act. He drew strength from his favourite's self-confidence. Rochester had bent before greatness and listened more than once, even in the hour of his triumph, to the counsels of wiser men. But on the conceit of Villiers the warnings of Abbot, the counsels of Bacon, were lavished in vain. He saw no course but his own; and the showy, audacious temper of the man made that course always a showy and audacious one. It was this that made the choice of the new favourite more memorable than the choice of Carr. At a moment when conciliation and concession were most needed on the part of the Crown, the character of Villiers made concession and conciliation impossible. To James his new adviser seemed the weapon he wanted to smite with trenchant edge the resistance of the realm. He never dreamed that the haughty young favourite, on whose neck he loved to loll, and whose cheek he slobbered with kisses, was to drag down in his fatal career the throne of the Stuarts.

The Spanish marriage.

As yet the temper of Villiers was as little known to the country as to the king. But the setting up of a new favourite on the ruin of the old had a significance which no Englishman could miss. It proved beyond question that the system of personal rule which was embodied in these dependent ministers was no passing caprice, but the settled purpose of the king. And never had such immense results hung on his resolve. Great as was the importance of the struggle at home, it was for a while to be utterly overshadowed by the greatness of the struggle which was opening abroad. The dangers which Cecil had foreseen in Germany were fast drawing to a head. Though he had failed to put England in a position to meet them, the dying statesman remained true to his policy. In 1612 he brought about a marriage between the king's daughter, Elizabeth, and the heir of the Elector Palatine, who was the leading prince in the Protestant Union. Such a marriage was a pledge that England would not tamely stand by if the Union was attacked; while the popularity of the match showed how keenly England was watching the dangers of German Protestantism, and how ready it was to defend it. But the step was hardly taken when Cecil's death left James free to pursue a policy of his own. The king was as anxious as his minister to prevent an outbreak of strife; and his daughter's bridal gave him a personal interest in the question. But he was far from believing with Cecil that the support of England was necessary for effective action. On the contrary, his quick, shallow intelligence held that it had found a way by which the Crown might at once exert weight abroad and be rendered independent of the nation at home. This was by a joint action with Spain. Weakened as were the resources of Spain by her struggle in the Netherlands, she was known to be averse from the opening of new troubles in Germany; and James might fairly reckon on her union with him in the work of peace. Her influence with the German branch of the House of Austria, as well as the weight her opinion had with every Catholic power, made her efforts even more important than those of James with the Calvinists. And that such a union could be brought about the king never doubted. His son was growing to manhood; and for years Spain had been luring James to a closer friendship by hints of the Prince's marriage with an Infanta. Such a match would not only gratify the pride of a sovereign who in his earlier days in his little kingdom had been overawed by the great Catholic monarchy, and on whose imagination it still exercised a spell, but it would proclaim to the world the union of the powers in the work of peace, while it provided James with the means of action. For poor as Spain really was, she was still looked upon as the richest state in the world; and the king believed that the bride would bring with her a dowry of some half-a-million. Such a dowry would set him free from the need of appealing to his Parliament, and give him the means of acting energetically on the Rhine.

The policy of Spain.

That there were difficulties in the way of such a policy, that Spain would demand concessions to the English Catholics, that the marriage would give England a Catholic queen, that the future heir of its crown must be trained by a Catholic mother, above all that the crown would be parted by plans such as these yet more widely from the sympathy of the nation, James could not but know. What he might have known as clearly, had he been a wise man instead of a merely clever man, was that, however such a bargain might suit himself, it was hardly likely to suit Spain. Spain was asked in effect to supply a bankrupt king with the means of figuring as the protector of Protestantism in Germany, while the only consideration offered to her was the hand of Prince Charles. But it never occurred to James to look at his schemes in any other light than his own. On the dissolution of the Parliament of 1614 he addressed a proposal of marriage to the Spanish court. Whatever was its ultimate purpose, Spain was careful to feed hopes which secured, so long as they lasted, better treatment for the Catholics, and which might be used to hold James from any practical action on behalf of the Protestants in Germany. Her cordiality increased as she saw, in spite of her protests, the crisis approaching. One member of the Austrian house, Ferdinand, had openly proclaimed and carried out his purpose of forcibly suppressing heresy in the countries he ruled, the Tyrol, Carinthia, Carniola, and Styria; and his succession to the childless Matthias in the rest of the Austrian dominions would infallibly be followed by a similar repression. To the Protestants of the Duchy, of Bohemia, of Hungary, therefore, the accession of Ferdinand meant either utter ruin or civil war, and a civil war would spread like wildfire along the Danube to the Rhine. But Matthias was resolved on bringing about the recognition of Ferdinand as his successor; and Spain saw that the time was come for effectually fettering James. If troubles must arise, religion and policy at once dictated the use which Spain would have to make of them. She could not support heretics, and she had very good reasons for supporting their foes. The great aim of her statesmen was to hold what was left of the Low Countries against either France or the Dutch, and now that she had lost the command of the sea, the road overland from her Italian dominions along the Rhine through Franche Comté to the Netherlands was absolutely needful for this purpose. But this road led through the Palatinate; and if war was to break out Spain must either secure the Palatinate for herself or for some Catholic prince on whose good-will she could rely. That the Dutch would oppose such a scheme was inevitable; but James alone could give fresh strength to the Dutch; and James could be duped into inaction by playing with his schemes for a marriage with the Infanta. In 1617 therefore negotiations for this purpose were formally opened between the courts of London and Madrid.

Ralegh's death.

Anger and alarm spread through England as the nation learned that James aimed at placing a Catholic queen upon its throne. Even at the court itself the cooler heads of statesmen were troubled by this disclosure of the king's projects. The old tradition of Cecil's policy lingered among a powerful party which had its representatives among the royal ministers; and powerless as these were to influence the king's course, they still believed they could impede it. If by any means war could be stirred up between England and Spain the marriage-treaty would fall to ruin, and James be forced into union with the Protestants abroad and into some reconciliation with the Parliament at home. The wild project by which they strove to bring war about may have sprung from a brain more inventive than their own. Of the great statesmen and warriors of Elizabeth's day one only remained. At the opening of the new reign Sir Walter Ralegh had been convicted on a charge of treason; but though unpardoned the sentence was never carried out, and he had remained ever since a prisoner in the Tower. As years went by the New World, where he had founded Virginia and where he had gleaned news of a Golden City, threw more and more a spell over his imagination; and at this moment he disclosed to James his knowledge of a gold-mine on the Oronoco, and prayed that he might sail thither and work its treasures for the king. No Spanish settlement, he said, had been made there; and like the rest of the Elizabethans he took no heed of the Spanish claims to all lands in America, whether settled or no. The king was tempted by the bait of gold; but he had no mind to be tricked out of his friendship with Spain; he exacted a pledge against any attack on Spanish territory, and told Ralegh that the shedding of Spanish blood would cost him his head. The threat told little on a man who had risked his head again and again; who believed in the tale he told; and who knew that if war could be brought about between England and Spain a new career was open to him. He found the coast occupied by Spanish troops; and while evading direct orders to attack, he sent his men up the country. They plundered a Spanish town, found no gold-mine, and soon came broken and defeated back. Ralegh's son had fallen in the struggle; but, heart-broken as he was by the loss and disappointment, the natural daring of the man saw a fresh resource. He proposed to seize the Spanish treasure ships as he returned, to sail with their gold to England, and like Drake to turn the heads of nation and king by the immense spoil. But the temper of the buccaneers was now strange to English seamen; his men would not follow him; and he was brought home to face his doom. James at once put his old sentence in force; and the death of Ralegh on the scaffold atoned for the affront to Spain.

The troubles in Bohemia.

The failure of Ralegh came at a critical moment in German history. In 1617, while he was traversing the Southern seas, Ferdinand was presented by Matthias to the Diet of Bohemia, and acknowledged by it as successor to that kingdom. As had been foreseen, he at once began the course of forcible suppression of Protestantism which had been successful in his other dominions. But the Bohemian nobles were not men to give up their faith without a fight for it; and in May 1618 they rose in revolt, flung Ferdinand's deputies out of the window of the palace at Prague, and called the country to arms. The long-dreaded crisis had come for Germany; but, as if with a foresight of the awful sufferings that the struggle was to bring, the Germans strove to look on it as a local revolt. The Lutheran princes longed only "to put the fire out"; the Calvinistic Union refused aid to the Bohemians; the Catholic League remained motionless. What partly accounted for the inaction of the Protestants was the ability of the Bohemians to hold their own. They were a match for all Ferdinand's efforts; through autumn and winter they held him easily at bay. In the spring of 1619 they even marched upon Vienna and all but surprised their enemy within his capital. But at this juncture the death of Matthias changed the face of affairs. Ferdinand became master of the whole Austrian heritage in Germany, and he offered himself as candidate for the vacant Imperial crown. Union among the Protestants might have hindered his accession, and with it the terrible strife which he was to bring upon the Empire. But an insane quarrel between Lutherans and Calvinists paralyzed their efforts; and in August 1619 Ferdinand became Emperor. Bohemia knew that its strength was insufficient to check a foe such as this; and two days before his formal election to the Empire its nobles declared the realm vacant, and chose Frederick, the young Elector-Palatine, as their king.

Outbreak of the Thirty Years War.

Frederick accepted the crown; but he was no sooner enthroned at Prague than the Bohemians saw themselves foiled in the hopes which had dictated their choice. They had trusted that Frederick's election would secure them support from the Calvinist Union, of which he was the leading member, and from James, whose daughter was his wife. But support from the Union was cut off by the jealousy of the French Government, which saw with suspicion the upgrowth of a great Calvinistic power, stretching from Bohemia to its own frontier, and pushing its influence through its relations with the Huguenot party into the very heart of France. James on the other hand was bitterly angered at Frederick's action. He could not recognize the right of subjects to depose a prince, or support Bohemia in what he looked on as revolt, or Frederick in what he believed to be the usurpation of a crown. By envoy after envoy he called on his son-in-law to lay down his new royalty, and to return to the Palatinate. His refusal of aid to the Protestant Union helped the pressure of France in paralyzing its action, while he threatened war against Holland, the one power which was earnest in the Palatine's cause. It was in vain that in England both court and people were unanimous in a cry for war, or that Archbishop Abbot from his sick-bed implored James to strike one blow for Protestantism. James still called on Frederick to withdraw from Bohemia, and relied in such a case on the joint efforts of England and Spain for a re-establishment of peace. But no consent to his plans could be wrung from Frederick; and the spring of 1620 saw Spain ready to throw aside the mask. The time had come for securing her road to the Netherlands, as well as for taking her old stand as a champion of Catholicism. Rumours of her purpose had already stolen over the Channel, and James was brought at last to suffer Sir Horace Vere to take some English volunteers to the Palatinate. But the succour came too late. Spinola, the Spanish general in the Low Countries, was ordered to march to the aid of the Emperor; and the famous Spanish battalions were soon moving up the Rhine. Their march turned the local struggle in Bohemia into a European war. The whole face of affairs was changed as by enchantment. The hesitation of the Union was ended by the needs of self-defence; but it could only free its hands for action against the Spaniards by signing a treaty of neutrality with the Catholic League. The treaty sealed the fate of Bohemia. It enabled the army of the League under Maximilian of Bavaria to march down the valley of the Danube; Austria was forced to submit unconditionally to Ferdinand; and in August, as Spinola reached the frontier of the Palatinate, the joint army of Ferdinand and the League prepared to enter Bohemia.

The Parliament of 1621.

On James the news of these events burst like a thunderbolt. He had been duped; and for the moment he bent before the burst of popular fury which the danger to German Protestantism called forth throughout the land. The cry for a Parliament, the necessary prelude to a war, overpowered the king's secret resistance; and the Houses were again called together. But before they could meet the game of Protestantism was lost. Spinola beat the troops of the Union back upon Worms, and occupied with ease the bulk of the Palatinate. On the 8th of November the army of the League forced Frederick to battle before the walls of Prague; and before the day was over he was galloping off, a fugitive, to North Germany. Such was the news that met the Houses on their assembly at Westminster in January 1621. The instinct of every Englishman told him that matters had now passed beyond the range of mediation or diplomacy. Armies were moving, fierce passions were aroused, schemes of vast ambition and disturbance were disclosing themselves; and at such a moment the only intervention possible was an intervention of the sword. The German princes called on James to send them an army. "The business is gone too far to be redressed with words only," said the Danish king, who was prepared to help them. "I thank God we hope, with the help of his Majesty of Great Britain and the rest of our friends, to give unto the Count Palatine good conditions. If ever we are to do any good for the liberty of Germany and religion now is the time." But this appeal met offers of "words only" and Denmark withdrew from the strife in despair. James in fact was as confident in his diplomatic efforts as ever; but even he saw at last that they needed the backing of some sort of armed force, and it was to procure this backing that he called for supplies from the Parliament.

Impeachment of the monopolists.

The Commons were bitterly chagrined. They had come together, trusting that their assembly meant such an attitude on the part of the Crown as would have rallied the Protestants of Germany round

England, and have aided the enterprise of the Dane. Above all they hoped for war with the power which had at once turned the strife to its own profit, whose appearance in the Palatinate had broken the strength of German Protestantism, and set the League free to crush Frederick at Prague. They found only demands for supplies, and a persistence in the old efforts to patch up a peace. Fresh envoys were now labouring to argue the Emperor into forgiveness of Frederick, and to argue the Spaniards into an evacuation of Frederick's dominions. With such aims not only was no war against the Spaniard to be thought of, but his good-will must be sought by granting permission for the export of arms from England to Spain. The Commons could only show their distrust of such a policy by a small vote of supplies and refusal of further aid in the future. But if their resentment could find no field in foreign affairs, it found a field at home. The most crying constitutional grievance arose from the revival of monopolies, in spite of the pledge of Elizabeth to suppress them. To the Crown they brought little profit; but they gratified the king by their extension of the sphere of his prerogative, and they put money into the pockets of his greedy dependants. A parliamentary right which had slept ever since the reign of Henry the Sixth, the right of the Lower House to impeach great offenders at the bar of the Lords, was revived against the monopolists; and James was driven by the general indignation to leave them to their fate. But the practice of monopolies was only one sign of the corruption of the court. Sales of peerages, sales of high offices of State, had raised a general disgust; and this disgust showed itself in the impeachment of the highest among the officers of State.

Fall of Bacon.

At the accession of James the rays of royal favour, so long looked for in vain, had broken slowly upon Francis Bacon. He became successively Solicitor and Attorney-General; the year of Shakspere's death saw him called to the Privy Council; he verified Elizabeth's prediction by becoming Lord Keeper. At last the goal of his ambition was reached. He had attached himself to the rising fortunes of Buckingham, and in 1618 the favour of Buckingham made him Lord Chancellor. He was raised to the peerage as Baron Verulam, and created, at a later time, Viscount St. Albans. But the nobler dreams for which these meaner honours had been sought escaped Bacon's grasp. His projects still remained projects, while to retain his hold on office he was stooping to a miserable compliance with the worst excesses of Buckingham and his master. The years during which he held the Chancellorship were, in fact, the most disgraceful years of a disgraceful reign. They saw the execution of Ralegh, the sacrifice of the Palatinate, the exaction of benevolences, the multiplication of monopolies, the supremacy of Buckingham. Against none of the acts of folly and wickedness which distinguished James's government did Bacon do more than protest; in some of the worst, and above all in the attempt to coerce the judges into prostrating the law at the king's feet, he took a personal part. But even his protests were too much for the young favourite, who regarded him as the mere creature of his will. It was in vain that Bacon flung himself on the Duke's mercy, and begged him to pardon a single instance of opposition to his caprice. A Parliament was impending, and Buckingham resolved to avert from himself the storm which was gathering by sacrificing to it his meaner dependants.

To ordinary eyes the Chancellor was at the summit of human success. Jonson had just sung of him as one "whose even thread the Fates spin round and full out of their choicest and their whitest wool" when the storm burst. The Commons charged Bacon with corruption in the exercise of his office. It had been customary among Chancellors to receive gifts from successful suitors after their suit was ended. Bacon, it is certain, had taken such gifts from men whose suits were still unsettled; and though his judgement may have been unaffected by them, the fact of their reception left him with no valid defence. He at once pleaded guilty to the charge. "I do plainly and ingenuously confess that I am guilty of corruption, and do renounce all defence. I beseech your Lordships," he added, "to be merciful to a broken reed." Though the heavy fine laid on him was remitted by the Crown, he was deprived of the Great Seal and declared incapable of holding office in the State or sitting in Parliament. Fortunately for his after fame Bacon's life was not to close in this cloud of shame. His fall restored him to that position of real greatness from which his ambition had so long torn him away. "My conceit of his person," says Ben Jonson, "was never increased towards him by his place or honours. But I have and do reverence him for his greatness that was only proper to himself, in that he seemed to me ever by his work one of the greatest men, and most worthy of admiration, that had been in many ages. In his adversity I ever prayed that God would give him strength; for greatness he could not want." Bacon's intellectual activity was never more conspicuous than in the last four years of his life. He began a digest of the laws and a history of England under the Tudors, revised and expanded his essays, and dictated a jest-book. He had presented "Novum Organum" to James in the year before his fall; in the year after it he produced his "Natural and Experimental History." Meanwhile he busied himself with experiments in physics which might carry out the principles he was laying down in these works; and it was while studying the effect of cold in preventing animal putrefaction that he stopped his coach to stuff a fowl with snow and caught the fever which ended in his death.

James clings to Spain.

James was too shrewd to mistake the importance of Bacon's impeachment; but the hostility of Buckingham to the Chancellor, and Bacon's own confession of his guilt, made it difficult to resist his condemnation. Energetic too as its measures were against corruption and monopolists, the Parliament respected scrupulously the king's prejudices in other matters; and even when checked by an adjournment, resolved unanimously to support him in any earnest effort for the Protestant cause. A warlike speech from a member at the close of the session in June roused an enthusiasm which recalled the days of Elizabeth. The Commons answered the appeal by a unanimous vote, "lifting their hats as high as they could hold them," that for the recovery of the Palatinate they would adventure their fortunes, their estates, and their lives. "Rather this declaration," cried a leader of the country party when it was read by the Speaker, "than ten thousand men already on the march." For the moment indeed the energetic declaration seemed to give vigour to the royal policy. James had aimed throughout at the restitution of Bohemia to Ferdinand, and at inducing the Emperor, through the mediation of Spain, to abstain from any retaliation on the Palatinate. He now freed himself for a moment from the trammels of diplomacy, and enforced a cessation of the attack on his son-in-law's dominions by a threat of war. The suspension of arms lasted through the summer of 1621; but threats could do no more. Frederick still refused to make the concessions which James pressed on him, and the army of the League advancing from Bohemia drove the forces of the Elector out of the upper or eastern portion of the Palatinate. Again the general restoration which James was designing had been thrown further back than ever by a Catholic advance; but the king had no mind to take up the challenge. He was only driven the more on his old policy of mediation through the aid of Spain. An end was put to all appearance of hostilities. The negotiations for the marriage with the Infanta, which had never ceased, were pressed more busily. Gondomar, the Spanish ambassador, who had become all-powerful at the English Court, was assured that no effectual aid should be sent to the Palatinate. The English fleet, which was cruising by way of menace off the Spanish coast, was called home. The king dismissed those of his ministers who still opposed a Spanish policy; and threatened on trivial pretexts a war with the Dutch, the one great Protestant power that remained in alliance with England, and was ready to back the Elector.

Dissolution of the Parliament.

But he had still to reckon with his Parliament; and the first act of the Parliament on its reassembling in November was to demand a declaration of war with Spain. The instinct of the nation was wiser than the statecraft of the king. Ruined and enfeebled as she really was, Spain to the world at large still seemed the champion of Catholicism. It was the entry of her troops into the Palatinate which had widened the local war in Bohemia into a struggle for the suppression of Protestantism along the Rhine; above all it was Spanish influence, and the hopes held out of a marriage of his son with a Spanish Infanta, which were luring the king into his fatal dependence on the great enemy of the Protestant cause. But the Commons went further than a demand for war. It was impossible any longer to avoid a matter so perilous to English interests, and in their petition the Houses coupled with their demands for war the demand of a Protestant marriage for their future king. Experience proved in later years how dangerous it was for English freedom that the heir to the Crown should be brought up under a Catholic mother; but James was beside himself at the presumption of the Commons in dealing with mysteries of State. "Bring stools for the Ambassadors," he cried in bitter irony as their committee appeared before him. He refused the petition, forbade any further discussion of State policy, and threatened the speakers with the Tower. "Let us resort to our prayers," a member said calmly as the king's letter was read, "and then consider of this great business." The temper of the House was seen in a Protestation with which it met the royal command to abstain from discussion. It resolved "That the liberties, franchises, privileges, and jurisdictions of Parliament are the ancient and undoubted birthright and inheritance of the subjects of England; and that the arduous and urgent affairs concerning the king, State, and defence of the realm, and of the Church of England, and the making and maintenance of laws, and redress of grievances, which daily happen within this realm, are proper subjects and matter of council and debate in Parliament. And that in the handling and proceeding of those businesses every member of the House hath, and of right ought to have, freedom of speech to propound, treat, reason, and bring to conclusion the same." The king answered the Protestation by a characteristic outrage. He sent for the Journals of the House, and with his own hand tore out the pages which contained it. "I will govern," he said, "according to the common weal, but not according to the common will." A few days after, on the nineteenth of December, he dissolved the Parliament.

Spain holds back.

"It is the best thing that has happened in the interests of Spain and of the Catholic religion since Luther began preaching," wrote the Count of Gondomar to his master, in his joy that all danger of war had passed away. "I am ready to depart," Sir Henry Savile on the other hand murmured on his death-bed, "the rather that having lived in good times I foresee worse." In the obstinacy with which he clung to his Spanish policy James stood indeed absolutely alone; for not only the old nobility and the statesmen who preserved the tradition of the age of Elizabeth, but even his own ministers, with the exception of Buckingham and the Treasurer, Cranfield, were at one with the Commons in their distrust of Spain. But James persisted in his plans. By the levy of a fresh benevolence he was able to keep Vere's force on foot for a few months while his diplomacy was at work in Germany and at Madrid. The Palatinate indeed was lost in spite of his despatches; but he still trusted to bring about its restitution to the Elector through his influence with Spain. It was to secure this influence that he pressed for a closer union with the great Catholic power. What really bound him to such a foreign policy was his policy at home. If James cared for the restoration of the Palatinate, he cared more for the system of government he had carried out since 1610; and with that system, as he well knew, Parliaments were incompatible. But a policy of war would at once throw him on the support of Parliaments; and the experience of 1621 had shown him at what a price that support must be bought. From war too, as from any policy which implied a decided course of action, the temper of James shrank. What he clung to was a co-operation with Spain in which the burden of enforcing peace on the German disputants should fall exclusively on that power. Of such a co-operation the marriage of his son Charles with the Infanta, which had so long been held out as a lure to his vanity, was to be the sign. But the more James pressed for this consummation of his projects, the more Spain held back. She too was willing to co-operate with James so long as such a co-operation answered her own purposes. Her statesmen had not favoured the war in Germany; even now they were willing to bring it to a close by the restoration of the Palatinate. But they would not abandon the advantages which the war had given to Catholicism; and their plan was to restore the Palatinate not to Frederick but to his son, and to bring up that son as a Catholic at Vienna. Of such a simple restoration of the religious and political balance in the Empire as James was contemplating, the statesmen of Madrid thought no more than they thought of carrying out the scheme of a marriage with his son. Spain had already gained all she wanted from the marriage-negotiations. They had held James from action; they had now made action even less possible by supplying a fresh ground of quarrel with the House of Commons. Had the match been likely to secure the conversion of England, or even a thorough toleration for Catholics, it might have been possible to consent to the union of a Spanish princess with a heretic. But neither result seemed probable: and the Spanish Court saw no gain in such a union as would compensate it for the loss of the Palatinate or the half-million which James counted on as the dowry of the bride.

End of the Spanish marriage.

But the more Spain hung back the hotter grew the impatience of Buckingham and James. At last the young favourite proposed to force the Spaniard's hand by the appearance of Prince Charles himself at Madrid. To the wooer in person Buckingham believed Spain would not dare to refuse either Infanta or Palatinate. James was too shrewd to believe in such a delusion, but in spite of his opposition the Prince quitted England in disguise in 1623, and at the beginning of March he appeared with Buckingham at Madrid to claim his promised bride. It was in vain that the Spanish Court rose in its demands; for every new demand was met by fresh concessions on the part of England. The abrogation of the penal laws against the worship of Catholics in private houses, a Catholic education for the Prince's children, a Catholic household for the Infanta, the erection of a Catholic church for her at Court, to which access should be free for all comers, were stipulations no sooner asked than they were granted. "We are building a chapel to the devil," said James when the last condition was laid before him; but he swore to the treaty and forced his councillors to swear to it. The marriage, however, was no nearer than before. The one thing which would have made it possible was a conversion of Charles to Catholicism; and though the Prince listened silently to arguments on the subject he gave no sign of becoming a Catholic. The aim of the Spanish ministers was to break off the match without a quarrel. They could only throw themselves on a policy of delay, and with this view the court theologians decided that the Infanta must in any case stay in Spain for a year after its conclusion till the conditions were fully carried out. Against such a condition Charles remonstrated in vain. And meanwhile the influence of the new policy on the war in Germany was hard to see. The Catholic League and its army under the command of Count Tilly won triumph after triumph over their divided foes. The reduction of Heidelberg and Mannheim completed the conquest of the Palatinate, whose Elector fled helplessly to Holland, while his Electoral dignity was transferred by the Emperor to the Duke of Bavaria. But there was still no sign of the hoped-for intervention on the part of Spain. At last the pressure of Charles on the subject of the Palatinate brought about a disclosure of the secret of Spanish policy. "It is a maxim of state with us," the Count of Olivares confessed, as the Prince demanded an energetic interference in Germany, "that the King of Spain must never fight against the Emperor. We cannot employ our forces against the Emperor." "If you hold to that," replied the Prince, "there is an end of all." Quitting Madrid he found a fleet at Santander, and on the fifth of October he again landed with Buckingham on the shores of England.

Prince Charles.

His return was the signal for a burst of national joy. All London was alight with bonfires in her delight at the failure of the Spanish match, and of the collapse, humiliating as it was, of a policy which had so long trailed English honour at the chariot-wheels of Spain. War seemed at last inevitable; for not only did James's honour call for some effort to win back the Palatinate for his daughter's children, but the resentment of Charles and Buckingham was ready to bear down any reluctance of the king. From the moment of their return indeed the direction of English affairs passed out of the hands of James into those of the favourite and the Prince. Charles started on his task of government with the aid of a sudden burst of popularity. To those who were immediately about him the journey to Madrid had revealed the strange mixture of obstinacy and weakness in the Prince's character, the duplicity which lavished promises because it never purposed to be bound by any, the petty pride that subordinated every political consideration to personal vanity or personal pique. Charles had granted demand after demand till the very Spaniards lost faith in his concessions. With rage in his heart at the failure of his efforts, he had renewed his betrothal on the very eve of his departure only that he might insult the Infanta by its contemptuous withdrawal as soon as he was safe at home. But to England at large the baser features of his character were still unknown. The stately reserve, the personal dignity and decency of manners which distinguished the Prince, contrasted favourably with the gabble and indecorum of his father. The courtiers indeed who saw him in his youth would often pray God that "he might be in the right way when he was set; for if he were in the wrong he would prove the most wilful of any king that ever reigned." But the nation was willing to take his obstinacy for firmness; as it took the pique which inspired his course on the return from Spain for patriotism and for the promise of a nobler rule.

The Parliament of 1624.

At the back of Charles stood the favourite Buckingham. The policy of James had recoiled upon its author. In raising his favourites to the height of honour James had looked to being at last an independent king. He had broken with parliaments, he had done away with the old administrative forms of government, that his personal rule might act freely through these creatures of his will. And now that his policy had reached its end, his will was set aside more ruthlessly than ever by the very instrument he had created to carry it out. In his zeal to establish the greatness of the monarchy he had brought on the monarchy a humiliation such as it had never known. Church, or Baronage, or Commons had many times in our history forced a king to take their policy for his own; but never had a mere minister of the Crown been able to force his policy on a king. This was what Buckingham set himself to do. The national passion, the Prince's support, his own quick energy, bore down the hesitation and reluctance of James. The king still clung desperately to peace. He still shrank from parliaments. But Buckingham overrode every difficulty. In February 1624 James was forced to meet a Parliament, and to concede the point on which he had broken with the last by laying before it the whole question of the Spanish negotiation. Buckingham and the Prince gave their personal support to a demand of the Houses for a rupture of the treaties with Spain and a declaration of war. A subsidy was eagerly voted; and as if to mark a new departure in the policy of the Stuarts, the persecution of the Catholics, which had long been suspended out of deference to Spanish intervention, began with new vigour. The favourite gave a fresh pledge of his constitutional aims by consenting to a new attack on a minister of the Crown. The Lord Treasurer, Cranfield, Earl of Middlesex, had done much by his management of the finances to put the royal revenues on a better footing. But he was the head of the Spanish party; and he still urged the king to cling to Spain and to peace. Buckingham and

Charles therefore looked coldly on while he was impeached for corruption and dismissed from office.

Buckingham's plans.

Though James was swept along helplessly by the tide, his shrewdness saw clearly the turn that affairs were taking; and it was only by hard pressure that the favourite succeeded in wresting his consent to Cranfield's disgrace. "You are making a rod for your own back," said the king. But Buckingham and Charles persisted in their plans of war. That these were utterly different from the plans of the Parliament troubled them little. What money the Commons had granted, they had granted on condition that the war should be exclusively a war against Spain, and a war waged as exclusively by sea. Their good sense shrank from plunging into the tangled and intricate medley of religious and political jealousies which was turning Germany into a hell. What they saw to be possible was to aid German Protestantism by lifting off it the pressure of the armies of Spain. That Spain was most assailable on the sea the ministers at Madrid knew as well as the leaders of the Commons. What they dreaded was not a defeat in the Palatinate, but the cutting off of their fleets from the Indies and a war in that new world which they treasured as the fairest flower of their crown. A blockade of Cadiz or a capture of Hispaniola would have produced more effect at the Spanish council-board than a dozen English victories on the Rhine. But such a policy had little attraction for Buckingham. His flighty temper exulted in being the arbiter of Europe, in weaving fanciful alliances, in marshalling imaginary armies. A treaty was concluded with Holland, and negotiations set on foot with the Lutheran princes of North Germany, who had looked coolly on at the ruin of the Elector Palatine, but were scared at last into consciousness of their own danger. Yet more important negotiations were opened for an alliance with France. To restore the triple league of France, England, and Holland was to restore the system of Elizabeth. Such a league would in fact have been strong enough to hold in check the House of Austria and save German Protestantism, while it would have hindered France from promoting and profiting by German disunion, as it did under Richelieu. But, as of old, James could understand no alliance that rested on merely national interests. A dynastic union seemed to him the one sure basis for joint action; and the plan for a French alliance became a plan for marriage with a French princess.

The French marriage.

The plan suited the pride of Charles and of Buckingham. But the first whispers of it woke opposition in the Commons. They saw the danger of a Roman Catholic queen. They saw yet more keenly the danger of pledges of toleration given to a foreign government, pledges which would furnish it with continual pretexts for interfering in the civil government of the country. Such an interference would soon breed on either side a mood for war. Before making these grants therefore they had called for a promise that no such pledges should be given, and as a subsidy hung on his consent James had solemnly promised this. But it was soon found that France was as firm on this point as Spain; and that toleration for the Catholics was a necessary condition of any marriage-treaty. The pressure of Buckingham and Charles was again brought to bear upon the king. The promise was broken and the marriage-treaty was signed. Its difficulties were quick to disclose themselves. It was impossible to call Parliament again together at winter tide, while such perfidy was fresh; and the subsidies, which had been counted on, could not be asked for. But a hundred schemes were pushed busily on; and twelve thousand Englishmen were gathered under an adventurer, Count Mansfield, to march to the Rhine. They reached Holland only to find themselves without supplies and to die of famine and disease.

Death of James.

If the blow fell lightly on the temper of the favourite, it fell heavily on the king. James was already sinking to the grave, and in the March of 1625 he died with the consciousness of failure. Even his sanguine temper was broken at last. He had struggled with the Parliament, and the Parliament was stronger than ever. He had broken with Puritanism, and England was growing more Puritan every day. He had claimed for the Crown authority such as it had never known, and the Commons had impeached and degraded his ministers. He had raised up dependants to carry out a purely personal rule, and it was a favourite who was now treading his will under foot. He had staked everything on his struggle with English freedom, and the victory of English freedom was well-nigh won. James had himself destroyed that enthusiasm of loyalty which had been the main strength of the Tudor throne. He had disenchanted his people of their blind faith in the monarchy by a policy both at home and abroad which ran counter to every national instinct. He had alienated alike the noble, the gentleman, and the trader. In his feverish desire for personal rule he had ruined the main bulwarks of the monarchy. He had destroyed the authority of the Council. He had accustomed men to think lightly of the ministers of the Crown, to see them browbeaten by favourites, and driven from office for corruption. He had degraded the judges and weakened the national reverence for their voice as an expression of law. He had turned the Church into a mere engine for carrying out the royal will. And meanwhile he had raised up in the very face of the throne a power which was strong enough to cope with it. He had quarrelled with and insulted the Houses as no English sovereign had ever done before; and all the while the authority he boasted of was passing without his being able to hinder it to the Parliament which he outraged. There was shrewdness as well as anger in his taunt at its "ambassadors." A power had at last risen up in the Commons with which the monarchy was to reckon. In spite of the king's petulant outbreaks Parliament had asserted with success its exclusive right of taxation. It had suppressed monopolies. It had reformed abuses in the courts of law. It had impeached and driven from office the highest ministers of the Crown. It had asserted its privilege of freely discussing all questions connected with the welfare of the realm. It had claimed to deal with the question of religion. It had even declared its will on the sacred "mystery" of foreign policy. The utter failure of the schemes of James at home can only be realized by comparing the attitude of the Houses at his death with their attitude during the last years of Elizabeth. Nor was his failure less abroad than at home. He had found England among the greatest of European powers. He had degraded her into a satellite of Spain. And now from a satellite he had dropped to the position of a dupe. In one plan alone could he believe himself successful. If his son had missed the hand of a Spanish Infanta, he had gained the hand of a daughter of France. But the one success of James was the most fatal of all his blunders; for in the marriage with Henrietta Maria lay the doom of his race. It was the fierce and despotic temper of the Frenchwoman that was to nerve Charles more than all to his fatal struggle against English liberty. It was her bigotry—as the Commons foresaw—that undermined the Protestantism of her sons. It was when the religious and the political temper of Henrietta mounted the throne in James the Second that the full import of the French marriage was seen in the downfall of the Stuarts.

CHAPTER V

CHARLES I. AND THE PARLIAMENT

1625-1629

Charles the First.

Had Charles mounted the throne on his return from Spain his accession would have been welcomed by a passionate burst of enthusiasm. He had aired himself as a staunch Protestant who had withstood Catholic seductions, and had come to nerve his father to a policy at one with the interests of religion and with the national will. But the few months that had passed since the last session of Parliament had broken the spell of this heroic attitude. The real character of the part which Charles had played in Spain was gradually becoming known. It was seen that he had been as faithless to Protestantism as his revenge had made him faithless to the Infanta. Nor had he shown less perfidy in dealing with England itself. In common with his father, he had promised that his marriage with a princess of France should in no case be made conditional on the relaxation of the penal laws against the Catholics. It was suspected, and the suspicion was soon to be changed into certainty, that in spite of this promise such a relaxation had been stipulated, and that a foreign power had again been given the right of intermeddling in the civil affairs of the realm. The general distrust of the new king was intensified by the conduct of the war. In granting its subsidies the Parliament of 1624 had restricted them to the purposes of a naval war, and that a war with Spain. It had done this after discussing and rejecting the wider schemes of the favourite for an intervention of England by land in the war of the Palatinate. But the grants once made, Buckingham's plans had gone on without a check. Alliances had been formed, subsidies promised to Denmark, and twelve thousand men actually despatched to join the armies on the Rhine. It was plain that the policy of the Crown was to be as unswayed by the will of the nation as in the days of King James. What it was really to be swayed by was the self-sufficient incapacity of the young favourite.

The king's policy.

A few months of action had shown Buckingham to England as he really was, vain, flighty, ingenious, daring, a brilliant but shallow adventurer, without political wisdom or practical ability, as little of an administrator as of a statesman. While projects without number were seething and simmering in his restless brain, while leagues were being formed and armies levied on paper, the one practical effort of the new minister had ended in the starvation of thousands of Englishmen on the sands of Holland. If English policy was once more to become a real and serious thing, it was plain that the great need of the nation was the dismissal of Buckingham. But Charles clung to Buckingham more blindly than his father had done. The shy reserve, the slow stubborn temper of the new king found relief in the frank gaiety of the favourite, in his rapid suggestions, in the defiant daring with which he set aside all caution and opposition. James had looked on Buckingham as his pupil. Charles clung to him as his friend. Nor was the new king's policy likely to be more national in Church affairs than in affairs of state. The war had given a new impulse to religious enthusiasm. The patriotism of the Puritan was strengthening his bigotry. To the bulk of Englishmen a fight with Spain meant a fight with Catholicism; and the fervour against Catholicism without roused a corresponding fervour against Catholicism within the realm. To Protestant eyes every English Catholic seemed a traitor at home, a traitor who must be watched and guarded against as the most dangerous of foes. A Protestant who leant towards Catholic usage or Catholic dogma was yet more formidable. To him men felt as towards a secret traitor in their own ranks. But it was to men with such leanings that Charles seemed disposed to show favour. Bishop Laud was recognized as the centre of that varied opposition to Puritanism, whose members were loosely grouped under the name of Arminians; and Laud now became the king's adviser in ecclesiastical matters. With Laud at its head the new party grew in boldness as well as numbers. It naturally sought for shelter for its religious opinions by exalting the power of the Crown; and its union of political error with theological heresy seemed to the Puritan to be at last proclaimed to the world when Montague, a court chaplain, ventured to slight the Reformed Churches of the Continent in favour of the Church of Rome, and to advocate in his sermon the Real Presence in the Sacrament and a divine right in kings.

The Parliament of 1625.

The Houses had no sooner met in the May of 1625 than their temper in religious matters was clear to every observer. "Whatever mention does break forth of the fears and dangers in religion and the increase of Popery," wrote a member who was noting the proceedings of the Commons, "their affections are much stirred." The first act of the Lower House was to summon Montague to its bar and to commit him to prison. In their grants to the Crown they showed no ill-will indeed, but they showed caution. They suspected that the pledge of making no religious concessions to France had been broken. They knew that the conditions on which the last subsidy had been granted had been contemptuously set aside. In his request for a fresh grant Charles showed the same purpose of carrying out his own policy without any regard for the national will by simply asking for supplies for the war without naming a sum or giving any indication of what war it was to support. The reply of the Commons was to grant a hundred and forty thousand pounds. A million would hardly cover the king's engagements, and Charles was bitterly angered. He was angered yet more by the delay in granting the permanent revenue of the Crown. The Commons had no wish to refuse their grant of tonnage and poundage, or the main customs duties, which had ever since Edward the Fourth's day been granted to each new sovereign for his life. But the additional impositions laid by James on these duties required further consideration, and to give time for a due arrangement of this vexed question the grant of the customs was made for a year only. But the limitation at once woke the jealousy of Charles. He looked on it as a restriction of the rights of the Crown, refused to accept the grant on such a condition, and adjourned the Houses. When they met again at Oxford it was in a sterner temper, for Charles had shown his defiance of Parliament by promoting Montague, who had been released on bond, to a royal chaplaincy, and by levying the disputed customs without authority of law. "England," cried Sir Robert Phelips, "is the last monarchy that yet retains her liberties. Let them not perish now." But the Commons had no sooner announced their resolve to consider public grievances before entering on other business than they were met in August by a dissolution.

The descent on Cadiz.

To the shallow temper of Buckingham the cautious firmness of the Commons seemed simply the natural discontent which follows on ill success. If he dissolved the Houses, it was in the full belief that their constitutional demands could be lulled by a military triumph. His hands were no sooner free than he sailed for the Hague to conclude a general alliance against the House of Austria, while a fleet of ninety vessels and ten thousand soldiers left Plymouth in October for the coast of Spain. But these vast projects broke down before Buckingham's administrative incapacity. The plan of alliance proved fruitless. After an idle descent on Cadiz the Spanish expedition returned broken with mutiny and disease; and the enormous debt which had been incurred in its equipment forced the favourite to advise a new summons of the Houses in the coming year. But he was keenly alive to the peril in which his failure had plunged him, and to a coalition which had been formed between his rivals at Court and the leaders of the last Parliament. The older nobles looked to his ruin to restore the power of the Council; and in this the leaders of the Commons went with them. Buckingham's reckless daring led him to anticipate the danger by a series of blows which should strike terror into his opponents. The Councillors were humbled by the committal of Lord Arundel to the Tower. Sir Robert Phelips, Coke, and four other leading patriots were made sheriffs of their counties, and thus prevented from sitting in the coming Parliament.

Eliot.

But their exclusion only left the field free for a more terrible foe. If Hampden and Pym are the great figures which embody the later national resistance, the earlier struggle for Parliamentary liberty centres in the figure of Sir John Eliot. Of an old family which had settled under Elizabeth near the fishing hamlet of St. Germans, and whose stately mansion gives its name of Port Eliot to a little town on the Tamar, he had risen to the post of Vice-Admiral of Devonshire under the patronage of Buckingham, and had seen his activity in the suppression of piracy in the Channel rewarded by an unjust imprisonment. He was now in the first vigour of manhood, with a mind exquisitely cultivated and familiar with the poetry and learning of his day, a nature singularly lofty and devout, a fearless and vehement temper. There was a hot impulsive element in his nature which showed itself in youth in his drawing sword on a neighbour who denounced him to his father, and which in later years gave its characteristic fire to his eloquence. But his intellect was as clear and cool as his temper was ardent. What he believed in was the English Parliament. He saw in it the collective wisdom of the realm; and in that wisdom he put a firmer trust than in the statecraft of kings. In the general enthusiasm which followed on the failure of the Spanish marriage, Eliot had stood almost alone in pressing for a recognition of the rights of Parliament as a preliminary to any real reconciliation with the Crown. He fixed, from the very outset of his career, on the responsibility of the royal ministers to Parliament as the one critical point for English liberty.

The Parliament of 1626.

It was to enforce the demand of this that he availed himself of Buckingham's sacrifice of the Treasurer, Cranfield, to the resentment of the Commons. "The greater the delinquent," he urged, "the greater the delict. They are a happy thing, great men and officers, if they be good, and one of the greatest blessings of the land: but power converted into evil is the greatest curse that can befall it." But the Parliament of 1626 had hardly met when Eliot came to the front to threaten a greater criminal than Cranfield. So menacing were his words, as he called for an enquiry into the failure before Cadiz, that Charles himself stooped to answer threat with threat. "I see," he wrote to the House, "you especially aim at the Duke of Buckingham. I must let you know that I will not allow any of my servants to be questioned among you, much less such as are of eminent place and near to me." A more direct attack on a right already acknowledged in the impeachment of Bacon and Cranfield could hardly be imagined, but Eliot refused to move from his constitutional ground. The king was by law irresponsible, he "could do no wrong." If the country therefore was to be saved from a pure despotism, it must be by enforcing the responsibility of the ministers who counselled and executed his acts. Eliot persisted in denouncing Buckingham's incompetence and corruption, and the Commons ordered the subsidy which the Crown had demanded to be brought in "when we shall have presented our grievances, and received his Majesty's answer thereto." Charles summoned them to Whitehall, and commanded them to cancel the condition. He would grant them "liberty of counsel, but not of control"; and he closed the interview with a significant threat. "Remember," he said, "that Parliaments are altogether in my power for their calling, sitting, and dissolution: and therefore, as I find the fruits of them to be good or evil, they are to continue or not to be." But the will of the Commons was as resolute as the will of the king. Buckingham's impeachment was voted and carried to the Lords.

Impeachment of Buckingham.

The favourite took his seat as a peer to listen to the charge with so insolent an air of contempt that one of the managers appointed by the Commons to conduct it turned sharply on him. "Do you jeer, my Lord!" said Sir Dudley Digges. "I can show you when a greater man than your Lordship—as high as you in place and power, and as deep in the king's favour—has been hanged for as small a crime as these articles contain." But his arrogance raised a more terrible foe than Sir Dudley Digges. The "proud carriage" of the Duke provoked an attack from Eliot which marks a new era in Parliamentary speech. From the first the vehemence and passion of his words had contrasted with the grave, colourless reasoning of older speakers. His opponents complained that Eliot aimed to "stir up affections." The quick emphatic sentences he substituted for the cumbrous periods of the day, his rapid argument, his vivacious and caustic allusions, his passionate appeals, his fearless invective, struck a new note in English eloquence. The frivolous ostentation of Buckingham, his very figure blazing with jewels and gold, gave point to the fierce attack. "He has broken those nerves and sinews of our land, the stores and treasures of the king. There needs no search for it. It is too visible. His profuse expenses, his superfluous feasts, his magnificent buildings, his riots, his excesses, what are they but the visible evidences of an express exhausting of the state, a chronicle of the immensity of his waste of the revenues of the Crown?" With the same terrible directness Eliot reviewed the Duke's greed and corruption, his insatiate ambition, his seizure of all public authority, his neglect of every public duty, his abuse for selfish ends of the powers he had accumulated. "The pleasure of his Majesty, his known directions, his public acts, his acts of council, the decrees of courts—all must be made inferior to this man's will. No right, no interest may withstand him. Through the power of state and justice he has dared ever to strike at his own ends." "My Lords," he ended, after a vivid parallel between Buckingham and Sejanus, "you see the man! What have been his actions, what he is like, you know! I leave him to your judgement. This only is conceived by us, the knights, citizens, and burgesses of the Commons House of Parliament, that by him came all our evils, in him we find the causes, and on him must be the remedies! Pereat qui perdere cuncta festinat! Opprimatur ne omnes opprimat!"

Dissolution of the Parliament.

In calling for Buckingham's removal the Houses were but exercising a right or a duty which was inherent in their very character of counsellors of the Crown. There had never been a time from the earliest days of the English Parliament when it had not called for the dismissal of evil advisers. What had in older time been done by risings of the baronage had been done since the Houses gathered at Westminster by their protests as representatives of the realm. They were far from having dreamed as yet of the right which Parliament exercises to-day of naming the royal ministers, nor had they any wish to meddle with the common administration of government. It was only in exceptional instances of evil counsel, when some favourite like Buckingham broke the union of the nation and the king, that they demanded a change. To Charles however their demand seemed a claim to usurp his sovereignty. His reply was as fierce and sudden as the attack of Eliot. He hurried to the House of Peers to avow as his own the deeds with which Buckingham was charged; while Eliot and Digges were called from their seats and committed prisoners to the Tower. The Commons however refused to proceed with public business till their members were restored; and after a ten-days' struggle Eliot was released. But his release was only a prelude to the close of the Parliament. "Not one moment," the king replied to the prayer of his Council for delay; and a final remonstrance in which the Commons begged him to dismiss Buckingham from his service for ever was met on the sixteenth of June by their instant dissolution. The remonstrance was burnt by royal order; Eliot was deprived of his Vice-Admiralty; and on the old pretext alleged by James for evading the law, the pretext that what it forbade was the demand of forced loans and not of voluntary gifts to the Crown, the subsidies which the Parliament had refused to grant till their grievances were redressed were levied in the arbitrary form of benevolences.

The Forced Loan.

But the tide of public resistance was slowly rising. Refusals to give anything "save by way of Parliament" came in from county after county. When the subsidy-men of Middlesex and Westminster were urged to comply, they answered with a tumultuous shout of "A Parliament! a Parliament! else no subsidies!" Kent stood out to a man. In Bucks the very justices neglected to ask for the "free gift." The freeholders of Cornwall only answered that, "if they had but two kine, they would sell one of them for supply to his Majesty—in a Parliamentary way." The failure of the voluntary benevolence forced Charles to pass from evasion into open defiance of the law. He met it in 1627 by the levy of a forced loan. It was in vain that Chief Justice Crewe refused to acknowledge that such loans were legal. The law was again trampled under foot, as in the case of his predecessor, Coke; and Crewe was dismissed from his post. Commissioners were named to assess the amount which every landowner was bound to lend, and to examine on oath all who refused. Every means of persuasion, as of force, was resorted to. The pulpits of the Laudian clergy resounded with the cry of "passive obedience." Dr. Mainwaring preached before Charles himself, that the king needed no Parliamentary warrant for taxation, and that to resist his will was to incur eternal damnation. Soldiers were quartered on recalcitrant boroughs. Poor men who refused to lend were pressed into the army or navy. Stubborn tradesmen were flung into prison. Buckingham himself undertook the task of overawing the nobles and the gentry. Among the bishops, the Primate and Bishop Williams of Lincoln alone resisted the king's will. The first was suspended on a frivolous pretext, and the second was disgraced. But in the country at large resistance was universal. The northern counties in a mass set the Crown at defiance. The Lincolnshire farmers drove the Commissioners from the town. Shropshire, Devon, and Warwickshire "refused utterly." Eight peers, with Lord Essex and Lord Warwick at their head, declined to comply with the exaction as illegal. Two hundred country gentlemen, whose obstinacy had not been subdued by their transfer from prison to prison, were summoned before the Council; and John Hampden, as yet only a young Buckinghamshire squire, appeared at the board to begin that career of patriotism which has made his name dear to Englishmen. "I could be content to lend," he said, "but fear to draw on myself that curse in Magna Charta, which should be read twice a year against those who infringe it." So close an imprisonment in the Gate House rewarded his protest "that he never afterwards did look like the same man he was before."

Charles and France.

The fierce energy with which Buckingham pressed the forced loan was no mere impulse of angry tyranny. Never was money so needed by the Crown. The blustering and blundering of the favourite had at last succeeded in plunging him into war with his own allies. England had been told that the friendship of France, a friendship secured by the king's marriage with a French princess, was the basis on which Charles was building up his great European alliance against Spain. She now suddenly found herself at war with Spain and France together. The steps by which this result had been brought about throw an amusing light on the capacity of the young king and his minister. The occupation of the Palatinate had forced France to provide for its own safety. Spain already fronted her along the Pyrenees and the border of the Netherlands; if the Palatinate was added to the Spanish possession of Franche-Comté, it would close France in on the east as well as the north and the south. War therefore was being forced on the French monarchy when Charles and Buckingham sought its alliance against Spain; and nothing hindered an outbreak of hostilities but a revolt of the Protestant town of Rochelle. Lewis the Thirteenth pleaded the impossibility of engaging in such a struggle so long as the Huguenots could rise in his rear; and he called on England to help him by lending ships to blockade Rochelle into submission in time for action in the spring of 1625. The Prince and Buckingham brought James to assent; but Charles had no sooner mounted the throne than he shrank from sending ships against a Protestant city, and secretly instigated the crews to mutiny against their captains on an order to sail. The vessels, it was trusted, would then arrive too late to take part in the siege. Unluckily for this intrigue they arrived to find the city still in arms, and it was the appearance of English ships among their enemies which forced the men of Rochelle to submit. While Englishmen were angered by the use of English vessels against Protestantism, France resented the king's attempt to evade his pledge. Its Court resented yet more the hesitation which Charles showed in face of his Parliament in fulfilling the promise he had given in the marriage-treaty of tolerating Catholic worship; and its resentment was embittered by an expulsion from the realm of the French attendants on the new Queen, a step to which Charles was at last driven by their insolence and intrigues. On the other hand, French statesmen were offended by the seizure of French ships charged with carrying materials of war to the Spaniards, and by an attempt of the English sovereign to atone for his past attack on Rochelle by constituting himself mediator of a peace on behalf of the Huguenots.

The siege of Rochelle.

But though grounds of quarrel multiplied every day, the French minister, Richelieu, had no mind for strife. He was now master of the Catholic faction which had fed the dispute between the Crown and the Huguenots with the aim of bringing about a reconciliation with Spain; he saw that in the European conflict which lay before him the friendship or the neutrality of England was all but essential; and though he gathered a fleet in the Channel and took a high tone of remonstrance, he strove by concession after concession to avert war. But on war Buckingham was resolved. Of policy in any true sense of the word the favourite knew nothing; for the real interest of England or the balance of Europe he cared little; what he saw before him was the chance of a blow at a power he had come to hate, and the chance of a war which would make him popular at home. The mediation of Charles in favour of Rochelle had convinced Richelieu that the complete reduction of that city was a necessary prelude to any effective intervention in Germany. If Lewis was to be master abroad, he must first be master at home. But it was hard for lookers-on to read the Cardinal's mind or to guess with what a purpose he resolved to exact submission from the Huguenots. In England, where the danger of Rochelle seemed a fresh part of the Catholic attack upon Protestantism throughout the world, the enthusiasm for the Huguenots was intense; and Buckingham resolved to take advantage of this enthusiasm to secure such a triumph for the royal arms as should silence all opposition at home. It was for this purpose that the forced loan was pushed on; and in July 1627 a fleet of a hundred vessels sailed under Buckingham's command for the relief of Rochelle. But imposing as was his force, Buckingham showed himself as incapable a soldier as he had proved a statesman. The troops were landed on the Isle of Rhé, in front of the harbour; but after a useless siege of the Castle of St. Martin, the English soldiers were forced in October to fall back along a narrow causeway to their ships, and two thousand fell in the retreat without the loss of a single man to their enemies.

The Parliament of 1628.

The first result of the failure at Rhé was the summoning of a new Parliament. Overwhelmed as he was with debt and shame, Charles was forced to call the Houses together again in the spring of 1628. The elections promised ill for the Court. Its candidates were everywhere rejected. The patriot leaders were triumphantly returned. To have suffered in the recent resistance to arbitrary taxation was the sure road to a seat. It was this question which absorbed all others in men's minds. Even Buckingham's removal was of less moment than the redress of personal wrongs; and some of the chief leaders of the Commons had not hesitated to bring Charles to consent to summon Parliament by promising to abstain from attacks on Buckingham. Against such a resolve Eliot protested in vain. But on the question of personal liberty the tone of the Commons when they met in March was as vehement as that of Eliot. "We must vindicate our ancient liberties," said Sir Thomas Wentworth in words soon to be remembered against himself: "we must reinforce the laws made by our ancestors. We must set such a stamp upon them, as no licentious spirit shall dare hereafter to invade them." Heedless of sharp and menacing messages from the king, of demands that they should take his "royal word" for their liberties, the House bent itself to one great work, the drawing up a Petition of Right. The statutes that protected the subject against arbitrary taxation, against loans and benevolences, against punishment, outlawry, or deprivation of goods, otherwise than by lawful judgement of his peers, against arbitrary imprisonment without stated charge, against billeting of soldiery on the people or enactment of martial law in time of peace, were formally recited. The breaches of them under the last two sovereigns, and above all since the dissolution of the last Parliament, were recited as formally. At the close of this significant list, the Commons prayed "that no man hereafter be compelled to make or yield any gift, loan, benevolence, tax, or such like charge, without common consent by Act of Parliament. And that none be called to make answer, or to take such oaths, or to be confined or otherwise molested or disputed concerning the same, or for refusal thereof. And that no freeman may in such manner as is before mentioned be imprisoned or detained. And that your Majesty would be pleased to remove the said soldiers and mariners, and that your people may not be so burthened in time to come. And that the commissions for proceeding by martial law may be revoked and annulled, and that hereafter no commissions of like nature may issue forth to any person or persons whatsoever to be executed as aforesaid, lest by colour of them any of your Majesty's subjects be destroyed and put to death, contrary to the laws and franchises of the land. All which they humbly pray of your most excellent Majesty, as their rights and liberties, according to the laws and statutes of the realm. And that your Majesty would also vouchsafe to declare that the awards, doings, and proceedings to the prejudice of your people in any of the premisses shall not be drawn hereafter into consequence or example. And that your Majesty would be pleased graciously for the further comfort and safety of your people to declare your royal will and pleasure, that in the things aforesaid all your officers and ministers shall serve you according to the laws and statutes of this realm, as they tender the honour of your Majesty and the prosperity of the kingdom."

The Petition of Right.

It was in vain that the Lords strove to conciliate Charles by a reservation of his "sovereign power." "Our petition," Pym quietly replied, "is for the laws of England, and this power seems to be another power distinct from the power of the law." The Lords yielded, but Charles gave an evasive reply; and the failure of the more moderate counsels for which his own had been set aside called Eliot again to the front. In a speech of unprecedented boldness he moved the presentation to the king of a Remonstrance on the state of the realm. But at the moment when he again touched on Buckingham's removal as the preliminary of any real improvement the Speaker of the House interposed. "There was a command laid on him," he said, "to interrupt any that should go about to lay an aspersion on the king's ministers." The breach of their privilege of free speech produced a scene in the Commons such as St. Stephen's had never witnessed before. Eliot sate abruptly down amidst the solemn silence of the House. "Then appeared such a spectacle of passions," says a letter of the time, "as the like had seldom been seen in such an assembly: some weeping, some expostulating, some prophesying of the fatal ruin of our kingdom, some playing the divines in confessing their sins and country's sins which drew these judgements upon us, some finding, as it were, fault with those that wept. There were above an hundred weeping eyes, many who offered to speak being interrupted and silenced by their own passions." Pym himself rose only to sit down choked with tears. At last Sir Edward Coke found words to blame himself for the timid counsels which had checked Eliot at the beginning of the Session, and to protest "that the author and source of all those miseries was the Duke of Buckingham." Shouts of assent greeted the resolution to insert the Duke's name in the Remonstrance. But at this moment the king's obstinacy gave way. A fresh expedition, which had been sent to Rochelle, returned unsuccessful; and if the siege was to be raised far greater and costlier efforts must be made. And that the siege should be raised Buckingham was still resolved. All his energies were now enlisted in this project; and to get supplies for his fleet he bent the king to consent in June to the Petition of Right. As Charles understood it, indeed, the consent meant little. The one point for which he really cared was the power of keeping men in prison without bringing them to trial or assigning causes for their imprisonment. On this he had consulted his judges; and they had answered that his consent to the Petition left his rights untouched; like other laws, they said, the Petition would have to be interpreted when it came before them, and the prerogative remained unaffected. As to the rest, while waiving all claim to levy taxes not granted by Parliament, Charles still reserved his right to levy impositions paid customarily to the Crown, and amongst these he counted tonnage and poundage. Of these reserves however the Commons knew nothing. The king's consent won a grant of subsidy, and such a ringing of bells and lighting of bonfires from the people "as were never seen but upon his Majesty's return from Spain."

Death of Buckingham.

But, like all the king's concessions, it came too late to effect the end at which he aimed. The Commons persisted in presenting their Remonstrance. Charles received it coldly and ungraciously; while Buckingham, who had stood defiantly at his master's side as he was denounced, fell on his knees to speak. "No, George!" said the king as he raised him; and his demeanour gave emphatic proof that the Duke's favour remained undiminished. "We will perish together, George," he added at a later time, "if thou dost." He had in fact got the subsidies which he needed; and it was easy to arrest all proceedings against Buckingham by proroguing Parliament at the close of June. The Duke himself cared little for a danger which he counted on drowning in the blaze of a speedy triumph. He had again gathered a strong fleet and a fine body of men, and his ardent fancy already saw the harbour of Rochelle forced and the city relieved. No shadow of his doom had fallen over the brilliant favourite when he set out in August to take command of the expedition. But a lieutenant in the army, John Felton, soured by neglect and wrongs, had found in the Remonstrance some imaginary sanction for the revenge he plotted; and, mixing with the throng which crowded the hall at Portsmouth, he stabbed Buckingham to the heart. Charles flung himself on his bed in a passion of tears when the news reached him; but outside the Court it was welcomed with a burst of joy. Young Oxford bachelors, grave London Aldermen, vied with each other in drinking healths to Felton. "God bless thee, little David," cried an old woman, as the murderer passed manacled by; "the Lord comfort thee," shouted the crowd, as the Tower gates closed on him. The very forces in the Duke's armament at Portsmouth shouted to the king, as he witnessed their departure, a prayer that he would "spare John Felton, their sometime fellow-soldier." But whatever national hopes the fall of Buckingham had aroused were quickly dispelled. Weston, a creature of the Duke, became Lord Treasurer, and his system remained unchanged. "Though our Achan is cut off," said Eliot, "the accursed thing remains."

The Laudian Clergy.

It seemed as if no act of Charles could widen the breach which his reckless lawlessness had made between himself and his subjects. But there was one thing dearer to England than free speech in Parliament, than security for property, or even personal liberty; and that one thing was, in the phrase of the day, "the Gospel." The gloom which at the outset of this reign we saw settling down on every Puritan heart had deepened with each succeeding year. The great struggle abroad had gone more and more against Protestantism, and at this moment the end of the cause seemed to have come. In Germany Lutheran and Calvinist alike lay at last beneath the heel of the Catholic House of Austria. The fall of Rochelle, which followed quick on the death of Buckingham, seemed to leave the Huguenots of France at the feet of a Roman Cardinal. In such a time as this, while England was thrilling with excitement at the thought that her own hour of deadly peril might come again, as it had come in the year of the Armada, the Puritans saw with horror the quick growth of Arminianism at home. Laud was now Bishop of London as well as the practical administrator of Church affairs, and to the excited Protestantism of the country Laud and the Churchmen whom he headed seemed a danger more really formidable than the Popery which was making such mighty strides abroad. To the Puritans they were traitors, traitors to God and their country at once. Their aim was to draw the Church of England farther away from the Protestant Churches, and nearer to the Church which Protestants regarded as

Babylon. They aped Roman ceremonies. Cautiously and tentatively they were introducing Roman doctrine. But they had none of the sacerdotal independence which Rome had at any rate preserved. They were abject in their dependence on the Crown. Their gratitude for the royal protection which enabled them to defy the religious instincts of the realm showed itself in their erection of the most dangerous pretensions of the monarchy into religious dogmas. Their model, Bishop Andrewes, had declared James to have been inspired by God. They preached passive obedience to the worst tyranny. They declared the person and goods of the subject to be at the king's absolute disposal. They were turning religion into a systematic attack on English liberty, nor was their attack to be lightly set aside. Up to this time they had been little more than a knot of courtly parsons, for the mass of the clergy, like their flocks, were steady Puritans; but the well-known energy of Laud and the open patronage of the Court promised a speedy increase of their numbers and their power. It was significant that upon the prorogation of 1628 Montague had been made a bishop, and Mainwaring, who had called Parliaments ciphers in the state, had been rewarded with a fat living. Instances such as these would hardly be lost on the mass of the clergy, and sober men looked forward to a day when every pulpit would be ringing with exhortations to passive obedience, with denunciations of Calvinism and apologies for Rome.

The Avowal.

Of all the members of the House of Commons Eliot was least fanatical in his natural bent, but the religious crisis swept away for the moment all other thoughts from his mind. "Danger enlarges itself in so great a measure," he wrote from the country, "that nothing but Heaven shrouds us from despair." When the Commons met again in January 1629, they met in Eliot's temper. The first business called up was that of religion. The House refused to consider any question of supplies, or even that of tonnage and poundage, which still remained unsettled though Charles had persisted in levying these duties without any vote of Parliament, till the religious grievance was discussed. "The Gospel," Eliot burst forth, "is that Truth in which this kingdom has been happy through a long and rare prosperity. This ground therefore let us lay for a foundation of our building, that that Truth, not with words, but with actions we will maintain!" "There is a ceremony," he went on, "used in the Eastern Churches, of standing at the repetition of the Creed, to testify their purpose to maintain it, not only with their bodies upright, but with their swords drawn. Give me leave to call that a custom very commendable!" The Commons answered their leader's challenge by a solemn avowal. They avowed that they held for truth that sense of the Articles as established by Parliament, which by the public act of the Church, and the general and current exposition of the writers of their Church, had been delivered unto them. It is easy to regard such an avowal as a mere outburst of Puritan bigotry, and the opposition of Charles as a defence of the freedom of religious thought. But the real importance of the avowal both to king and Commons lay in its political significance. In the mouth of the Commons it was a renewal of the claim that all affairs of the realm, spiritual as well as temporal, were cognizable in Parliament. To Charles it seemed as if the Commons were taking to themselves, in utter defiance of his rights as governor of the Church, "the interpretation of articles of religion; the deciding of which in doctrinal points," to use his own words, "only appertaineth to the clergy and Convocation." To use more modern phrases, the king insisted that the nation should receive its creed at the hands of the priesthood and the Crown. England in the avowal of Parliament asserted that the right to determine the belief of a nation lay with the nation itself.

Dissolution of the Parliament.

But the debates over religion were suddenly interrupted. In granting the Petition of Right we have seen that Charles had no purpose of parting with his power of arbitrary arrest or of levying customs. Both practices in fact went on as before, and the goods of merchants who refused to pay tonnage and poundage were seized as of old. At the reopening of the Session indeed the king met the Commons with a proposal that they should grant him tonnage and poundage and pass silently over what had been done by his officers. But the House was far from assenting to the interpretation which Charles had put on the Petition, and it was resolved to vindicate what it held to be the law. It deferred all grant of customs till the wrong done in the illegal levy of them was redressed, and summoned the farmers of those dues to the bar. But though they appeared, they pleaded the king's command as a ground for their refusal to answer. The House was proceeding to a protest, when on the second of March the Speaker signified that he had received an order to adjourn. Dissolution was clearly at hand, and the long-suppressed indignation broke out in a scene of strange disorder. The Speaker was held down in the chair, while Eliot, still clinging to his great principle of ministerial responsibility, denounced the new Treasurer as the adviser of the measure. "None have gone about to break Parliaments," he added in words to which after events gave a terrible significance, "but in the end Parliaments have broken them." The doors were locked, and in spite of the Speaker's protests, of the repeated knocking of the usher at the door, and the gathering tumult within the House itself, the loud "Aye, Aye!" of the bulk of the members supported Eliot in his last vindication of English liberty. By successive resolutions the Commons declared whomsoever should bring in innovations in religion, or whatever minister endorsed the levy of subsidies not granted in Parliament, "a capital enemy to the kingdom and commonwealth," and every subject voluntarily complying with illegal acts and demands "a betrayer of the liberty of England and an enemy of the same."

CHAPTER VI

THE PERSONAL GOVERNMENT

1629-1635

The policy of Charles.

At the opening of his third Parliament Charles had hinted in ominous words that the continuance of Parliament at all depended on its compliance with his will. "If you do not your duty," said the king, "mine would then order me to use those other means which God has put into my hand." When the threat failed to break the resistance of the Commons the ominous words passed into a settled policy. "We have showed," said a proclamation which followed on the dissolution of the Houses, on the tenth of March, "by our frequent meeting our people our love to the use of Parliament. Yet the late abuse having for the present drawn us unwillingly out of that course, we shall account it presumption for any to prescribe any time unto us for Parliament."

No Parliament in fact met for eleven years. But it would be unfair to charge the king at the outset of this period with any definite scheme of establishing a tyranny, or of changing what he conceived to be the older constitution of the realm. He "hated the very name of Parliaments"; but in spite of his hate he had as yet no purpose of abolishing them. His belief was that England would in time recover its senses, and that then Parliament might reassemble without inconvenience to the Crown. In the interval, however long it might be, he proposed to govern single-handed by the use of "those means which God had put into his hands." Resistance indeed he was resolved to put down. The leaders of the country party in the last Parliament were thrown into prison; and Eliot died, the first martyr of English liberty, in the Tower. Men were forbidden to speak of the reassembling of a Parliament. But here the king stopped. The opportunity which might have suggested dreams of organized despotism to a Richelieu suggested only means of filling his exchequer to Charles. He had in truth neither the grander nor the meaner instincts of a born tyrant. He did not seek to gain an absolute power over his people, because he believed that his absolute power was already a part of the constitution of the country. He set up no standing army to secure it, partly because he was poor, but yet more because his faith in his position was such that he never dreamed of any effectual resistance. He believed implicitly in his own prerogative, and he never doubted that his subjects would in the end come to believe in it too. His system rested not on force, but on a moral basis, on an appeal from opinion ill informed to opinion, as he looked on it, better informed. What he relied on was not the soldier, but the judge. It was for the judges to show from time to time the legality of his claims, and for England at last to bow to the force of conviction.

Peace.

He was resolute indeed to free the Crown from its dependence on Parliament; but his expedients for freeing the Crown from a dependence against which his pride as a sovereign revolted were simply peace and economy. With France an accommodation had been brought about in 1629 by the fall of Rochelle. The terms which Richelieu granted to the defeated Huguenots showed the real drift of his policy; and the reconciliation of the two countries set the king's hands free to aid Germany in her hour of despair. The doom of the Lutheran princes of the north had followed hard on the ruin of the Calvinistic princes of the south. The selfish neutrality of Saxony and Brandenburg received a fitting punishment in their helplessness before the triumphant advance of the Emperor's troops. His general, Wallenstein, encamped on the Baltic; and the last hopes of German Protestantism lay in the resistance of Stralsund. The danger called the Scandinavian powers to its aid. Denmark and Sweden leagued to resist Wallenstein; and Charles sent a squadron to the Elbe while he called on Holland to join in a quadruple alliance against the Emperor. Richelieu promised to support the alliance with a fleet: and even the withdrawal of Denmark, bribed into neutrality by the restitution of her possessions on the mainland, left the force of the league an imposing one. Gustavus of Sweden remained firm in his purpose of entering Germany, and appealed for aid to both England and France. But at this moment the dissolution of the Parliament left

Charles penniless. He at once resolved on a policy of peace, refused aid to Gustavus, withdrew his ships from the Baltic, and opened negotiations with Spain, which brought about a treaty at the end of 1630 on the virtual basis of an abandonment of the Palatinate. Ill luck clung to Charles in peace as in war. He had withdrawn from his efforts to win back the dominions of his brother-in-law at the very moment when those efforts were about to be crowned with success. The treaty with Spain was hardly concluded when Gustavus landed in Germany and began his wonderful career of victory. Charles at once strove to profit by his success; and in 1631 he suffered the Marquis of Hamilton to join the Swedish king with a force of Scotch and English regiments. After some service in Silesia, this force aided in the battle of Breitenfeld and followed Gustavus in his reconquest of the Palatinate. But the conqueror demanded, as the price of its restoration to Frederick, that Charles should again declare war upon Spain; and this was a price that the king would not pay. The danger in Germany was over; the power of France and of Holland threatened the supremacy of England on the seas; and even had these reasons not swayed him to friendship with Spain, Charles was stubborn not to plunge into a combat which would again force him to summon a Parliament.

Financial measures.

What absorbed his attention at home was the question of the revenue. The debt was a large one; and the ordinary income of the Crown, unaided by Parliamentary supplies, was inadequate to meet its ordinary expenditure. Charles himself was frugal and laborious; and the economy of Weston, the new Lord Treasurer, whom he raised to the earldom of Portland, contrasted advantageously with the waste and extravagance of the government under Buckingham. But economy failed to close the yawning gulf of the Treasury, and the course into which Charles was driven by the financial pressure showed with how wise a prescience the Commons had fixed on the point of arbitrary taxation as the chief danger to constitutional freedom. It is curious to see to what shifts the royal pride was driven in its effort at once to fill the Exchequer, and yet to avoid, as far as it could, any direct breach of constitutional law in the imposition of taxes by the sole authority of the Crown. The dormant powers of the prerogative were strained to their utmost. The right of the Crown to force knighthood on the landed gentry was revived, in order to squeeze them into composition for the refusal of it. Fines were levied on them for the redress of defects in their title-deeds. A Commission of the Forests exacted large sums from the neighbouring landowners for their encroachments on Crown lands. Three hundred thousand pounds were raised by this means in Essex alone. London, the special object of courtly dislike, on account of its stubborn Puritanism, was brought within the sweep of royal extortion by the enforcement of an illegal proclamation which James had issued, prohibiting its extension. Every house throughout the large suburban districts in which the prohibition had been disregarded was only saved from demolition by the payment of three years' rental to the Crown. The Treasury gained a hundred thousand pounds by this clever stroke, and Charles gained the bitter enmity of the great city whose strength and resources were fatal to him in the coming war. Though the Catholics were no longer troubled by any active persecution, and the Lord Treasurer was in heart a Papist, the penury of the Exchequer forced the Crown to maintain the old system of fines for "recusancy."

Fines and monopolies.

Vexatious measures of extortion such as these were far less hurtful to the state than the conversion of justice into a means of supplying the royal necessities by means of the Star Chamber. The jurisdiction of the King's Council had been revived by Wolsey as a check on the nobles; and it had received great developement, especially on the side of criminal law, during the Tudor reigns. Forgery, perjury, riot, maintenance, fraud, libel, and conspiracy, were the chief offences cognizable in this court, but its scope extended to every misdemeanour, and especially to charges where, from the imperfection of the common law, or the power of offenders, justice was baffled in the lower courts. Its process resembled that of Chancery: it usually acted on an information laid before it by the King's Attorney. Both witnesses and accused were examined on oath by special interrogatories, and the Court was at liberty to adjudge any punishment short of death. The possession of such a weapon would have been fatal to liberty under a great tyrant; under Charles it was turned simply to the profit of the Exchequer. Large numbers of cases which would ordinarily have come before the Courts of Common Law were called before the Star Chamber, simply for the purpose of levying fines for the Crown. The same motive accounts for the enormous penalties which were exacted for offences of a trivial character. The marriage of a gentleman with his niece was punished by the forfeiture of twelve thousand pounds, and fines of four and five thousand pounds were awarded for brawls between lords of the Court. Fines such as these however affected a smaller range of sufferers than the financial expedient to which Weston had recourse in the renewal of monopolies. Monopolies, abandoned by Elizabeth, extinguished by Act of Parliament under James, and denounced with the assent of Charles himself in the Petition of Right, were again set on foot, and on a scale far more gigantic than had been seen before; the companies who undertook them paying a fixed duty on their profits as well as a large sum for the original concession of the monopoly. Wine, soap, salt, and almost every article of domestic consumption fell into the hands of monopolists, and rose in price out of all proportion to the profit gained by the Crown. "They sup in our cup," Colepepper said afterwards in the Long Parliament, "they dip in our dish, they sit by our fire; we find them in the dye-fat, the wash bowls, and the powdering tub. They share with the cutler in his box. They have marked and sealed us from head to foot."

Customs and benevolences.

In spite of the financial expedients we have described the Treasury would have remained unfilled had not the king persisted in those financial measures which had called forth the protest of the Parliament. The exaction of customs duties went on as of old at the ports. The resistance of the London merchants to their payment was roughly put down by the Star Chamber; and an alderman who complained bitterly that men were worse off in England than in Turkey was ruined by a fine of two thousand pounds. Writs for benevolences, under the old pretext of gifts, were issued for every shire. But the freeholders of the counties were more difficult to deal with than London aldermen. When those of Cornwall were called together at Bodmin to contribute to a voluntary gift, half the hundreds refused, and the yield of the rest came to little more than two thousand pounds. One of the Cornishmen has left an amusing record of the scene which took place before the Commissioners appointed for assessment of the gift. "Some with great words and threatenings, some with persuasions," he says, "were drawn to it. I was like to have been complimented out of my money; but knowing with whom I had to deal, I held, when I talked with them, my hands fast in my pockets."

General prosperity.

By means such as these the financial difficulty was in some measure met. During Weston's five years of office the debt, which had mounted to sixteen hundred thousand pounds, was reduced by one half. On the other hand the annual revenue of the Crown was raised from half-a-million to eight hundred thousand. Nor was there much sign of active discontent. Vexatious indeed and illegal as were the proceedings of the Crown, there seems in these earlier years of personal rule to have been little apprehension of any permanent danger to freedom in the country at large. To those who read the letters of the time there is something inexpressibly touching in the general faith of their writers in the ultimate victory of the Law. Charles was obstinate, but obstinacy was too common a foible amongst Englishmen to rouse any vehement resentment. The people were as stubborn as their king, and their political sense told them that the slightest disturbance of affairs must shake down the financial fabric which Charles was slowly building up, and force him back on subsidies and a Parliament. Meanwhile they would wait for better days, and their patience was aided by the general prosperity of the country. The great Continental wars threw wealth into English hands. The intercourse between Spain and Flanders was carried on solely in English ships, and the English flag covered the intercourse of Portugal with its colonies in Africa, India, and the Pacific. The long peace was producing its inevitable results in an extension of commerce and a rise of manufactures in the towns of the West Riding of Yorkshire. Fresh land was being brought into cultivation, and a great scheme was set on foot for reclaiming the Fens. The new wealth of the country gentry, through the increase of rent, was seen in the splendour of the houses which they were raising. The contrast of this peace and prosperity with the ruin and bloodshed of the Continent afforded a ready argument to the friends of the king's system. So tranquil was the outer appearance of the country that in Court circles all sense of danger had disappeared. "Some of the greatest statesmen and privy councillors," says May, "would ordinarily laugh when the word 'liberty of the subject' was named." There were courtiers bold enough to express their hope that "the king would never need any more Parliaments."

Wentworth.

But beneath this outer calm "the country," Clarendon honestly tells us while eulogizing the Peace, "was full of pride and mutiny and discontent." Thousands were quitting England for America. The gentry held aloof from the Court. "The common people in the generality and the country freeholders would rationally argue of their own rights and the oppressions which were laid upon them." If Charles was content to deceive himself, there was one man among his ministers who saw that the people were right in their policy of patience, and that unless other measures were taken the fabric of despotism would fall at the first breath of adverse fortune. Sir Thomas Wentworth, a great Yorkshire landowner and one of the representatives of his county in Parliament, had stood during the Parliament of 1628 among the more prominent members of the Country party in the Commons. But he was no Eliot. He had no faith in Parliaments, save as means of checking exceptional misgovernment. He had no belief in the general wisdom of the realm, or in its value, when represented by the Commons, as a means of bringing about good government. Powerful as his mind was, it was arrogant and contemptuous; he knew his own capacity for rule, and he looked with scorn on the powers or wits of meaner men. He was a born administrator; and, like Bacon, he panted for an opportunity of displaying his talent in what then seemed the only sphere of political action. From the first moment of his appearance in public his passionate desire had been to find employment in the service of the Crown. At the close of the preceding reign he was already connected with the Court, he had secured a seat in Yorkshire for one of the royal ministers, and was believed to be on the high road to a peerage. But the consciousness of political ability which spurred his ambition roused the jealousy of Buckingham; and the haughty pride of Wentworth was flung by repeated slights into an attitude of opposition, which his eloquence—grander in its sudden outbursts, though less earnest and sustained than that of Eliot—soon rendered formidable. His intrigues at Court roused Buckingham to crush by a signal insult the rival whose genius he instinctively dreaded. While sitting in his court as sheriff of Yorkshire, Wentworth received the announcement of his dismissal from office and of the gift of his post to Sir John Savile, his rival in the county. "Since they will thus weakly breathe on me a seeming disgrace in the public face of my country," he said, with a characteristic outburst of contemptuous pride, "I shall crave leave to wipe it away as openly, as easily!" His whole conception of a strong and able rule revolted against the miserable government of the favourite, his maladministration at home, his failures and disgraces abroad. Wentworth's aim was to force on the king, not such a freedom as Eliot longed for, but such a system as the Tudors had clung to, where a large and noble policy placed the sovereign naturally at the head of the people, and where Parliaments sank into mere aids to the Crown. But before this could be, Buckingham and the system of blundering misrule that he embodied must be cleared away. It was with this end that Wentworth sprang to the front of the Commons in urging the Petition of Right. Whether in that crisis of his life some nobler impulse, some true passion for the freedom he was to trample under foot, mingled with his thirst for revenge, it is hard to tell. But his words were words of fire. "If he did not faithfully insist for the common liberty of the subject to be preserved whole and entire," it was thus he closed one of his speeches on the Petition, "it was his desire that he might be set as a beacon on a hill for all men else to wonder at."

Wentworth as minister.

It is as such a beacon that his name has stood from that time to this. He had shown his powers to good purpose; and at the prorogation of the Parliament he passed into the service of the Crown. He became President of the Council of the North, a court set up in limitation of the common law, and which wielded almost unbounded authority beyond the Humber. In 1629 the death of

Buckingham removed the obstacle that stood between his ambition and the end at which it had aimed throughout. All pretence to patriotism was set aside; Wentworth was admitted to the royal Council; and as he took his seat at the board he promised to "vindicate the Monarchy for ever from the conditions and restraints of subjects." So great was the faith in his zeal and power which he knew how to breathe into his royal master that he was at once raised to the peerage, and placed with Laud in the first rank of the king's councillors. Charles had good ground for this rapid confidence in his new minister. In Wentworth the very genius of tyranny was embodied. He soon passed beyond the mere aim of restoring the system of the Tudors. He was far too clear-sighted to share his master's belief that the arbitrary power which Charles was wielding formed any part of the old constitution of the country, or to dream that the mere lapse of time would so change the temper of Englishmen as to reconcile them to despotism. He knew that absolute rule was a new thing in England, and that the only way of permanently establishing it was not by reasoning, or by the force of custom, but by the force of fear. His system was the expression of his own inner temper; and the dark gloomy countenance, the full heavy eye, which meet us in Strafford's portrait are the best commentary on his policy of "Thorough." It was by the sheer strength of his genius, by the terror his violence inspired amid the meaner men whom Buckingham had left, by the general sense of his power, that he had forced himself upon the Court. He had none of the small arts of a courtier. His air was that of a silent, proud, passionate man; and when he first appeared at Whitehall his rough uncourtly manners provoked a smile in the royal circle. But the smile soon died into a general hate. The Queen, frivolous and meddlesome as she was, detested him; his fellow-ministers intrigued against him, and seized on his hot speeches against the great lords, his quarrels with the royal household, his transports of passion at the very Council-table, to ruin him in his master's favour. The king himself, while steadily supporting him against his rivals, was utterly unable to understand his drift. Charles valued him as an administrator, disdainful of private ends, crushing great and small with the same haughty indifference to men's love or hate, and devoted to the one aim of building up the power of the Crown. But in his purpose of preparing for the great struggle with freedom which he saw before him, of building up by force such a despotism in England as Richelieu was building up in France, and of thus making England as great in Europe as France had been made by Richelieu, he could look for little sympathy and less help from the king.

Ireland under the Stuarts.

Wentworth's genius turned impatiently to a sphere where it could act alone, untrammelled by the hindrances it encountered at home. His purpose was to prepare for the coming contest by the provision of a fixed revenue, arsenals, fortresses, and a standing army, and it was in Ireland that he resolved to find them. Till now this miserable country had been but a drain on the resources of the Crown. Under the administration of Mountjoy's successor, Sir Arthur Chichester, an able and determined effort had been made for the settlement of the conquered province by the general introduction of a purely English system of government, justice, and property. Every vestige of the old Celtic constitution of the country was rejected as "barbarous." The tribal authority of the chiefs was taken from them by law. They were reduced to the position of great nobles and landowners, while their tribesmen rose from subjects into tenants, owing only fixed and customary dues and services to their lords. The tribal system of property in common was set aside, and the communal holdings of the tribesmen turned into the copyholds of English law. In the same way the chieftains were stripped of their hereditary jurisdiction, and the English system of judges and trial by jury substituted for their proceedings under Brehon or customary law. To all these changes the Celts opposed the tenacious obstinacy of their race. Irish juries, then as now, refused to convict. Glad as the tribesmen were to be freed from the arbitrary exactions of their chiefs, they held them for chieftains still. The attempt made by Chichester, under pressure from England, to introduce the English uniformity of religion ended in utter failure; for the Englishry of the Pale remained as Catholic as the native Irishry; and the sole result of the measure was to build up a new Irish people out of both on the common basis of religion. Much however had been done by the firm yet moderate government of the Deputy, and signs were already appearing of a disposition on the part of the people to conform gradually to the new usages, when the English Council under James suddenly resolved upon and carried through the revolutionary measure which is known as the Colonization of Ulster. In 1610 the pacific and conservative policy of Chichester was abandoned for a vast policy of spoliation. Two-thirds of the north of Ireland was declared to have been confiscated to the Crown by the part that its possessors had taken in a recent effort at revolt; and the lands which were thus gained were allotted to new settlers of Scotch and English extraction. In its material results the Plantation of Ulster was undoubtedly a brilliant success. Farms and homesteads, churches and mills, rose fast amidst the desolate wilds of Tyrone. The Corporation of London undertook the colonization of Derry, and gave to the little town the name which its heroic defence has made so famous. The foundations of the economic prosperity which has raised Ulster high above the rest of Ireland in wealth and intelligence were undoubtedly laid in the confiscation of 1610. Nor did the measure meet with any opposition at the time save that of secret discontent. The evicted natives withdrew sullenly to the lands which had been left them by the spoiler, but all faith in English justice had been torn from the minds of the Irishry, and the seed had been sown of that fatal harvest of distrust and disaffection which was to be reaped through tyranny and massacre in the age to come.

Wentworth in Ireland.

But the bitter memories of conquest and spoliation only pointed out Ireland to Wentworth as the best field for his experiment. The balance of Catholic against Protestant might be used to make both parties dependent on the royal authority; the rights of conquest which in Wentworth's theory vested the whole land in the absolute possession of the Crown gave him scope for his administrative ability; and for the rest he trusted, and trusted justly, to the force of his genius and of his will. In the summer of 1633 he sailed as Lord Deputy to Ireland, and five years later his aim seemed almost realized. "The king," he wrote to Laud, "is as absolute here as any prince in the world can be." The government of the new deputy indeed was a rule of terror. Archbishop Usher, with almost every name which we can respect in the island, was the object of his insult and oppression. His tyranny strode over all legal bounds. Wentworth is the one English statesman of all time who may be said to have had no sense of law; and his scorn of it showed itself in his coercion of juries as of parliaments. The highest of the Irish nobles learned to tremble when a few insolent words, construed as mutiny, were enough to bring Lord Mountnorris before a council of war, and to inflict on him a sentence of death. But his tyranny aimed at public ends, and in Ireland the heavy hand of a single despot delivered the mass of the people at any rate from the local despotism of a hundred masters. The Irish landowners were for the first time made to feel themselves amenable to the law. Justice was enforced, outrage was repressed, the condition of the clergy was to some extent raised, the sea was cleared of the pirates who infested it. The foundation of the linen manufacture which was to bring wealth to Ulster, and the first developement of Irish commerce, date from the Lieutenancy of Wentworth. Good government however was only a means with him for further ends. The noblest work to be done in Ireland was the bringing about a reconciliation between Catholic and Protestant, and an obliteration of the anger and thirst for vengeance which had been raised by the Ulster Plantation. Wentworth, on the other hand, angered the Protestants by a toleration of Catholic worship and a suspension of the persecution which had feebly begun against the priesthood, while he fed the irritation of the Catholics by urging in 1635 a new Plantation of Connaught. His purpose was to encourage a disunion which left both parties dependent for support and protection on the Crown. It was a policy which was to end in bringing about the horrors of the Irish revolt, the vengeance of Cromwell, and the long series of atrocities on both sides which make the story of the country he ruined so terrible to tell. But for the hour it left Ireland helpless in his hands. He doubled the revenue. He raised an army. To provide for its support he ventured, in spite of the panic with which Charles heard of his project, to summon in 1634 an Irish Parliament. His aim was to read a lesson to England and the king by showing how completely that dreaded thing, a Parliament, could be made an organ of the royal will; and his success was complete. The task of overawing an Irish Parliament indeed was no very difficult one. Two-thirds of its House of Commons consisted of the representatives of wretched villages which were pocket-boroughs of the Crown, while absent peers were forced to entrust their proxies to the Council to be used at its pleasure. But precautions were hardly needed. The two Houses trembled at the stern master who bade their members not let the king "find them muttering, or to speak it more truly, mutinying in corners," and voted with a perfect docility the means of maintaining an army of five thousand foot and five hundred horse. Had the subsidy been refused, the result would have been the same. "I would undertake," wrote Wentworth, "upon the peril of my head, to make the king's army able to subsist and provide for itself among them without their help."

Laud.

While Strafford was thus working out his system of "Thorough" on one side of St. George's Channel, it was being carried out on the other by a mind inferior indeed to his own in genius, but almost equal to it in courage and tenacity. Cold, pedantic, superstitious as he was (he notes in his diary the entry of a robin-redbreast into his study as a matter of grave moment), William Laud rose out of the mass of court-prelates by his industry, his personal unselfishness, his remarkable capacity for administration. At a later period, when immersed in State business, he found time to acquire so complete a knowledge of commercial affairs that the London merchants themselves owned him a master in matters of trade. Of statesmanship indeed he had none. The shrewdness of James had read the very heart of the man when Buckingham pressed for his first advancement to the see of St. David's. "He hath a restless spirit," said the old king, "which cannot see when things are well, but loves to toss and change, and to bring matters to a pitch of reformation floating in his own brain. Take him with you, but by my soul you will repent it." But Laud's influence was really derived from this oneness of purpose. He directed all the power of a clear, narrow mind and a dogged will to the realization of a single aim. His resolve was to raise the Church of England to what he conceived to be its real position as a branch, though a reformed branch, of the great Catholic Church throughout the world; protesting alike against the innovations of Rome and the innovations of Calvin, and basing its doctrines and usages on those of the Christian communion in the centuries which preceded the Council of Nicæa. The first step in the realization of such a theory was the severance of whatever ties had hitherto united the English Church to the Reformed Churches of the Continent. In Laud's view episcopal succession was of the essence of a Church; and by their rejection of bishops the Lutheran and Calvinistic Churches of Germany and Switzerland had ceased to be Churches at all. The freedom of worship therefore which had been allowed to the Huguenot refugees from France, or the Walloons from Flanders, was suddenly withdrawn; and the requirement of conformity with the Anglican ritual drove them in crowds from the southern ports to seek toleration in Holland. The same conformity was required from the English soldiers and merchants abroad, who had hitherto attended without scruple the services of the Calvinistic churches. The English ambassador in Paris was forbidden to visit the Huguenot conventicle at Charenton.

Laud and the Puritans.

As Laud drew further from the Protestants of the Continent, he drew, consciously or unconsciously, nearer to Rome. His theory owned Rome as a true branch of the Church, though severed from that of England by errors and innovations against which the Primate vigorously protested. But with the removal of these obstacles reunion would naturally follow; and his dream was that of bridging over the gulf which ever since the Reformation had parted the two Churches. The secret offer of a cardinal's hat proved Rome's sense that Laud was doing his work for her; while his rejection of it, and his own reiterated protestations, prove equally that he was doing it unconsciously. Union with the great body of Catholicism indeed he regarded as a work which only time could bring about, but for which he could prepare the Church of England by raising it to a higher standard of Catholic feeling and Catholic practice. The great obstacle in his way was the Puritanism of nine-tenths of the English people, and on Puritanism he made war without mercy. Till 1633 indeed his direct range of action was limited to his own diocese of London, though his influence with the king enabled him in great measure to shape the general course of the government in ecclesiastical matters. But on the death of Abbot Laud was raised to the Archbishopric of Canterbury, and no sooner had his elevation placed him at the head of the English Church, than he turned the High Commission into a standing attack on the Puritan ministers. Rectors and vicars were scolded, suspended, deprived for "Gospel preaching." The use of the surplice, and the ceremonies most offensive to Puritan feeling, were enforced in every parish. The lectures founded in towns, which were the favourite posts of Puritan preachers, were rigorously suppressed. They found a refuge among the country gentlemen, and the Archbishop withdrew from the country gentlemen the privilege of keeping chaplains, which they had till then enjoyed. As parishes became vacant the High Church bishops had long been filling them with men who denounced Calvinism, and declared passive obedience to the sovereign to be part of the law of God. The Puritans felt the stress of this process, and endeavoured to meet it by buying up the appropriations of livings, and securing through feoffees a succession of Protestant ministers in the parishes of which they were patrons: but in 1633 Laud cited the feoffees into the Star Chamber, and roughly put an end to them.

Sunday pastimes.

Nor was the persecution confined to the clergy. Under the two last reigns the small pocket-Bibles called the Geneva Bibles had become universally popular amongst English laymen; but their marginal notes were found to savour of Calvinism, and their importation was prohibited. The habit of receiving the communion in a sitting posture had become common, but kneeling was now enforced, and hundreds were excommunicated for refusing to comply with the injunction. A more galling means of annoyance was found in the different views of the two religious parties on the subject of Sunday. The Puritans identified the Lord's day with the Jewish Sabbath, and transferred to the one the strict observances which were required for the other. The Laudian clergy, on the other hand, regarded it simply as one among the holidays of the Church, and encouraged their flocks in the pastimes and recreations after service which had been common before the Reformation. The Crown under James had taken part with the latter, and had issued a "Book of Sports" which recommended certain games as lawful and desirable on the Lord's day. On the other hand judges of assize and magistrates had issued orders against Sunday "wakes" and "profanation of God's Sabbath." The general religious sense of the country was undoubtedly tending to a stricter observance of the day, when Laud brought the contest to a sudden issue. He summoned the Chief-Justice, Richardson, who had issued the orders in the western shires, to the Council-table, and rated him so violently that the old man came out complaining he had been all but choked by a pair of lawn sleeves. He then ordered every minister to read the declaration in favour of Sunday pastimes from the pulpit. One Puritan minister had the wit to obey, and to close the reading with the significant hint, "You have heard read, good people, both the commandment of God and the commandment of man! Obey which you please." But the bulk refused to comply with the Archbishop's will. The result followed at which Laud no doubt had aimed. Puritan ministers were cited before the High Commission, and silenced or deprived. In the diocese of Norwich alone thirty parochial clergymen were expelled from their cures.

Laud and the clergy.

The suppression of Puritanism in the ranks of the clergy was only a preliminary to the real work on which the Archbishop's mind was set, the preparation for Catholic reunion by the elevation of the clergy to a Catholic standard in doctrine and ritual. Laud publicly avowed his preference of an unmarried to a married priesthood. Some of the bishops, and a large part of the new clergy who occupied the posts from which the Puritan ministers had been driven, advocated doctrines and customs which the Reformers had denounced as sheer Papistry; the practice, for instance, of auricular confession, a Real Presence in the Sacrament, or prayers for the dead. One prelate, Montagu, was in heart a convert to Rome. Another, Goodman, died acknowledging himself a Papist. Meanwhile Laud was indefatigable in his efforts to raise the civil and political status of the clergy to the point which it had reached ere the fatal blow of the Reformation fell on the priesthood. Among the archives of his see lies a large and costly volume in vellum, containing a copy of such records in the Tower as concerned the privileges of the clergy. Its compilation was entered in the Archbishop's diary as one among the "twenty-one things which I have projected to do if God bless me in them," and as among the fifteen to which before his fall he had been enabled to add his emphatic "done." The power of the Bishops' Courts, which had long fallen into decay, revived under his patronage. In 1636 he was able to induce the king to raise a prelate,

Juxon, Bishop of London, to the highest civil post in the realm, that of Lord High Treasurer. "No Churchman had it since Henry the Seventh's time," Laud comments proudly. "I pray God bless him to carry it so that the Church may have honour, and the State service and content by it. And now, if the Church will not hold up themselves, under God I can do no more."

Laud and ritual.

And as Laud aimed at a more Catholic standard of doctrine in the clergy, so he aimed at a nearer approach to the pomp of Catholicism in public worship. His conduct in his own house at Lambeth brings out with singular vividness the reckless courage with which he threw himself across the religious instincts of a time when the spiritual aspect of worship was overpowering in most minds its æsthetic and devotional sides. Men noted as a fatal omen an accident which marked his first entry into Lambeth; for the overladen ferry-boat upset in the passage of the river, and though the horses and servants were saved, the Archbishop's coach remained at the bottom of the Thames. But no omen, carefully as he might note it, brought a moment's hesitation to the bold, narrow mind of the new Primate. His first act, he boasted, was the setting about a restoration of his chapel; and, as Laud managed it, his restoration was a simple undoing of all that had been done there by his predecessors since the Reformation. With characteristic energy he aided with his own hands in the replacement of the painted glass in its windows, and racked his wits in piecing the fragments together. The glazier was scandalized by the Primate's express command to repair and set up again the "broken crucifix" in the east window. The holy table was removed from the centre, and set altarwise against the eastern wall, with a cloth of arras behind it, on which was embroidered the history of the Last Supper. The elaborate woodwork of the screen, the rich copes of the chaplain, the silver candlesticks, the credence table, the organ and the choir, the stately ritual, the bowings at the sacred name, the genuflexions to the altar made the chapel at last such a model of worship as Laud desired. If he could not exact an equal pomp of devotion in other quarters, he exacted as much as he could. Bowing to the altar was introduced into all cathedral churches. A royal injunction ordered the removal of the communion table, which for the last half-century or more had in almost every parish church stood in the middle of the nave, back to its pre-Reformation position in the chancel, and secured it from profanation by a rail. The removal implied, and was understood to imply, a recognition of the Real Presence, and a denial of the doctrine which Englishmen generally held about the Lord's Supper. But, strenuous as was the resistance which the Archbishop encountered, his pertinacity and severity warred it down. Parsons who denounced the change from their pulpits were fined, imprisoned, and deprived of their benefices. Churchwardens who refused or delayed to obey the injunction were rated at the Commission-table, and frightened into compliance.

The Puritan panic.

In their last Remonstrance to the king the Commons had denounced Laud as the chief assailant of the Protestant character of the Church of England; and every year of his Primacy showed him bent upon justifying the accusation. His policy was no longer the purely Conservative policy of Parker or Whitgift; it was aggressive and revolutionary. His "new counsels" threw whatever force there was in the feeling of conservatism into the hands of the Puritan, for it was the Puritan who seemed to be defending the old character of the Church of England against its Primate's attacks. But backed as Laud was by the power of the Crown, the struggle became more hopeless every day. While the Catholics owned that they had never enjoyed a like tranquillity, while the fines for recusancy were reduced and their worship suffered to go on in private houses, the Puritan saw his ministers silenced or deprived, his Sabbath profaned, the most sacred act of his worship brought near, as he fancied, to the mass. Roman doctrine met him from the pulpit, Roman practices met him in the Church. It was plain that the purpose of Laud aimed at nothing short of the utter suppression of Puritanism, in other words, of the form of religion which was dear to the mass of Englishmen. Already indeed there were signs of a change of temper which might have made a bolder man pause. Thousands of "the best," scholars, merchants, lawyers, farmers, were flying over the Atlantic to seek freedom and purity of religion in the wilderness. Great landowners and nobles were preparing to follow. Ministers were quitting their parsonages rather than abet the royal insult to the sanctity of the Sabbath. The Puritans who remained among the clergy were giving up their homes rather than consent to the change of the sacred table into an altar, or to silence in their protests against the new Popery. The noblest of living Englishmen refused to become the priest of a Church whose ministry could only be "bought with servitude and forswearing."

Milton at Horton.

We have seen John Milton leave Cambridge, self-dedicated "to that same lot, however mean or high, to which time leads me and the will of Heaven." But the lot to which these called him was not the ministerial office to which he had been destined from his childhood. In later life he told bitterly the story how he had been "Church-outed by the prelates." "Coming to some maturity of years, and perceiving what tyranny had invaded in the Church, that he who would take orders must subscribe slave, and take an oath withal, which unless he took with a conscience that would retch he must either straight perjure or split his faith, I thought it better to prefer a blameless silence before the sacred office of speaking, bought and begun with servitude and forswearing." In spite therefore of his father's regrets, he retired in 1633 to a new home which the scrivener had found at Horton, a village in the neighbourhood of Windsor, and quietly busied himself with study and verse. The poetic impulse of the Renascence had been slowly dying away under the Stuarts. The stage was falling into mere coarseness and horror. Shakspere had died quietly at Stratford in Milton's childhood; the last and worst play of Ben Jonson appeared in the year of his settlement at Horton; and though Ford and Massinger still lingered on, there were no successors for them but Shirley and Davenant. The philosophic and meditative taste of the age had produced indeed poetic schools of its own: poetic satire had become fashionable in Hall, better known afterwards as a bishop, and had been carried on vigorously by George Wither; the so-called "metaphysical" poetry, the vigorous and pithy expression of a cold and prosaic good sense, began with Sir John Davies and buried itself in fantastic affectations in Donne; religious verse had become popular in the gloomy allegories of

Quarles and the tender refinement which struggles through a jungle of puns and extravagances in George Herbert. But what poetic life really remained was to be found only in the caressing fancy and lively badinage of lyric singers like Herrick, whose grace is untouched by passion and often disfigured by coarseness and pedantry; or in the school of Spenser's more direct successors, where Browne in his pastorals and the two Fletchers, Phineas and Giles, in their unreadable allegories, still preserved something of their master's sweetness, if they preserved nothing of his power.

His early poems.

Milton was himself a Spenserian; he owned to Dryden in later years that "Spenser was his original," and in some of his earliest lines at Horton he dwells lovingly on "the sage and solemn tones" of the "Faerie Queen," its "forests and enchantments drear, where more is meant than meets the ear." But of the weakness and affectation which characterized Spenser's successors he had not a trace. In the "Allegro" and "Penseroso," the first results of his retirement at Horton, we catch again the fancy and melody of the Elizabethan verse, the wealth of its imagery, its wide sympathy with nature and man. There is a loss perhaps of the older freedom and spontaneity of the Renascence, a rhetorical rather than passionate turn in the young poet, a striking absence of dramatic power, and a want of subtle precision even in his picturesque touches. Milton's imagination is not strong enough to identify him with the world which he imagines; he stands apart from it, and looks at it as from a distance, ordering it and arranging it at his will. But if in this respect he falls both in his earlier and later poems below Shakspere or Spenser, the deficiency is all but compensated by his nobleness of feeling and expression, the severity of his taste, his sustained dignity, and the perfectness and completeness of his work. The moral grandeur of the Puritan breathes, even in these lighter pieces of his youth, through every line. The "Comus," which he planned as a masque for some festivities which the Earl of Bridgewater was holding at Ludlow Castle, rises into an almost impassioned pleading for the love of virtue.

Puritan fanaticism.

The historic interest of Milton's "Comus" lies in its forming part of a protest made by the more cultured Puritans at this time against the gloomier bigotry which persecution was fostering in the party at large. The patience of Englishmen, in fact, was slowly wearing out. There was a sudden upgrowth of virulent pamphlets of the old Martin Marprelate type. Men, whose names no one asked, hawked libels, whose authorship no one knew, from the door of the tradesman to the door of the squire. As the hopes of a Parliament grew fainter, and men despaired of any legal remedy, violent and weak-headed fanatics came, as at such times they always come, to the front. Leighton, the father of the saintly archbishop of that name, had given a specimen of their tone at the outset of this period by denouncing the prelates as men of blood, Episcopacy as Antichrist, and the Popish Queen as a daughter of Heth. The "Histriomastix" of Prynne, a lawyer distinguished for his constitutional knowledge, but the most obstinate and narrow-minded of men, marked the deepening of Puritan bigotry under the fostering warmth of Laud's persecution. The book was an attack on players as the ministers of Satan, on theatres as the Devil's chapels, on hunting, maypoles, the decking of houses at Christmas with evergreens, on cards, music, and false hair. The attack on the stage was as offensive to the more cultured minds among the Puritan party as to the Court itself; Selden and Whitelock took a prominent part in preparing a grand masque by which the Inns of Court resolved to answer its challenge, and in the following year Milton wrote his masque of "Comus" for Ludlow Castle. To leave Prynne however simply to the censure of wiser men than himself was too sensible a course for the angry Primate. No man was ever sent to prison before or since for such a sheer mass of nonsense; but a passage in the book was taken as a reflection on the Queen, who had purposed to take part in a play at the time of its publication; and the sentence showed the hard cruelty of the Primate's temper. In 1634 Prynne was dismissed from the bar, deprived of his university degree, and set in the pillory. His ears were clipped from his head, and the stubborn lawyer was then taken back to prison to be kept there during the king's pleasure.

With such a world around them we can hardly wonder that men of less fanatical turn than Prynne gave way to despair. But it was in this hour of despair that the Puritans won their noblest triumph. They "turned," to use Canning's words in a far truer and grander sense than that which he gave to them, "they turned to the New World to redress the balance of the Old." It was during the years which followed the close of the third Parliament of Charles that a great Puritan migration founded the States of New England.

Virginia.

Ralegh's settlement on the Virginian coast, the first attempt which Englishmen had made to claim North America for their own, had soon proved a failure. The introduction of tobacco and the potato into Europe dates from his voyage of discovery, but the energy of his colonists was distracted by the delusive dream of gold, the hostility of the native tribes drove them from the coast, and it is through the gratitude of later times for what he strove to do, rather than for what he did, that Raleigh, the capital of North Carolina, preserves his name. The first permanent settlement on the Chesapeake was effected in the beginning of the reign of James the First, and its success was due to the conviction of the settlers that the secret of the New World's conquest lay simply in labour. Among the hundred and five colonists who originally landed, forty-eight were gentlemen, and only twelve were tillers of the soil. Their leader, John Smith, however, not only explored the vast Bay of Chesapeake and discovered the Potomac and the Susquehannah, but held the little company together in the face of famine and desertion till the colonists had learned the lesson of toil. In his letters to the colonizers at home he set resolutely aside the dream of gold. "Nothing is to be expected thence," he wrote of the new country, "but by labour"; and supplies of labourers, aided by a wise allotment of land to each colonist, secured after five years of struggle the fortunes of Virginia. "Men fell to building houses and planting corn"; the very streets of Jamestown, as their capital was called from the reigning sovereign, were sown with tobacco; and in fifteen years the colony numbered five thousand souls.

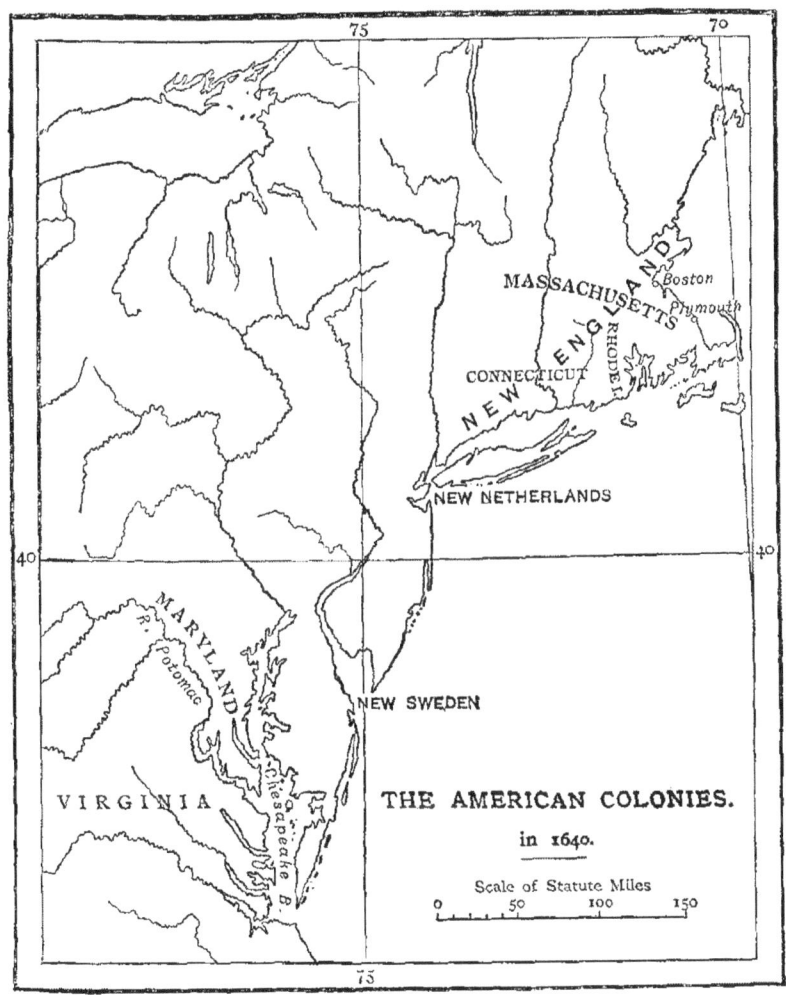

The Pilgrim Fathers.

Only a few years after the settlement of Smith in Virginia, the church of Brownist or Independent refugees, whom we saw driven in Elizabeth's reign to Amsterdam, resolved to quit Holland and find a home in the wilds of the New World. They were little disheartened by the tidings of suffering which came from the Virginian settlement. "We are well weaned," wrote their minister, John Robinson, "from the delicate milk of the mother-country, and inured to the difficulties of a strange land: the people are industrious and frugal. We are knit together as a body in a most sacred covenant of the Lord, of the violation whereof we make great conscience, and by virtue whereof we hold ourselves strictly tied to all care of each other's good and of the whole. It is not with us as with men whom small things can discourage." Returning from Holland to Southampton, they started in two small vessels for the new land: but one of these soon put back, and only its companion, the *Mayflower*, a bark of a hundred and eighty tons, with forty-one emigrants and their families on board, persisted in prosecuting its voyage. In 1620 the little company of the "Pilgrim Fathers," as after-times loved to call them, landed on the barren coast of Massachusetts at a spot to which they gave the name of Plymouth, in memory of the last English port at which they touched. They had soon to face the long hard winter of the north, to bear sickness and famine: even when these years of toil and suffering had passed there was a time when "they knew not at night where to have a bit in the morning." Resolute and industrious as they were, their progress was very slow; and at the end of ten years they numbered only three hundred souls. But small as it was, the colony was now firmly established and the struggle for mere existence was over. "Let it not be grievous unto you," some of their brethren had written from England to the poor emigrants in the midst of their sufferings, "that you have been instrumental to break the ice for others. The honour shall be yours to the world's end."

The Puritan migration.

From the moment of their establishment the eyes of the English Puritans were fixed on this little Puritan settlement in North America. Through the early years of Charles projects were being canvassed for the establishment of a new settlement beside the little Plymouth; and the aid which the merchants of Boston in Lincolnshire gave to the realization of this project was acknowledged in the name of its capital. At the moment when he was dissolving his third Parliament Charles granted the charter which established the colony of Massachusetts; and by the Puritans at large the grant was at once regarded as a Providential call. Out of the failure of their great constitutional struggle and the pressing danger to "godliness" in England rose the dream of a land in the West where religion and liberty could find a safe and lasting home. The Parliament was hardly dissolved when "conclusions" for the establishment of a great colony on the other side of the Atlantic were circulating among gentry and traders, and descriptions of the new country of Massachusetts were talked over in every Puritan household. The proposal was welcomed with the quiet, stern enthusiasm which marked the temper of the time; but the words of a well-known emigrant show how hard it was even for the sternest enthusiasts to tear themselves from their native land. "I shall call that my country," wrote the younger Winthrop in answer to feelings of this sort, "where I may most glorify God and enjoy the presence of my dearest friends." The answer was accepted, and the Puritan emigration began on a scale such as England had never before seen. The two hundred who first sailed for Salem were soon followed by John Winthrop with eight hundred men; and seven hundred more followed ere the first year of personal government had run its course. Nor were the emigrants, like the earlier colonists of the South, "broken men," adventurers, bankrupts, criminals; or simply poor men and artisans, like the Pilgrim Fathers of the *Mayflower*. They were in great part men of the professional and middle classes; some of them men of large landed estate, some zealous clergymen like Cotton, Hooker, and Roger Williams, some shrewd London lawyers, or young scholars from Oxford. The bulk were God-fearing farmers from Lincolnshire and the Eastern counties. They desired in fact "only the best" as sharers in their enterprise; men driven forth from their fatherland not by earthly want, or by the greed of gold, or by the lust of adventure, but by the fear of God, and the zeal for a godly worship. But strong as was their zeal, it was not without a wrench that they tore themselves from their English homes. "Farewell, dear England!" was the cry which burst from the first little company of emigrants as its shores faded from their sight. "Our hearts," wrote Winthrop's followers to the brethren whom they had left behind, "shall be fountains of tears for your everlasting welfare, when we shall be in our poor cottages in the wilderness."

New England.

For a while, as the first terrors of persecution died down, there was a lull in the emigration. But no sooner had Laud's system made its pressure felt than again "godly people in England began to apprehend a special hand of Providence in raising this plantation" in

Massachusetts; "and their hearts were generally stirred to come over." It was in vain that weaker men returned to bring news of hardships and dangers, and told how two hundred of the newcomers had perished with their first winter. A letter from Winthrop told how the rest toiled manfully on. "We now enjoy God and Jesus Christ," he wrote to those at home, "and is not that enough? I thank God I like so well to be here as I do not repent my coming. I would not have altered my course though I had foreseen all these afflictions. I never had more content of mind." With the strength and manliness of Puritanism, its bigotry and narrowness crossed the Atlantic too. Roger Williams, a young minister who held the doctrine of freedom of conscience, was driven from the new settlement to become a preacher among the settlers of Rhode Island. The bitter resentment stirred in the emigrants by persecution at home was seen in their abolition of Episcopacy and their prohibition of the use of the Book of Common Prayer. The intensity of its religious sentiments turned the colony into a theocracy. "To the end that the body of the Commons may be preserved of honest and good men, it was ordered and agreed that for the time to come no man shall be admitted to the freedom of the body politic but such as are members of some of the churches within the bounds of the same." But the fiercer mood which persecution was begetting in the Puritans only welcomed this bigotry. As years went by and the contest grew hotter at home, the number of emigrants rose fast. Three thousand new colonists arrived from England in a single year. Between the sailing of Winthrop's expedition and the assembling of the Long Parliament, in the space, that is, of ten or eleven years, two hundred emigrant ships had crossed the Atlantic, and twenty thousand Englishmen had found a refuge in the West.

CHAPTER VII

THE RISING OF THE SCOTS

1635-1640

England in 1635.

When Weston died in 1635 six years had passed without a Parliament, and the Crown was at the height of its power. Its financial difficulties seemed coming to an end. The long peace, the rigid economy of administration, the use of forgotten rights and vexatious monopolies, had now halved the amount of debt, while they had raised the revenue to a level with the royal expenditure. Charles had no need of subsidies; and without the need of subsidies he saw no ground for again encountering the opposition of Parliament. The religious difficulty gave him as little anxiety. If Laud was taking harsh courses with the Puritans, he seemed to be successful in his struggle with Puritanism. The most able among its ministers were silenced or deprived. The most earnest of its laymen were flying over seas. But there was no show of opposition to the reforms of the Primate or the High Commission. In the two dependent kingdoms all appeared to be going well. In Scotland Charles had begun quietly to carry further his father's schemes for religious uniformity; but there was no voice of protest. In Ireland Wentworth could point to a submissive Parliament and a well-equipped army, ready to serve the king on either side St. George's Channel. The one solitary anxiety of Charles, in fact, lay in the aspect of foreign affairs. The union of Holland and of France had done the work that England had failed to do in saving German Protestantism from the grasp of the House of Austria. But if their union was of service to Germany, it brought danger to England. France was its ancient foe. The commercial supremacy of the Dutch was threatening English trade. The junction of their fleets would at once enable them to challenge the right of dominion which England claimed over the Channel. And at this moment rumours came of a scheme of partition by which the Spanish Netherlands were to be shared between the French and the Dutch, and by which Dunkirk was at once to be attacked and given into the hands of France.

Ship-money.

To suffer the extension of France along the shores of the Netherlands had seemed impossible to English statesmen from the days of Elizabeth. To surrender the command of the Channel was equally galling to the national pride. Even Weston, fond as he was of peace, had seen the need of putting a strong fleet upon the seas; and in 1634 Spain engaged to defray part of the expense of equipping such a fleet in the hope that the king's demand would bring on war with Holland and with France. But money had to be found at home, and as Charles would not hear of the gathering of a Parliament means had to be got by a new stretch of prerogative. The legal research of Noy, one of the law-officers of the Crown, found precedents among the records in the Tower for the provision of ships for the king's use by the port-towns of the kingdom, and for the furnishing of their equipment by the maritime counties. The precedents dated from times when no permanent fleet existed, and when sea warfare could only be waged by vessels lent for the moment by the various ports. But they were seized as a means of equipping a permanent navy without cost to the Exchequer; the first demand of ships was soon commuted into a demand of money for the provision of ships; and the writs for the payment of ship-money which were issued to London and other coast-towns were enforced by fine and imprisonment. The money was paid, and in 1635 a fleet put to sea. The Spaniards however were too poor to fulfil their share of the bargain; they sent neither money nor vessels; and Charles shrank from a contest single-handed with France and the Dutch. But with the death of the Earl of Portland a bolder hand seized the reins of power. To Laud as to Wentworth the system of Weston had hardly seemed government at all. In the correspondence which passed between the two ministers the king was censured as over-cautious, the Star Chamber as feeble, the judges as over-scrupulous. "I am for Thorough," the one writes to the other in alternate fits of impatience at the slow progress they are making. Wentworth was anxious that his good work might not "be spoiled on that side." Laud echoed the wish, while he envied the free course of the Lord Lieutenant. "You have a good deal of humour here," he writes, "for your proceeding. Go on a' God's name. I have done with expecting of Thorough on this side."

The new ship-money.

With feelings such as these Laud no sooner took the direction of affairs than a more vigorous and unscrupulous impulse made itself felt. Far from being drawn from his projects by the desertion of Spain, Charles was encouraged to carry them out by his own efforts. It was determined to strengthen the fleet; and funds for this purpose were raised by an extension of the levy of ship-money. The pretence of precedents was thrown aside, and Laud resolved to find a permanent revenue in the conversion of the "ship-money," till now levied on ports and the maritime counties, into a general tax imposed by the royal will upon the whole country. The sum expected from the tax was no less than a quarter of a million a year. "I know no reason," Wentworth had written significantly, "but you may as well rule the common lawyers in England as I, poor beagle, do here"; and the judges no sooner declared the new impost to be legal than he drew the logical deduction from their decision. "Since it is lawful for the king to impose a tax for the equipment of the navy, it must be equally so for the levy of an army: and the same reason which authorizes him to levy an army to resist, will authorize him to carry that army abroad that he may prevent invasion. Moreover what is law in England is law also in Scotland and Ireland. The decision of the judges will therefore make the king absolute at home and formidable abroad. Let him only abstain from war for a few years that he may habituate his subjects to the payment of that tax, and in the end he will find himself more powerful and respected than any of his predecessors." "The debt of the Crown being taken off," he wrote to Charles, "you may govern at your will."

John Hampden.

But there were men who saw the danger to freedom in this levy of ship-money as clearly as Wentworth himself. The bulk of the country party abandoned all hope of English freedom. There was a sudden revival of the emigration to New England; and men of blood and fortune now prepared to seek a new home in the West. Lord Warwick secured the proprietorship of the Connecticut valley. Lord Saye and Sele and Lord Brooke began negotiations for transporting themselves to the New World. Oliver Cromwell is said, by a doubtful tradition, to have only been prevented from crossing the seas by a royal embargo. It is more certain that John Hampden purchased a tract of land on the Narragansett. No visionary danger would have brought the soul of Hampden to the thought of flight. He was sprung of an ancient line, which had been true to the House of Lancaster in the Wars of the Roses, and whose fidelity had been rewarded by the favour of the Tudors. On the brow of the Chilterns an opening in the woods has borne the name of "the Queen's Gap" ever since Griffith Hampden cleared an avenue for one of Elizabeth's visits to his stately home. His grandson, John, was born at the close of the Queen's reign; the dissipations of youth were cut short by an early marriage at twenty-five to a wife he loved; and the young squire settled down to a life of study and religion. His wealth and lineage opened to him a career such as other men were choosing at the Stuart court. Few English commoners had wider possessions; and under James it was easy to purchase a peerage by servility and hard cash. "If my son will seek for his honour," wrote his mother from the court, "tell him now to come, for here are multitudes of lords a-making!" But Hampden had nobler aims than a peerage. From the first his choice was made to stand by the side of those who were struggling for English freedom; and at the age of twenty-six he took his seat in the memorable Parliament of 1621. Young as he was, his ability at once carried him to the front; he was employed in "managing conferences with the Lords" and other weighty business, and became the friend of Eliot and of Pym. He was again returned to the two first Parliaments of Charles; and his firm refusal to contribute to forced loans at the close of the second marked the quiet firmness of his temper. "I could be content to lend," he replied to the demand of the Council, "but for fear to draw on myself that curse in Magna Charta which should be read twice a year against those that do infringe it." He was rewarded with so close an imprisonment in the Tower, "that he never afterwards did look the same man he was before." But a prison had no force to bend the steady patriotism of John Hampden, and he again took a prominent part in the Parliament of 1628, especially on the religious questions which came under debate.

With the dissolution of this Parliament Hampden again withdrew to his home, the home that, however disguised by tasteless changes without, still stands unaltered within on a rise of the Chilterns, its Elizabethan hall girt round with galleries and stately staircases winding up beneath shadowy portraits in ruffs and farthingales. Around are the quiet undulations of the chalk-country, billowy heavings and sinkings as of some primæval sea suddenly hushed into motionlessness, soft slopes of grey grass or brown-red corn falling gently to dry bottoms, woodland flung here and there in masses over the hills. A country of fine and lucid air, of far shadowy distances, of hollows tenderly veiled by mist, graceful everywhere with a flowing unaccentuated grace, as though Hampden's own temper had grown out of it. As we look on it, we recall the "flowing courtesy to all men," the "seeming humility and submission of judgement," the "rare affability and temper in debate," that woke admiration and regard even in the fiercest of his opponents. But beneath the outer grace of Hampden's demeanour lay a soul of steel. Buried as he seemed in the affections of his home, the great patriot waited patiently for the hour of freedom that he knew must come. Around him gathered the men that were to stand by his side in the future struggle. He had been the bosom friend of Eliot till the victim of the king's resentment lay dead in the Tower. He was now the bosom-friend of Pym. His mother had been a daughter of the great Cromwell house at Hinchinbrook, and he was thus closely linked by blood to Oliver Cromwell and connected with Oliver St. John. The marriages of two daughters united him to the Knightleys and the Lynes. Selden and Whitelock were among his closest counsellors. It was in steady commune with these that the years passed by, while outer eyes saw in him only a Puritan squire of a cultured sort, popular among his tenantry and punctual at Quarter-Sessions, with "an exceeding propenseness to field sports" and "busy in the embellishment of his estate, of which he was very fond."

Hampden and ship-money.

At last the quiet patience was broken by the news of the ship-money, and of a writ addressed to the High Sheriff, Sir Peter Temple of Stave, ordering him to raise £4500 on the county of Buckingham. Hampden's resolve was soon known. In the January of 1636 a return was made of the payments for ship-money from the village of Great Kimble at the foot of the Chilterns round which his chief property lay, and at the head of those who refused to pay stood the name of John Hampden. For a while matters moved slowly; and it was not till the close of June that a Council warrant summoned the High Sheriff to account for arrears. Hampden meanwhile had been taking counsel in the spring with Whitelock and others of his friends concerning the means of bringing the matter to a legal issue. Charles was as eager to appeal to the law as Hampden himself; but he followed his father's usage in privately consulting the judges on the subject of his claim, and it was not till the February of 1637 that their answer asserted its legality. The king at once made their opinion public in the faith that all resistance would cease. But the days were gone by when the voice of the judges was taken submissively for law by Englishmen. They had seen the dismissal of Coke and of Crewe. They knew that in matters of the prerogative the judges admitted a right of interference and of dictation on the part of the Crown. "The judges," Sir Harbottle Grimston could say in the Long Parliament, "the judges have overthrown the law, as the bishops religion!" What Hampden aimed at was not the judgement of such judges, but an open trial where England might hear, in spite of the silence of Parliament, a discussion of this great inroad on its freedom. His wishes were realized at last by the issue in May of a writ from the Exchequer, calling on him to show cause why payment of ship-money for his lands should not be made.

Charles and Scotland.

The news of Hampden's resistance thrilled through the country at a moment when men were roused by news of resistance in the north. Since the accession of James Scotland had bent with a seeming tameness before aggression after aggression. Its pulpits had been bridled. Its boldest ministers had been sent into exile. Its General Assembly had been brought to submission by the Crown. Its Church had been forced to accept bishops, if not with all their old powers, still with authority as permanent superintendents of the diocesan synods. The ministers and elders had been deprived of their right of excommunicating offenders, save with a bishop's sanction. A Court of High Commission enforced the supremacy of the Crown. But with this enforcement of his royal authority James was content. He had no wish for a doctrinal change, or for the bringing about of a strict uniformity with the Church of England. It was in vain that Laud in his earlier days invited James to draw his Scotch subjects "to a nearer conjunction with the liturgy and canons of this nation." "I sent him back again," said the shrewd old king, "with the frivolous draft he had drawn. For all that, he feared not my anger, but assaulted me again with another ill-fangled platform to make that stubborn Kirk stoop more to the English platform; but I durst not play fast and loose with my word. He knows not the stomach of that people." The earlier policy of Charles followed his father's line of action. It effected little save a partial restoration of Church-lands, which the lords were forced to surrender. But Laud's vigorous action made itself felt. His first acts were directed rather to points of outer observance than to any attack on the actual fabric of Presbyterian organization. The estates were induced to withdraw the control of ecclesiastical apparel from the Assembly, and to commit it to the Crown; and this step was soon followed by a resumption of their episcopal costume on the part of the Scotch bishops. When the Bishop of Moray preached before Charles in his rochet, on the king's visit to Edinburgh in 1633, it was the first instance of its use since the Reformation. The innovation was followed by the issue of a Royal warrant which directed all ministers to use the surplice in divine worship.

The new Liturgy.

The enforcement of the surplice woke Scotland from its torpor, and alarm at once spread through the country. Quarterly meetings were held in parishes with fasting and prayer to consult on the dangers which threatened religion, and ministers who conformed to the new ceremonies were rebuked and deserted by their congregations. The popular discontent soon found leaders in the Scotch nobles. Threatened in power by the attempts of the Crown to narrow their legal jurisdiction, in purse by projects for the resumption and restoration to the Church of the bishops' lands, irritated by the restoration of the prelates to their old rank, by their reintroduction to Parliament and the Council, by the nomination of Archbishop Spottiswood to the post of Chancellor, and above all by the setting up again the worrying bishops' courts, the nobles with Lord Lorne at their head stood sullenly aloof from the new system. But Charles was indifferent to the discontent which his measures were rousing. Under Laud's pressure he was resolved to put an end to the Presbyterian character of the Scotch Church altogether, and to bring it to a uniformity with the Church of England in organization and ritual. With this view a book of Canons was issued in 1636 on the sole authority of the king. These Canons placed the government of the Church absolutely in the hands of its bishops; and made a bishop's licence necessary for instruction and for the publication of books. The authority of the prelates indeed was jealously subordinated to the supremacy of the Crown. No Church Assembly might be summoned but by the king, no alteration in worship or discipline introduced but by his permission. As daring a stretch of the prerogative superseded what was known as Knox's Liturgy—the book of Common Order drawn up on the Genevan model by that Reformer, and generally used throughout Scotland—by a new Liturgy based on the English Book of Common Prayer.

Its rejection.

The Liturgy and Canons had been Laud's own handiwork; in their composition the General Assembly had neither been consulted nor recognized; and taken together they formed the code of a political and ecclesiastical system which aimed at reducing Scotland to an utter subjection to the Crown. To enforce them on the land was to effect a revolution of the most serious kind. The books however were backed by a royal injunction, and Laud flattered himself that the revolution had been wrought. But the patience of Scotland found an end at last. In the summer of 1637, while England was waiting for the opening of the great cause of ship-money, peremptory orders from the king forced the clergy of Edinburgh to introduce the new service into their churches. On the 23rd of July the Prayer-Book was used at the church of St. Giles. But the book was no sooner opened than a murmur ran through the congregation, and the murmur grew into a formidable riot. The church was cleared, and the service read; but the rising discontent frightened the judges into a decision that the royal writ enjoined the purchase, not the use, of the Prayer-Book, and its use was at once discontinued. The angry orders which came from England for its restoration were met by a shower of protests from every part of Scotland. The ministers of Fife pleaded boldly the want of any confirmation of the book by a General Assembly. "This Church," they exclaimed, "is a free and independent Church, just as this kingdom is a free and independent kingdom." The Duke of Lennox alone took sixty-eight petitions with him to the Court; while ministers, nobles, and gentry poured into Edinburgh to organize a national resistance.

The temper of England.

The effect of these events in Scotland was at once seen in the open demonstration of discontent south of the border. The prison with which Laud had rewarded Prynne's dumpy quarto had tamed his spirit so little that a new tract, written within its walls, denounced the bishops as devouring wolves and lords of Lucifer. A fellow-prisoner, John Bastwick, declared in his "Litany" that "Hell was broke loose, and the devils in surplices, hoods, copes, and rochets were come amongst us." Burton, a London clergyman silenced by the High Commission, called on all Christians to resist the bishops as "robbers of souls, limbs of the beast, and factors of Antichrist." Raving of this sort might well have been passed by, had not the general sympathy with Prynne and his fellow-pamphleteers, when Laud dragged them in 1637 before the Star Chamber as "trumpets of sedition," shown how fast the tide of general anger against the Government was rising. The three culprits listened with defiance to their sentence of exposure in the pillory and imprisonment for life; and the crowd who filled Palace Yard to witness their punishment groaned at the cutting off of their ears, and "gave a great shout" when Prynne urged that the sentence on him was contrary to law. A hundred thousand Londoners lined the road as they passed on the way to prison; and the journey of these "Martyrs," as the spectators called them, was like a triumphal progress. Startled as he was at the sudden burst of popular feeling, Laud remained dauntless as ever. Prynne's entertainers, as he passed through the country, were summoned before the Star Chamber, while the censorship struck fiercer blows at the Puritan press. But the real danger lay not in the libels of silly zealots, but in the attitude of Scotland, and in the effect which was being produced in England at large by the trial of Hampden. Wentworth was looking on from Ireland with cool insolence at the contest between a subject and the Crown. "Mr. Hampden," he wrote, "is a great brother; and the genius of that faction of people leads them always to oppose, both civilly and ecclesiastically, all that ever authority ordains." But England looked on with other eyes. "The eyes of all men," owns Clarendon, "were fixed upon him as their *Pater Patriæ* and the pilot who must steer the vessel through the tempests and storms that threatened it." In November and December 1637 the cause of ship-money was solemnly argued for twelve days before the full bench of judges. It was proved that the tax in past times had been levied only in cases of sudden emergency, and confined to the coast and port towns alone, and that even the show of legality had been taken from it by formal statute, and by the Petition of Right.

The judgement on ship-money.

The case was adjourned, but its discussion told not merely on England, but on the temper of the Scots. Charles had replied to their petitions by a simple order to all strangers to leave the capital. But the Council at Edinburgh was unable to enforce his order; and the nobles and gentry before dispersing to their homes petitioned against the bishops, resolved not to own the jurisdiction of their courts, and named in November 1637 a body of delegates, under the odd title of "the Tables." These delegates carried on through the winter a series of negotiations with the Crown. The negotiations were interrupted in the spring of 1638 by a renewed order for their dispersion, and for the acceptance of a Prayer-Book; while the judges in England delivered in June their long-delayed decision on Hampden's case. Two judges only pronounced in his favour; though three followed them on technical grounds. The majority, seven in number, laid down the broad principle that no statute prohibiting arbitrary taxation could be pleaded against the king's will. "I never read or heard," said Judge Berkeley, "that lex was rex, but it is common and most true that rex is lex." Finch, the Chief-Justice, summed up the opinions of his fellow-judges. "Acts of Parliament to take away the king's royal power in the defence of his kingdom are void," he said: "they are void Acts of Parliament to bind the king not to command the subjects, their persons, and goods, and I say their money too, for no Acts of Parliament make any difference."

The Covenant.

The case was ended; and Charles looked for the Puritans to give way. But keener eyes discerned that a new spirit of resistance had been stirred by the trial. The insolence of Wentworth was exchanged for a tone of angry terror. "I wish Mr. Hampden and others to his likeness," the Lord Deputy wrote bitterly from Ireland, "were well whipt into their right senses." Amidst the exultation of the Court over the decision of the judges, Wentworth saw clearly that Hampden's work had been done. Legal and temperate as his course had been, he had roused England to a sense of the danger to her freedom, and forced into light the real character of the royal claims. How stern and bitter the temper even of the noblest Puritans had become at last we see in the poem which Milton produced at this time, his elegy of "Lycidas." Its grave and tender lament is broken by a sudden flash of indignation at the dangers around the Church, at the "blind mouths that scarce themselves know how to hold a sheephook," and to whom "the hungry sheep look up, and are not fed," while "the grim wolf" of Rome "with privy paw daily devours apace, and nothing said!" The stern resolve of the people to demand justice on their tyrants spoke in his threat of the axe. Strafford and Laud, and Charles himself, had yet to reckon with "that two-handed engine at the door" which stood "ready to smite once, and smite no more." But stern as was the general resolve, there was no need for immediate action, for the difficulties which were gathering in the north were certain to bring a strain on the Government which would force it to seek support from the people. The king's demand for immediate submission, which reached Scotland while England was waiting for the Hampden judgement, in the spring of 1638, gathered the whole body of remonstrants together round "the Tables" at Stirling; and a protestation, read at Edinburgh, was followed, on Johnston of Warriston's suggestion, by a renewal of the Covenant with God which had been drawn up and sworn to in a previous hour of peril, when Mary was still plotting against Protestantism, and Spain was preparing its Armada. "We promise and swear," ran the solemn engagement at its close, "by the great name of the Lord our God, to continue in the profession and obedience of the said religion, and that we shall defend the same, and resist all their contrary errors and corruptions, according to our vocation and the utmost of that power which God has put into our hands all the days of our life."

Charles and Scotland.

The Covenant was signed in the churchyard of the Greyfriars at Edinburgh on the first of March, in a tumult of enthusiasm, "with such content and joy as those who, having long before been outlaws and rebels, are admitted again into covenant with God." Gentlemen and nobles rode with the document in their pockets over the country, gathering subscriptions to it, while the ministers pressed for a general consent to it from the pulpit. But pressure was needless. "Such was the zeal of subscribers that for a while many subscribed with tears on their cheeks"; some were indeed reputed to have "drawn their own blood and used it in place of ink to underwrite their names." The force given to Scottish freedom by this revival of religious fervour was seen in the new tone adopted by the Covenanters. The Marquis of Hamilton, who came as Royal Commissioner to put an end to the quarrel, was at once met by demands for an abolition of the Court of High Commission, the withdrawal of the Books of Canons and Common Prayer, a free Parliament, and a free General Assembly. He threatened war; but the threat proved fruitless, and even the Scotch Council pressed Charles to give fuller satisfaction to the people. "I will rather die," the king wrote to Hamilton, "than yield to these impertinent and damnable demands"; but it was needful to gain time. "The discontents at home," wrote Lord Northumberland to Wentworth, "do rather increase than lessen"; and Charles was without money or men. It was in vain that he begged for a loan from Spain on promise of declaring war against Holland, or that he tried to procure two thousand troops from Flanders, with which to occupy Edinburgh. The loan and troops were both refused, and some contributions offered by the English Catholics did little to recruit the Exchequer.

The Scotch Revolution.

Charles had directed the Marquis to delay any decisive breach till the royal fleet appeared in the Forth; but it was hard to equip a fleet at all. Scotland in fact was sooner ready for war than the king. The Scotch volunteers who had been serving in the Thirty Years War streamed home at the call of their brethren; and General Leslie, a veteran trained under Gustavus, came from Sweden to take the command of the new forces. A voluntary war tax was levied in every shire. Charles was so utterly taken by surprise that he saw no choice but to yield, if but for the moment, to the Scottish demands. Hamilton announced that the king allowed the Covenant, the service book was revoked; a pledge was given that the power of the bishops should be lessened; a Parliament was promised for the coming year; and a General Assembly summoned at once. The Assembly met at Glasgow in November 1638; it had been chosen according to the old form which James had annulled, and its 144 ministers were backed by 96 lay elders amongst whom all the leading Covenanters found a place. They had hardly met when, at the news of their design to attack the Bishops, Hamilton declared the Assembly dissolved. But the Church claimed its old freedom of meeting apart from any licence from kings; and by an almost unanimous vote the Assembly resolved to continue its session. Its acts were an undoing of all that the Stuarts had done. The two books of Canons and Common Prayer, the High Commission, the Articles of Perth, were all set aside as invalid. Episcopacy was abjured, the bishops were deposed from their office, and the system of Presbyterianism re-established in its fullest extent.

The Scotch War.

Scotland was fighting England's battle as well as her own. The bold assertion of a people's right to frame its own religion was a practical carrying out of the claim which had been made by the English Parliament of 1629. But Charles was as resolute to resist it now as then. He was firm in his resolve of war, and the strong remonstrances of his Scotch councillors against it were met by a fierce pressure from Wentworth and Laud. Both felt that the question had ceased to be one for Scotland only; they saw that a concession to the Scots must now be fatal to the political and ecclesiastical system they had built up in Ireland and England alike. In both countries those who opposed the Government were looking to the rising in the North. They were suspicious of correspondence between the Puritans in England and the Scotch leaders; and whether these suspicions were true or no, of the sympathy with which the proceedings at Edinburgh were watched south of the Border there could be little doubt. It was with the conviction that the whole Stuart system was at stake that the two ministers pressed for war. But angered as he was, Charles was a Scotchman, and a Scotch king; and he shrank from a march with English troops into his hereditary kingdom. He counted rather on the sympathy of the northern clans and of Huntly, on the impression produced by the appearance of Hamilton with a fleet in the Forth, and by the suspension of trade with Holland, than on any actual force of arms from the South. The 20,000 men he gathered at York were to serve rather as a demonstration, and to protect the border, than as an invading force. But again his plans broke down before the activity and resolution of the Scots. The news that Charles was gathering an army at York, and reckoning for support on the clans of the north, was answered in the spring of 1639 by the seizure of Edinburgh, Dumbarton, and Stirling; while 10,000 well-equipped troops under Leslie and the Earl of Montrose entered Aberdeen, and brought the Earl of Huntly a prisoner to the south. Instead of overawing the country, the appearance of the royal fleet in the Forth was the signal for Leslie's march with 20,000 men to the Border. Charles had hardly pushed across the Tweed, when the "old little crooked soldier," encamping on the hill of Dunse Law, a few miles from Berwick, fairly offered him battle.

Scotland and France.

The king's threats at once broke down. Charles had a somewhat stronger force than Leslie, but his men had no will to fight; and he was forced to evade a battle by consenting to the gathering of a free Assembly and of a Scotch Parliament. But he had no purpose of being bound by terms which had been wrested from him by rebel subjects. In his eyes the pacification at Berwick was a mere suspension of arms; and the king's summons of Wentworth from Ireland was a proof that violent measures were in preparation. The Scotch leaders were far from deceiving themselves as to the king's purpose; and in the struggle which they foresaw they sought aid from a power which Scotch tradition had looked on for centuries as the natural ally of their country. The jealousy between France and England had long been smouldering, and only the weakness of Charles and the caution of Richelieu had prevented its bursting into open flame. In the weary negotiations which the English king still carried on for the restoration of his nephew to the Palatinate, he had till now been counting rather on the friendly mediation of Spain with the Emperor than on any efforts of France or its Protestant allies. At this moment however a strange piece of fortune brought about a sudden change in his policy. A Spanish fleet, which had been attacked by the Dutch in the Channel, took refuge under the guns of Dover; and Spain appealed for its protection to the friendship of the king. But Charles saw in the incident a chance of winning the Palatinate without a blow. He at once opened negotiations with Richelieu. He offered to suffer the Spanish vessels to be destroyed, if France would pledge itself to restore his nephew. Richelieu on the other hand would only consent to his restoration if Charles would take an active part in the war. But the negotiations were suddenly cut short by the daring of the Dutch. In spite of the king's threats they attacked the Spanish fleet as it lay in English waters, and drove it broken to Ostend. Such an act of defiance could only embitter the enmity which Charles already felt towards France and its Dutch allies; and Richelieu grasped gladly at the Scotch revolt as a means of hindering England from joining in the war. His agents opened communications with the Scottish leaders; and applications for its aid were forwarded by the Scots to the French court.

The Short Parliament.

The discovery of this correspondence roused anew the hopes of the king. He was resolved not to yield to rebels; and the proceedings in Scotland since the pacification of Berwick seemed to him mere rebellion. A fresh General Assembly adopted as valid the acts of its predecessor. The Parliament only met to demand that the council should be responsible to it for its course of government. The king prorogued both that he might use the weapon which fortune had thrown into his hand. He never doubted that if he appealed to the country English loyalty would rise to support him against Scottish treason. He yielded at last to the counsels of Wentworth. Wentworth was still for war. He had never ceased to urge that the Scots should be whipped back to their border; and the king now avowed his concurrence in this policy by raising him to the earldom of Strafford, and from the post of Lord Deputy to that of Lord Lieutenant. Strafford agreed with Charles that a Parliament should be summoned, the correspondence laid before it, and advantage taken of the burst of indignation on which the king counted to procure a heavy subsidy. But he had foreseen that it might refuse all aid; and in such a case the Earl and the Council held that the King would have a right to fall back on "extraordinary means." Strafford himself hurried to Ireland to read a practical lesson to the English Parliament. In fourteen days he had procured four subsidies from the Irish Commons, and set on foot a force of 8000 men to take part in the attack on the Scots. He came back, flushed with his success, in time for the meeting of the Houses at Westminster in the middle of April 1640. But the lesson failed in its effect. Statesmen like Hampden and Pym were not fools enough to aid the great enemy of English freedom against men who had risen for freedom across the Tweed. Every member of the Commons knew that Scotland was fighting the battle of English liberty. All hope of bringing them to any attack upon the Scots proved fruitless. The intercepted letters were quietly set aside; and the Commons declared as of old that redress of grievances must precede any grant of supplies. No subsidy could be granted till security was had for religion, for property, and for the liberties of Parliament. An offer to relinquish ship-money proved fruitless; and after three weeks sitting the "Short Parliament" was dissolved. "Things must go worse before they go better" was the cool comment of St. John. But the country was strangely moved. After eleven years of personal rule, its hopes had risen again with the summons of the Houses to Westminster; and their rough dismissal after a three weeks sitting brought all patience to an end. "So great a defection in the kingdom," wrote Lord Northumberland, "hath not been known in the memory of man."

The Bishops' War.

Strafford alone stood undaunted. He had provided for the resolve of the Parliament by the decision of the Council that in such a case the king might resort to "extraordinary means"; and he now urged that by the act of the Commons Charles was "freed from all rule of government," and entitled to supply himself at his will. The Irish army, he said, was at the king's command, and Scotland could be subdued in a single summer. He was bent, in fact, on war; and he took command of the royal army, which again advanced to the north. But the Scots were as ready for war as Strafford. As early as March they had reassembled their army; and their Parliament commissioned the Committee of Estates, of which Argyle was the most influential member, to carry on the government. Encouraged by the refusal of the English Houses to grant supplies, they now published a new manifesto and resolved to meet the march of Strafford's army by an advance into England. On the twentieth of August the Scotch army crossed the Border; Montrose being the first to set foot on English soil. Forcing the passage of the Tyne in the face of an English detachment, they occupied Newcastle, and despatched from that town their proposals of peace. They prayed the king to consider their grievances, and "with the advice and consent of the Estates of England convened in Parliament, to settle a firm and desirable peace." The prayer was backed by preparations for a march upon York, where Charles had abandoned himself to despair. The warlike bluster of Strafford had broken utterly down the moment he attempted to take the field. His troops were a mere mob; and neither by threats nor prayers could the earl recall them to their duty. He was forced to own that two months were needed before they could be fit for action. Charles was driven again to open negotiations with the Scots, and to buy a respite in their advance by a promise of pay for their army and by leaving Northumberland and Durham in their hands as pledges for the fulfilment of his engagements. But the truce only met half his difficulties. Behind him England was all but in revolt. The Treasury was empty, and London and the East India merchants alike refused a loan. The London apprentices mobbed

Laud at Lambeth, and broke up the sittings of the High Commission at St. Paul's. The war was denounced everywhere as "the Bishops' War," and the new levies murdered officers whom they suspected of Papistry, broke down altar-rails in every church they passed, and deserted to their homes. To all but Strafford it was plain that the system of Charles had broken hopelessly down. Two peers, Lord Wharton and Lord Howard, ventured to lay before the king himself a petition for peace with the Scots; and though Strafford arrested and proposed to shoot them as mutineers, the English Council shrank from desperate courses. But if desperate courses were not taken, there was nothing for it but to give way. Penniless, without an army, with a people all but in revolt, the obstinate temper of the king still strove to escape from the humiliation of calling a Parliament. He summoned a Great Council of the Peers at York. But his project broke down before its general repudiation by the nobles; and with wrath and shame at his heart Charles was driven to summon again the Houses to Westminster.

CHAPTER VIII

THE LONG PARLIAMENT

1640-1644

John Pym.

If Strafford embodied the spirit of tyranny, John Pym, the leader of the Commons from the first meeting of the new Houses at Westminster, stands out for all after time as the embodiment of law. A Somersetshire gentleman of good birth and competent fortune, he entered on public life in the Parliament of 1614, and was imprisoned for his patriotism at its close. He had been a leading member in that of 1620, and one of the "twelve ambassadors" for whom James ordered chairs to be set at Whitehall. Of the band of patriots with whom he had stood side by side in the constitutional struggle against the earlier despotism of Charles he was almost the one survivor. Coke had died of old age; Cotton's heart was broken by oppression; Eliot had perished in the Tower; Wentworth had apostatized. But Pym remained, resolute, patient as of old; and as the sense of his greatness grew silently during the eleven years of deepening misrule, the hope and faith of better things clung almost passionately to the man who never doubted of the final triumph of freedom and the law. At their close, Clarendon tells us, in words all the more notable for their bitter tone of hate, "he was the most popular man, and the most able to do hurt, that have lived at any time." He had shown he knew how to wait, and when waiting was over he showed he knew how to act. On the eve of the Long Parliament he rode through England to quicken the electors to a sense of the crisis which had come at last; and on the assembling of the Commons he took his place, not merely as member for Tavistock, but as their acknowledged head. Few of the country gentlemen indeed who formed the bulk of the members, had sat in any previous House; and of the few none represented in so eminent a way the Parliamentary tradition on which the coming struggle was to turn. Pym's eloquence, inferior in boldness and originality to that of Eliot or Wentworth, was better suited by its massive and logical force to convince and guide a great party; and it was backed by a calmness of temper, a dexterity and order in the management of public business, and a practical power of shaping the course of debate, which gave a form and method to Parliamentary proceedings such as they had never had before.

His political theory.

Valuable however as these qualities were, it was a yet higher quality which raised Pym into the greatest, as he was the first, of Parliamentary leaders. Of the five hundred members who sate round him at St. Stephen's, he was the one man who had clearly foreseen, and as clearly resolved how to meet, the difficulties which lay before them. It was certain that Parliament would be drawn into a struggle with the Crown. It was probable that in such a struggle the House of Commons would be hampered, as it had been hampered before, by the House of Lords. The legal antiquarians of the older constitutional school stood helpless before such a conflict of co-ordinate powers, a conflict for which no provision had been made by the law, and on which precedents threw only a doubtful and conflicting light. But with a knowledge of precedent as great as their own, Pym rose high above them in his grasp of constitutional principles. He was the first English statesman who discovered, and applied, to the political circumstances around him, what may be called the doctrine of constitutional proportion. He saw that as an element of constitutional life Parliament was of higher value than the Crown; he saw too that in Parliament itself the one essential part was the House of Commons. On these two facts he based his whole policy in the contest which followed. When Charles refused to act with the Parliament, Pym treated the refusal as a temporary abdication on the part of the sovereign, which vested the executive power in the two Houses until new arrangements were made. When the Lords obstructed public business, he warned them that obstruction would only force the Commons "to save the kingdom alone." Revolutionary as these principles seemed at the time, they have both been recognized as bases of our constitution since the days of Pym. The first principle was established by the Convention and Parliament which followed on the departure of James the Second; the second by the acknowledgement on all sides since the Reform

Bill of 1832 that the government of the country is really in the hands of the House of Commons, and can only be carried on by ministers who represent the majority of that House.

His political genius.

It was thus that the work of Pym brought about a political revolution greater than any that England has ever experienced since his day. But the temper of Pym was the very opposite of the temper of a revolutionist. Few natures have ever been wider in their range of sympathy or action. Serious as his purpose was, his manners were genial and even courtly; he turned easily from an invective against Strafford to a chat with Lady Carlisle; and the grace and gaiety of his social tone, even when the care and weight of public affairs were bringing him to his grave, gave rise to a hundred silly scandals among the prurient royalists. It was this striking combination of genial versatility with a massive force in his nature which marked him out from the first moment of power as a born ruler of men. He proved himself at once the subtlest of diplomatists and the grandest of demagogues. He was equally at home in tracking the subtle intricacies of royalist intrigues, or in kindling popular passion with words of fire. Though past middle life when his work really began, for he was born in 1584, four years before the coming of the Armada, he displayed from the first meeting of the Long Parliament the qualities of a great administrator, an immense faculty for labour, a genius for organization, patience, tact, a power of inspiring confidence in all whom he touched, calmness and moderation under good fortune or ill, an immovable courage, an iron will. No English ruler has ever shown greater nobleness of natural temper or a wider capacity for government than the Somersetshire squire whom his enemies, made clear-sighted by their hate, greeted truly enough as "King Pym."

The meeting of the Parliament.

On the eve of the elections he rode with Hampden through the counties to rouse England to a sense of the crisis which had come. But his ride was hardly needed, for the summons of a Parliament at once woke the kingdom to a fresh life. The Puritan emigration to New England was suddenly and utterly suspended; "the change," said Winthrop, "made all men to stay in England in expectation of a new world." The public discontent spoke from every Puritan pulpit, and expressed itself in a sudden burst of pamphlets, the first-fruits of the thirty thousand which were issued in the twenty years that followed, and which turned England at large into a school of political discussion. The resolute looks of the members, as they gathered at Westminster on the third of November 1640, contrasted with the hesitating words of the king; and each brought from borough or county a petition of grievances. Fresh petitions were brought every day by bands of citizens or farmers. The first week was spent in receiving these petitions, and in appointing forty committees to examine and report on them, whose reports formed the grounds on which the Commons subsequently acted. The next work of the Commons was to deal with the agents of the royal system. It was agreed that the king's name should be spared; but in every county a list of officers who had carried out the plans of the Government was ordered to be prepared and laid before the House. But the Commons were far from dealing merely with these meaner "delinquents." They resolved to strike at the men whose counsels had wrought the evil of the past years of tyranny; and their first blow was at the leading ministers of the king.

Impeachment of Strafford.

Even Laud was not the centre of so great and universal a hatred as the Earl of Strafford. Strafford's guilt was more than the guilt of a servile instrument of tyranny, it was the guilt of "that grand apostate to the Commonwealth who," in the terrible words which closed Lord Digby's invective, "must not expect to be pardoned in this world till he be despatched to the other." He was conscious of his danger, but Charles forced him to attend the Court; and with characteristic boldness he resolved to anticipate attack by accusing the Parliamentary leaders of a treasonable correspondence with the Scots. He reached London a week after the opening of the Parliament; and hastened the next morning to an interview with the king. But he had to deal with men as energetic as himself. He was just laying his scheme before Charles when the news reached him that Pym was at the bar of the Lords with his impeachment for high treason. On the morning of the 11th of November the doors of the House of Commons had been locked, Strafford's impeachment voted, and carried by Pym with 300 members at his back to the bar of the Lords. The Earl hurried at once to the Parliament. "With speed," writes an eye-witness, "he comes to the House: he calls rudely at the door," and, "with a proud glooming look, makes towards his place at the board-head. But at once many bid him void the House, so he is forced in confusion to go to the door till he was called." He was only recalled to hear his committal to the Tower. He was still resolute to retort the charge of treason on his foes, and "offered to speak, but was commanded to be gone without a word." The keeper of the Black Rod demanded his sword as he took him in charge. "This done, he makes through a number of people towards his coach, no man capping to him, before whom that morning the greatest of all England would have stood uncovered."

Fall of the Ministers.

The blow was quickly followed up. Windebank, the Secretary of State, was charged with a corrupt favouring of recusants, and escaped to France; Finch, the Lord Keeper, was impeached, and fled in terror over sea. In December Laud was himself committed to the charge of the Usher. The shadow of what was to come falls across the pages of his diary, and softens the hard temper of the man into a strange tenderness. "I stayed at Lambeth till the evening," writes the Archbishop, "to avoid the gaze of the people. I went to evening prayer in my chapel. The Psalms of the day and chapter fifty of Isaiah gave me great comfort. God make me worthy of it, and fit to receive it. As I went to my barge, hundreds of my poor neighbours stood there and prayed for my safety and return to my house. For which I bless God and them." In February Sir Robert Berkeley, one of the judges who had held that ship-money was legal, was seized while sitting on the Bench and committed to prison. In the very first days of the Parliament a yet more emphatic proof of the downfall of the royal system had been given by the recall of Prynne and his fellow "martyrs" from their prisons, and by their entry in triumph into London, amidst the shouts of a great multitude who strewed laurels in their path.

Work of the Houses.

The effect of these rapid blows was seen in the altered demeanour of the king. Charles at once dropped his old tone of command. He ceased to protest against the will of the Commons, and looked sullenly on while one by one the lawless acts of his Government were undone. Ship-money was declared illegal; and the judgement in Hampden's case was annulled. In February 1641 a statute declaring "the ancient right of the subjects of this kingdom that no subsidy, custom, impost, or any charge whatsoever ought or may be laid or imposed upon any merchandise exported or imported by subjects, denizens, or aliens, without common consent in Parliament," put an end for ever to all pretensions to a right of arbitrary taxation on the part of the Crown. A Triennial Bill enforced the assembly of the Houses every three years, and bound the returning officers to proceed to election if no royal writ were issued to summon them.

Church reform.

The subject of religion was one of greater difficulty. In ecclesiastical as in political matters the aim of the parliamentary leaders was strictly conservative. Their purpose was to restore the Church of England to its state under Elizabeth, and to free it from the "innovations" introduced by Laud and his fellow-prelates. With this view commissioners were sent in January 1641 into every county "for the defacing, demolishing, and quite taking away of all images, altars, or tables turned altarwise, crucifixes, superstitious pictures, monuments, and reliques of idolatry out of all churches and chapels." But the bulk of the Commons as of the Lords were averse from any radical changes in the constitution or doctrine of the Church. All however were agreed on the necessity of reform; and one of the first acts of the Parliament was to appoint a Committee of Religion to consider the question. Within as without the House the general opinion was in favour of a reduction of the power and wealth of the prelates, as well as of the jurisdiction of the Church courts. Even among the bishops themselves the more prominent saw the need for consenting to an abolition of Chapters and Bishops' Courts, as well as to the election of a council of ministers in each diocese, which had been suggested by Archbishop Usher as a check on episcopal autocracy. A scheme to this effect was drawn up by Bishop Williams of Lincoln; but it was far from meeting the wishes of the general body of the Commons. The part which the higher clergy had taken in lending themselves to do political work for the Crown was fresh in the minds of all; and in addition to the changes which Williams proposed, Pym and Lord Falkland demanded a severance of the clergy from all secular or state offices, and an expulsion of the bishops from the House of Lords. Such a measure seemed needful to restore the independent action of the Peers; for the number and servility of the bishops were commonly strong enough to prevent the Upper House from taking any part which was disagreeable to the Crown.

The Bishops and Parliament.

Further the bulk of the Commons had no will to go. There were others indeed who were pressing hard to go further. A growing party demanded the abolition of Episcopacy altogether. The doctrines of Cartwright had risen into popularity under the persecution of Laud, and Presbyterianism was now a formidable force among the middle classes. Its chief strength lay in the eastern counties and in London, where a few clergymen such as Calamy and Marshall formed a committee for its diffusion; while in Parliament it was represented by Lord Brooke, Lord Mandeville, and Lord Saye and Sele. In the Commons Sir Harry Vane represented a more extreme party of reformers, the Independents of the future, whose sentiments were little less hostile to Presbyterianism than to Episcopacy, but who acted with the Presbyterians for the present, and formed a part of what became known as the "root and branch" party, from its demand for the utter extirpation of prelacy. The attitude of Scotland in the struggle against tyranny, and the political advantages of a religious union between the two kingdoms, gave force to the Presbyterian party; and the agitation which it set on foot found a vigorous support in the Scotch Commissioners who had been sent to treat of peace with the Parliament. Thoughtful men, too, were moved by a desire to knit the English Church more closely to the general body of Protestantism. Milton, who after the composition of his "Lycidas" had spent a year in foreign travel, returned to throw himself on this ground into the theological strife. He held it "an unjust thing that the English should differ from all churches as many as be reformed." In spite of this pressure however, and of a Presbyterian petition from London with fifteen thousand signatures which had been presented at the very opening of the Houses, the Parliament remained hostile to any change in the constitution of the Church. The Committee of Religion reported in favour of the reforms proposed by Falkland and Pym; and on the tenth of March 1641 a bill for the removal of bishops from the House of Peers passed the Commons almost unanimously.

Trial of Strafford.

As yet all had gone well. The king made no sign of opposition. He was known to be resolute against the abolition of Episcopacy; but he announced no purpose of resisting the removal of the bishops from the House of Peers. Strafford's life he was determined to save; but he threw no obstacle in the way of his impeachment. The trial of the Earl opened on the twenty-second of March. The whole of the House of Commons appeared in Westminster Hall to support it, and the passion which the cause excited was seen in the loud cries of sympathy or hatred which burst from the crowded benches on either side as Strafford for fifteen days struggled with a remarkable courage and ingenuity against the list of charges, and melted his audience to tears by the pathos of his defence. But the trial was suddenly interrupted. Though tyranny and misgovernment had been conclusively proved against the Earl, the technical proof of treason was weak. "The law of England," to use Hallam's words, "is silent as to conspiracies against itself," and treason by the Statute of Edward the Third was restricted to a levying of war against the king or a compassing of his death. The Commons endeavoured to strengthen their case by bringing forward the notes of a meeting of the Council in which Strafford had urged the use of his Irish troops "to reduce that kingdom to obedience"; but the Lords would only admit the evidence on condition of wholly reopening the case. Pym and Hampden remained convinced of the sufficiency of the impeachment; but the House broke loose from their control. Under the guidance of St. John and Lord Falkland the Commons resolved to abandon these judicial proceedings, and fall back on the resource of a Bill of Attainder. The bill passed the Lower House on the 21st of April by a majority of 204 to 59; and on the 29th it received the assent of the Lords. The course which the Parliament took has been bitterly censured by some whose opinion in such a matter is entitled to respect. But the crime of Strafford was none the less a crime that it did not fall within the scope of the Statute of Treasons. It is impossible indeed to provide for some of the greatest dangers which can happen to national freedom by any formal statute. Even now a minister might avail himself of the temper of a Parliament elected in some moment of popular panic, and, though the nation returned to its senses, might simply by refusing to appeal to the country govern in defiance of its will. Such a course would be technically legal, but such a minister would be none the less a criminal. Strafford's course, whether it fell within the Statute of Treasons or no, was from beginning to end an attack on the freedom of the whole nation. In the last resort a nation retains the right of self-defence, and a Bill of Attainder is the assertion of such a right for the punishment of a public enemy who falls within the scope of no written law.

The Army Plot.

The counsel of Pym and of Hampden had been prompted by no doubt of the legality of the attainder. But they looked on the impeachment as still likely to succeed, and they were anxious at this moment to conciliate the king. The real security for the permanence of the changes they had wrought lay in a lasting change in the royal counsels; and such a change it seemed possible to bring about. To save Strafford and Episcopacy Charles listened in the spring of 1641 to a proposal for entrusting the offices of state to the leaders of the Parliament. In this scheme the Earl of Bedford was to become Lord Treasurer, Pym Chancellor of the Exchequer, Holles Secretary of State, while Lords Essex, Mandeville, and Saye and Sele occupied various posts in the administration. Foreign affairs would have been entrusted to Lord Holland, whose policy was that of alliance with Richelieu and Holland against Spain, a policy whose adoption would have been sealed by the marriage of a daughter of Charles with the Prince of Orange. With characteristic foresight Hampden sought only the charge of the Prince of Wales. He knew that the best security for freedom in the after-time would be a patriot king.

Charles listened to this project with seeming assent; the only conditions he made were that Episcopacy should not be abolished, nor Strafford executed; and though the death of Lord Bedford put an end to it for the moment, the Parliamentary leaders seem still to have had hopes of their entry into the royal Council. But meanwhile Charles was counting the chances of a very different policy. The courtiers about him were rallying from their first panic. His French Queen, furious at what she looked on as insults to royalty, and yet more furious at the persecution of the Catholics, was spurring him to violent courses. And for violence there seemed at the moment an opportunity. In Ireland Strafford's army refused to disband itself. In Scotland the union of the nobles was already broken by the old spirit of faction; and in his jealousy of the power gained by his hereditary enemy, the Earl of Argyle, Lord Montrose had formed a party with other great nobles, and was pressing Charles to come and carry out a counter-revolution in the North. Above all the English army, which still lay at York, was discontented by its want of pay and by the favour shown to the Scottish soldiers in its front. The discontent was busily fanned by its officers; and a design was laid before Charles by which advantage might be taken of the humour of the army to march it upon London, to seize the Tower and free Strafford. With the Earl at their head, the soldiers could then overawe the Houses and free the king from his thraldom. Charles listened to the project; he refused any expression of assent; but he kept the secret, and suffered the plot to go on, while he continued the negotiations with the Parliamentary leaders.

Death of Strafford.

But he was now in the hands of men who were his match in intrigue as they were more than his match in quickness of action. In the beginning of May, it is said through a squabble among the conspirators, the army plot became known to Pym. The moment was a critical one. Much of the energy and union of the Parliament was already spent. The Lords were beginning to fall back into their old position of allies of the Court. They were holding at bay the bill for the expulsion of the bishops from their seats in Parliament which had been sent up by the Lower House, though the measure aimed at freeing the Peers as a legislative body by removing from among them a body of men whose servility made them mere tools of the Crown, while it averted—if but for the moment—the growing pressure for the abolition of episcopacy. Things were fast coming to a standstill, when the discovery of the army plot changed the whole situation. Waver as the Peers might, they had no mind to be tricked by the king and overawed by his soldiery. The Commons were stirred to their old energy, London itself was driven to panic at the thought of passing into the hands of a mutinous and unpaid army. The general alarm sealed Strafford's doom. In plotting for his release, the plotters had marked him out as a life which was the main danger to the new state of things. Strafford still hoped in his master; he had a pledge from Charles that his life should be saved; and on the first of May the king in a formal message to the Parliament had refused his assent to the Bill of Attainder. But the Queen had no mind that her husband should suffer for a minister whom she hated, and before her pressure the king gave way. On the tenth of May he gave his assent to the bill by commission, and on the twelfth Strafford passed to his doom. He died as he had lived. His friends warned him of the vast multitude gathered before the Tower to witness his fall. "I know how to look death in the face, and the people too," he answered proudly. "I thank God I am no more afraid of death, but as cheerfully put off my doublet at this time as ever I did when I went to bed." As the axe fell, the silence of the great multitude was broken by a universal shout of joy. The streets blazed with bonfires. The bells clashed out from every steeple. "Many," says an observer, "that came to town to see the execution rode in triumph back, waving their hats, and with all expressions of joy through every town they went, crying, 'His head is off. His head is off!'"

The Panic.

The failure of the attempt to establish a Parliamentary ministry, the discovery of the army plot, the execution of Strafford, were the turning points in the history of the Long Parliament. Till May 1641 there was still hope for an accommodation between the Commons and the Crown by which the freedom that had been won might have been taken as the base of a new system of government. But from that hour little hope of such an agreement remained. The Parliament could put no trust in the king. The air at Westminster, since the discovery of the army conspiracy, was full of rumours and panic; the creak of a few boards revived the memory of the Gunpowder Plot, and the members rushed out of the House of Commons in the full belief that it was undermined. On the other hand, Charles put by all thought of reconciliation. If he had given his assent to Strafford's death, he never forgave the men who had wrested his assent from him. From that hour he regarded his consent to the new measures as having been extorted by force, and to be retracted at the first opportunity. His opponents were quick to feel the king's resolve of a counter-revolution; and both Houses, in their terror, swore to defend the Protestant religion and the public liberties, an oath which was subsequently exacted from every one engaged in civil employment, and voluntarily taken by the great mass of the people. The same terror of a counter-revolution induced even Hyde and the "moderate men" in the Commons to bring in a bill providing that the present Parliament should not be dissolved but by its own consent; and the same commission which gave the king's assent to Strafford's attainder gave his assent to this bill for perpetuating the Parliament.

Charles in Scotland.

Of all the demands of the Parliament this was the first that could be called distinctly revolutionary. To consent to it was to establish a power permanently co-ordinate with the Crown. But Charles signed the bill without protest. He had ceased to look on his acts as those of a free agent; and he was already planning the means of breaking the Parliament. What had hitherto held him down was the revolt of Scotland and the pressure of the Scotch army across the border. But its payment and withdrawal could no longer be delayed. The death of Strafford was immediately followed by the conclusion of a pacification between the two countries; and the sum required for the disbanding of both armies was provided by a poll-tax. Meanwhile the Houses hastened to complete their task of reform. The civil and judicial jurisdiction of the Star Chamber and the Court of High Commission, the irregular jurisdictions of the Council of the North, the Duchy of Lancaster, the County of Chester, were summarily abolished with a crowd of lesser tribunals. The work was pushed hastily on, for haste was needed. On the sixth of August the two armies were alike disbanded; and the Scots were no sooner on their way homeward than the king resolved to prevent their return. In spite of prayers from the Parliament, he left London for Edinburgh, yielded to every demand of the Assembly and the Scotch Estates, attended the Presbyterian worship, lavished titles and favours on the Earl of Argyle and the patriot leaders, and gained for a while a popularity which spread dismay in the English Parliament. Their dread of his designs was increased when he was found to have been intriguing all the while with the Earl of Montrose—whose conspiracy had been discovered before the king's coming and rewarded with imprisonment in the castle of Edinburgh—and when Hamilton and Argyle withdrew suddenly from the capital, and charged Charles with a treacherous plot to seize and carry them out of the realm.

The Irish Rising.

The fright was fanned to frenzy by news which came suddenly from Ireland. The quiet of that unhappy country under Strafford's rule had been a mere quiet of terror. The Catholic Englishry were angered by the Deputy's breach of faith. Before his coming Charles had promised for a sum of £120,000 to dispense with the oath of supremacy, to suffer recusants to practise in the courts of law, and to put a stop to the constant extortion of their lands by legal process. The money was paid; but by the management of Wentworth, the "Graces" which it was to bring received no confirmation from the Irish Parliament. The Lord-Deputy's policy aimed at keeping the recusants still at the mercy of the Crown; what it really succeeded in doing was to rob them of any hope of justice or fair dealing from the government. The native Irishry were yet more bitterly outraged by his dealings in Connaught. Under pretext that as inhabitants of a conquered country Irishmen had no rights but by express grant from the Crown, the Deputy had wrested nearly a half of the lands in that province from their native holders with the view of founding a new English plantation. The new settlers were slow in coming, but the evictions and spoliation renewed the bitter wrath which had been stirred by the older plantation in Ulster. All however remained quiet till the fall of Strafford put an end to the semblance of rule. The disbanded soldiers of the army he had raised spread over the country, and stirred the smouldering disaffection into a flame. In

October 1641, a rising, organized with wonderful power and secrecy by Roger O'Moore and Owen Roe O'Neill, burst forth under Sir Phelim O'Neill in Ulster, where the confiscation of the Settlement had never been forgiven, and spread like wildfire over the centre and west of the island. Dublin was saved by a mere chance; but in the open country the rebellion went on unchecked. The trembling planters fled for shelter to the towns as the clansmen poured back over their old tribal lands, and rumour doubled and trebled the number of the slain. Tales of horror and outrage, such as maddened our own England when they reached us from Cawnpore, came day after day over the Irish Channel; and sworn depositions told how husbands were cut to pieces in presence of their wives, their children's brains dashed out before their faces, their daughters brutally violated and driven out naked to perish frozen in the woods.

Its effect on England.

Much of all this was no doubt the wild exaggeration of panic, and the research of later times has shown how fraud lent a terrible aid to panic in multiplying a hundredfold the tales of outrage. But there was enough in the revolt to carry terror to the hearts of Englishmen. It was unlike any earlier rising in its religious character. It was no longer a struggle, as of old, of Celt against Saxon, but of Catholic against Protestant. The Papists within the Pale joined hands in it with the wild kernes outside the Pale. When the governing body of the rebels met at Kells in the following spring they called themselves "Confederate Catholics," resolved to defend "the public and free exercise of the true and Catholic Roman religion." The panic waxed greater when it was found that they claimed to be acting by the king's commission, and in aid of his authority. They professed to stand by Charles and his heirs against all that should "directly and indirectly endeavour to suppress their royal prerogatives." They showed a Commission, purporting to have been issued by royal command at Edinburgh, and styled themselves "the king's army." The Commission was a forgery, but belief in it was quickened by the want of all sympathy with the national honour which Charles displayed. To him the revolt seemed a useful check on his opponents. "I hope," he wrote coolly, when the news reached him, "this ill news of Ireland may hinder some of these follies in England." In any case it would necessitate the raising of an army, and with an army at his command he would again be the master of the Parliament. The Parliament, on the other hand, saw in the Irish revolt, the news of which met them but a few days after their reassembly at the close of October, the disclosure of a vast scheme for a counter-revolution, of which the withdrawal of the Scotch army, the reconciliation of Scotland, the intrigues at Edinburgh were all parts. Its terror was quickened into panic by the exultation of the royalists at the king's return to London at the close of November, and by the appearance of a royalist party in the Parliament itself.

The new Royalists.

The new party had been silently organized by Hyde, the future Lord Clarendon. To Hyde and to the men who gathered round him enough seemed to have been done. They clung to the law, but the law had been vindicated. They bitterly resented the system of Strafford and of Laud; but the system was at an end. They believed that English freedom hung on the assembly of Parliament and on the loyal co-operation of the Crown with this Great Council of the Realm; but the assembly of Parliaments was now secured by the Triennial Bill, and the king professed himself ready to rule according to the counsels of Parliament. On the other hand they desired to preserve to the Crown the right and power it had had under the Tudors. They revolted from any attempt to give the Houses a share in the actual work of administration. On both political and religious grounds they were resolute to suffer no change in the relations of the Church to the State, or to weaken the prerogative of the Crown by the establishment of a Presbyterianism which asserted any sort of spiritual independence. More complex impulses told on the course of Lord Falkland. Falkland was a man learned and accomplished, the centre of a circle which embraced the most liberal thinkers of his day. He was a keen reasoner and an able speaker. But he was the centre of that Latitudinarian party which was slowly growing up in the reaction from the dogmatism of the time, and his most passionate longing was for liberty of religious thought. Such a liberty the system of the Stuarts had little burdened; what Laud pressed for was uniformity, not of speculation, but of practice and ritual. But the temper of Puritanism was a dogmatic temper, and the tone of the Parliament already threatened a narrowing of the terms of speculative belief for the Church of England. While this fear estranged Falkland from the Parliament, his dread of a conflict with the Crown, his passionate longing for peace, his sympathy for the fallen, led him to struggle for a king whom he distrusted, and to die in a cause that was not his own. Behind Falkland and Hyde soon gathered a strong force of supporters; chivalrous soldiers like Sir Edmund Verney ("I have eaten the king's bread and served him near thirty years, and will not do so base a thing as to forsake him"), as well as men frightened at the rapid march of change, or by the dangers which threatened Episcopacy and the Church. And with these stood the few but ardent partizans of the Court; and the time-servers who had been swept along by the tide of popular passion, but who had believed its force to be spent, and looked forward to a new triumph of the Crown.

The Remonstrance.

With a broken Parliament, and perils gathering without, Pym resolved to appeal for aid to the nation itself. The Grand Remonstrance which he laid before the House of Commons in November was in effect an appeal to the country at large. It is this purpose that accounts for its unusual form. The Remonstrance was more an elaborate State-Paper than a petition to the king. It told in a detailed narrative the work which the Parliament had done, the difficulties it had surmounted, and the new dangers which lay in its path. The Parliament had been charged with a design to abolish Episcopacy, it declared its purpose to be simply that of reducing the power of bishops. Politically it repudiated the taunt of revolutionary aims. It demanded only the observance of the existing laws against recusancy, securities for the due administration of justice, and the employment of ministers who possessed the confidence of Parliament. The new king's party fought fiercely against its adoption; debate followed debate; the sittings were prolonged till lights had to be brought in; and it was only at midnight, and by a majority of eleven, that the Remonstrance was finally adopted. On an attempt of the minority to offer a formal protest against a subsequent vote for its publication the slumbering passion broke out into a flame. "Some waved their hats over their heads, and others took their swords in their scabbards out of their belts, and held them by the pommels in their hands, setting the lower part on the ground." Only Hampden's coolness and tact averted a conflict. The Remonstrance was felt on both sides to be a crisis in the struggle. "Had it been rejected," said Cromwell as he left the House, "I would have sold to-morrow all I possess, and left England for ever!" It was presented to Charles on the first of December, and the king listened to it sullenly; but it kindled afresh the spirit of the country. London swore to live and die with the Parliament; associations were formed in every county for the defence of the Houses; and when the guard which the Commons had asked for in the panic of the army plot was withdrawn by the king, the populace crowded down to Westminster to take its place.

Cavaliers and Roundheads.

The gathering passion soon passed into actual strife. Pym and his colleagues saw that the disunion in their ranks sprang above all from the question of the Church. On the one side were the Presbyterian zealots who were clamouring for the abolition of Episcopacy. On the other were the conservative tempers who in the dread of such demands were beginning to see in the course of the Parliament a threat against the Church which they loved. To put an end to the pressure of the one party and the dread of the other Pym took his stand on the compromise suggested by the Committee of Religion in the spring. The bill for the removal of bishops from the House of Lords had been rejected by the Lords on the eve of the king's journey to Scotland. It was now again introduced. But, in spite of violent remonstrances from the Commons, the bill still hung fire among the Peers; and the delay roused the excited crowd of Londoners who gathered round Whitehall. The bishops' carriages were stopped, and the prelates themselves rabbled on their way to the House. At the close of December the angry pride of Williams induced ten of his fellow-bishops to declare themselves prevented from attendance in Parliament, and to protest against all acts done in their absence as null and void. Such a protest was utterly unconstitutional; and even on the part of the Peers who had been maintaining the bishops' rights it was met by the committal of the prelates who had signed it to the Tower. But the contest gave a powerful aid to the projects of the king. The courtiers declared openly that the rabbling of the bishops proved that there was "no free Parliament," and strove to bring about fresh outrages by gathering troops of officers and soldiers of fortune, who were seeking for employment in the Irish war, and pitting them against the crowds at Whitehall. The combatants pelted one another with nicknames which were soon to pass into history. To wear his hair long and flowing almost to the shoulder was at this time the mark of a gentleman, whether Puritan or anti-Puritan. Servants on the other hand or apprentices wore the hair closely cropped to the head. The crowds who flocked to Westminster were chiefly made up of London apprentices; and their opponents taunted them as "Roundheads." They replied by branding the courtiers about Whitehall as soldiers of fortune or "Cavaliers." The gentlemen who gathered round the king in the coming struggle were as far from being military adventurers as the gentlemen who fought for the Parliament were from being London apprentices; but the words soon passed into nicknames for the whole mass of royalists and patriots.

Seizure of the Five Members.

From nicknames the soldiers and apprentices soon passed to actual brawls; and the strife beneath its walls created fresh alarm in the Parliament. But Charles persisted in refusing it a guard. "On the honour of a king" he engaged to defend them from violence as completely as his own children, but the answer had hardly been given when his Attorney appeared at the bar of the Lords, and accused Hampden, Pym, Holles, Strode, and Haselrig of high treason in their correspondence with the Scots. A herald-at-arms appeared at the bar of the Commons, and demanded the surrender of the five members. All constitutional law was set aside by a charge which proceeded personally from the king, which deprived the accused of their legal right to a trial by their peers, and summoned them before a tribunal that had no pretence to a jurisdiction over them. The Commons simply promised to take the demand into consideration. They again requested a guard. "I will reply to-morrow," said the king. He had in fact resolved to seize the members in the House itself; and on the morrow, the 4th of January 1642, he summoned the gentlemen who clustered about Whitehall to follow him, and, embracing the Queen, whose violent temper had urged him to this outrage, promised her that in an hour he would return master of his kingdom. A mob of Cavaliers joined him as he left the palace, and remained in Westminster Hall as Charles, accompanied by his nephew, the Elector-Palatine, entered the House of Commons. "Mr. Speaker," he said, "I must for a time borrow your chair!" He paused with a sudden confusion as his eye fell on the vacant spot where Pym commonly sate: for at the news of his approach the House had ordered the five members to withdraw. "Gentlemen," he began in slow broken sentences, "I am sorry for this occasion of coming unto you. Yesterday I sent a Sergeant-at-arms upon a very important occasion to apprehend some that by my command were accused of high treason, whereunto I did expect obedience and not a message." Treason, he went on, had no privilege, "and therefore I am come to know if any of these persons that were accused are here." There was a dead silence, only broken by his reiterated "I must have them wheresoever I find them." He again paused, but the stillness was unbroken. Then he called out, "Is Mr. Pym here?" There was no answer; and Charles, turning to the Speaker, asked him whether the five members were there. Lenthall fell on his knees, and replied that he had neither eyes nor tongue to see or say anything save what the House commanded him. "Well, well," Charles angrily retorted, "'tis no matter. I think my eyes are as good as another's!" There was another long pause while he looked carefully over the ranks of members. "I see," he said at last, "my birds are flown, but I do expect you will send them to me." If they did not, he added, he would seek them himself; and with a closing protest that he never intended any force "he went out of the House," says an eye-witness, "in a more discontented and angry passion than he came in."

Charles withdraws from London.

Nothing but the absence of the five members and the calm dignity of the Commons had prevented the king's outrage from ending in bloodshed. "It was believed," says Whitelock, who was present at the scene, "that if the king had found them there, and called in his guards to have seized them, the members of the House would have endeavoured the defence of them, which might have proved a very unhappy and sad business." Five hundred gentlemen of the best blood in England would hardly have stood tamely by while the bravoes of Whitehall laid hands on their leaders in the midst of the Parliament. But Charles was blind to the danger of his course. The five members had taken refuge in the City, and it was there that on the next day the king himself demanded their surrender from the aldermen at Guildhall. Cries of "Privilege" rang round him as he returned through the streets: the writs issued for the arrest of the five were disregarded by the Sheriffs; and a proclamation issued four days later, declaring them traitors, passed without notice. Terror drove the Cavaliers from Whitehall, and Charles stood absolutely alone; for the outrage had severed him for the moment from his new friends in the Parliament, and from the ministers, Falkland and Colepepper, whom he had chosen among them. But, lonely as he was, Charles had resolved on war. The Earl of Newcastle was despatched to muster a royal force in the north; and on the tenth of January news that the five members were about to return in triumph to Westminster drove Charles from Whitehall. He retired to Hampton Court and to Windsor, while the Trained Bands of London and Southwark on foot, and the London watermen on the river, all sworn "to guard the Parliament, the Kingdom, and the King," escorted Pym and his fellow-members along the Thames to the House of Commons. Both sides prepared for a struggle which was now inevitable. The Queen sailed from Dover with the Crown jewels to buy munitions of war. The Cavaliers again gathered round the king, and the royalist press flooded the country with State papers drawn up by Hyde. On the other hand, the Commons resolved by vote to secure the great arsenals of the kingdom, Hull, Portsmouth, and the Tower; while mounted processions of freeholders from Buckinghamshire and Kent traversed London on their way to St. Stephen's, vowing to live and die with the Parliament.

Preparations for war.

The Lords were scared out of their policy of obstruction by Pym's bold announcement of the position taken by the House of Commons. "The Commons," said their leader, "will be glad to have your concurrence and help in saving the kingdom: but if they fail of it, it should not discourage them in doing their duty. And whether the kingdom be lost or saved, they shall be sorry that the story of this present Parliament should tell posterity that in so great a danger and extremity the House of Commons should be enforced to save the kingdom alone." The effect of these words was seen in the passing of the bill for excluding bishops from the House of Lords, the last act of this Parliament to which Charles gave his assent. The great point however was to secure armed support from the nation at large, and here both sides were in a difficulty. Previous to the innovations introduced by the Tudors, and which had been taken away by the bill against pressing soldiers, the king in himself had no power of calling on his subjects generally to bear arms, save for the purposes of restoring order or meeting foreign invasion. On the other hand no one contended that such a power has ever been exercised by the two Houses without the king; and Charles steadily refused to consent to a Militia bill, in which the command of the national force was given in every county to men devoted to the Parliamentary cause. Both parties therefore broke through constitutional precedent, the Parliament in appointing Lord Lieutenants of the Militia by ordinance of the two Houses, Charles in levying forces by royal commissions of array.

Outbreak of war.

But the king's great difficulty lay in procuring arms, and on the twenty-third of April he suddenly appeared before Hull, the magazine of the north, and demanded admission. The new governor, Sir John Hotham, fell on his knees, but refused to open the gates: and the avowal of his act by the Parliament was followed at the end of May by the withdrawal of the royalist party among its members from their seats at Westminster. Falkland, Colepepper, and Hyde, with thirty-two peers and sixty members of the House of Commons, joined Charles at York; and Lyttelton, the Lord Keeper, followed with the Great Seal. But one of their aims in joining the king was to put a check on his projects of war; and their efforts were backed by the general opposition of the country. A great meeting of the Yorkshire freeholders which Charles convened on Heyworth Moor ended in a petition praying him to be reconciled to the Parliament; and in spite of gifts of plate from the universities and nobles of his party arms and money were still wanting for his new levies. The two Houses, on the other hand, gained in unity and vigour by the withdrawal of the royalists. The militia was rapidly enrolled, Lord Warwick named to the command of the fleet, and a loan opened in the City to which the women brought even their wedding-rings. The tone of the two Houses rose with the threat of force. It was plain at last that nothing but actual compulsion could bring Charles to rule as a constitutional sovereign; and the last proposals of the Parliament demanded the powers of appointing and dismissing the ministers, of naming guardians for the royal children, and of virtually controlling military, civil, and religious affairs. "If I granted your demands," replied Charles, "I should be no more than the mere phantom of a king."

END OF VOL. V

Lightning Source UK Ltd.
Milton Keynes UK
UKHW010636011121
393187UK00001B/18